THE FOUR GOSPELS

Maurice Hogan SSC is a member of the Missionary Society of St Columban. Ordained in 1965, he has served as a missionary in Japan and more recently in Hong Kong. He was Professor of Sacred Scripture at the Pontifical University, St Patrick's College, Maynooth, and a former member of the Pontifical Biblical Commission (1996–2007). He is presently Director of World Missions Ireland (Pontifical Mission Societies).

THE FOUR GOSPELS

Following in the Footsteps of Jesus

Maurice Hogan ssc

VERITAS

Published 2015 by
Veritas Publications
7–8 Lower Abbey Street
Dublin 1, Ireland
publications@veritas.ie
www.veritas.ie

ISBN 978 1 84730 589 3
Copyright © Maurice Hogan, 2015

10 9 8 7 6 5 4 3 2 1

Cover designed by Barbara Croatto, Veritas
Printed in the Republic of Ireland by SPRINT-print, Dublin

Veritas books are printed on paper made from the wood pulp of managed forests. For every tree felled, at least one tree is planted, thereby renewing natural resources.

CONTENTS

PREFACE

In an interview shortly after being elected to the see of Peter, Pope Francis spoke of the necessity for the Church to find new paths to preach the Good News of Jesus Christ: 'Instead of being a Church that welcomes and receives by keeping the doors open,' he said, 'let us also be a Church that finds new roads, that is able to step out of itself and go to those who do not attend Mass, to those who have quit or are indifferent.' In our time, one of the particular problems facing the Church is the challenge of people distancing themselves from the practice of the faith. This manifests itself progressively in societies, like Ireland, that for centuries appeared to have been imbued with the Gospel.

'Cradle' Catholics who struggle to live out their faith often sense that it is undernourished and unable to sustain and challenge them as adults living in today's de-Christianised world. Years of experience have built up a relationship with Jesus. During their childhood years, a personal portrait of Jesus gradually took shape. It was formed first of all in their families, then later on by the teaching and example at school and in the local parish. Returning to the Gospels as adults may serve to confirm their expectations of Jesus and what following him entails. But it may also be challenging. Their image of Jesus may not be totally accurate – too much of themselves and their expectations may have crept in, or their image of discipleship may be immature and does not reflect their personal growth in other areas. The task is now to pass from an immature faith, or one supported by custom, to a mature faith expressed in clear personal decisions that witness to a vision of life that is deeper, richer and more satisfying than the surrounding superficialities.

In October 2012, Pope Benedict XVI inaugurated the Year of Faith to herald the New Evangelisation with the conviction that new methods and new forms of expression were needed to convey to people today the perennial truth of Jesus Christ. For the Christian, faith is first and foremost an encounter and relationship with Jesus Christ. The goal of the New Evangelisation is to create the possibility for such an encounter. This call for a new presentation means that the same Good News from the beginning is now proclaimed with a new enthusiasm, in a new language that is comprehensible in a new cultural situation, and with a new method that is capable of transmitting its deeper sense. However, there is no real evangelisation unless the name and teaching, the life and mystery of Jesus Christ of Nazareth, the Son of God, are proclaimed.

This is the theme of Pope Francis's Apostolic Exhortation *Evangelii Gaudium* ('The Joy of the Gospel'), promulgated in November 2013. The Good News of Jesus Christ, he says, is characterised by *joy* (mentioned one hundred and nine times), the result of a personal encounter with the risen Christ that gives life a whole new meaning, a whole new direction. Such a person is liberated from self-absorption and enabled to become fully human by reaching out to others to proclaim the Good News. A dignified and fulfilling life, he adds, becomes possible only by reaching out to others. This includes fellow Christians, to help them grow spiritually so that they can respond with joy to God's love manifested in Jesus Christ. It also includes the baptised but non-practising who no longer experience the consolation of the faith. They need conversion so that joy can be restored. But first and foremost it means reaching out to non-Christians who do not know Christ and to those who are searching for God in the hope of finding him. Christians can show them the beauty of the Christian life and the joy that flows from it. Missionary activity is therefore the first and primary task of the *whole* Church, each and every Christian by virtue of Baptism is called to spread the Good News: 'Each Christian and every community must discern the path that the Lord points out, but all of us are asked to obey his call to go forth from our own comfort zone in order to reach all the "peripheries" in need of the light of the Gospel' (no. 20). 'All the baptised, whatever their position in the Church or their level of instruction in the faith, are agents of evangelisation ... The new evangelisation calls for personal involvement on the part of each of the baptised' (no. 120).

Christians have at their disposal vast supernatural resources, though they do not always make use of them. Among the more prominent of these resources are the four Gospels that are capable of being appropriated as guides in the development of a mature Christian faith for all believers, lay and religious alike. The contemplation of Christ in the Gospels is also available to anybody who seeks a purpose in life, a reason to live and a reason to die. Many thoughtful adults at one time or another are confronted with the fundamental questions of living: where have I come from? Where am I going? How ought I to live as befits a human being? What is the meaning of life and death, suffering, injustice and evil in the world? Is there life beyond death, or is death the end of everything? Does God exist and if so what kind of God? The Gospels do provide answers to these and similar questions. This book is offered as a guide to anybody who wishes to take up each of the Gospels in turn, read through them, meditate on them, and pray them. One popular method of praying the Gospels is known as *lectio divina*.

Lectio divina is a reflective reading of the Word of God, a means of praying the Gospels that follows from meditation on given passages. It relies on the guidance of the Holy Spirit within the heart as each person reads a specific passage and pauses to seek out the deeper meaning that God wants to convey through his word. The Word of God then becomes a means of union with God. The various aspects listed below are distinguished to focus attention, but may not be separated. They can be reduced to two aspects: contemplation (receptivity, simply being in the presence of God); and activity (cooperating with God's grace to become the person God intends me to be). A person chooses a text from the Gospels, takes a word(s), phrase(s), scene(s), or a story, reads them slowly, and ponders them so that they invite him or her into dialogue with God.

1. **Reading/Listening**: reading a Gospel passage and listening 'with the ears of the heart' to attune oneself to the presence of God in his Word. It is read and re-read slowly, attentively, listening to hear a word or phrase that stands out and becomes God's Word for me.

2. **Explanation**: seeking help from biblical commentaries or footnotes to understand the original religious meaning of the text.

3. **Meditation**: reflecting, 'ruminating' on the word or passage, like Mary who 'treasured all these things and pondered them in her heart' (Lk 2:19). Through meditation I allow God's Word to touch me so that it affects me at my deepest levels. How am I challenged by this Word?

4. **Prayer**: both as dialogue with God and as a loving conversation with him. I allow myself to be touched and changed by the Word of God. This includes prayer for help to recognise and respond to the challenges discovered in the text.

5. **Contemplation**: silence before the God who is communicating and revealing himself to me. A wordless, quiet rest in the presence of the One who loves me.

6. **Consolation**: enjoying the experience of simply being in the presence of God. This creates the proper atmosphere for courageous choices.

7. **Discernment**: distinguishing the mind of God expressed in his Word so as to enable me to make proper choices both for personal living and as a member of Christ's Body, the Church.

8. **Choosing**: deciding on a *concrete* course of action inspired by the Word of God.

9. **Action**: in the light of my particular vocation in life, living out the Word of God in my daily life together with its social consequences.

The following pages are designed as a companion to the four Gospels, not as a replacement for encountering the Word of God. The hope is that they will encourage an ever-deepening appreciation of the inspiring pages of the Gospels, each of which is a literary and theological entity, a story meant to engage the reader as a person. That is why each Gospel should first be read as a whole, preferably in one or more sittings. All the elements that make up each of the Gospel narratives are carefully arranged to present a single, overall picture.

Anyone who writes on the Gospels today is indebted to a host of authors that cannot easily be quantified. I owe a debt of gratitude to the many scholars who have written on the four Gospels and whose contributions have influenced the approach outlined in these pages. Inexpensive editions of the New Testament are easily available nowadays. Among the many translations, the *Jerusalem Bible,* the *New Jerusalem Bible,* the *New English Bible,* the *New Revised Standard Version,* the *New American Bible* and the *New International Version,* may be recommended depending on each reader's taste or preference. The abbreviation of biblical books follows that of the *New Jerusalem Bible.* Biblical quotations are from the *Jerusalem Bible.*

Maurice Hogan SSC
St Columban's
Dalgan Park
Navan

CHAPTER ONE

INTRODUCTION

At the experiential centre of Christianity is God's love for us human beings: 'God's love for us was revealed when God sent into the world his only Son so that we could have life through him; this is the love I mean: not our love for God, but God's love for us when he sent his Son to be the sacrifice that takes our sins away' (1 Jn 4:9-10). The response to this love is Christian conversion and maturation, an event and a process grounded in the grace and challenge of God's love manifested in Jesus Christ. For where love is present, there is always the possibility of further growth and development. At no stage may one assume that there is no need for further advance along the road to a full conversion that is Christian maturity. In reality, the formation of the Christian disciple has different stages or moments of development that continue throughout life. Following the liturgical reforms of the Second Vatican Council, the restoration of the catechumenate[1] as part of the process of becoming a Catholic has been a major impetus for the re-examination of the meaning of conversion and its consequences for all Christians.

In the Old Testament, conversion implies a turning away from sin, evil and idolatry and a turning towards the living God so as to have fullness of life. In the New Testament it has more to do with an internal process that manifests itself in external effects – the inevitable and radical changes to one's way of living that follow from the internal acceptance of conversion. True conversion, then, involves both interior and exterior elements. In English, repentance/conversion is used interchangeably to translate the radical change envisaged by the biblical vocabulary.

The story of Jesus begins with the appearance of John the Baptist proclaiming 'a baptism of repentance for the forgiveness of sins' (Mk 1:4) as a proper preparation for the imminent coming of God's kingdom[2] in the person of Jesus Christ. This repentance must manifest itself in concrete deeds of goodness (Lk 3:8ff). Israel is summoned to a change of lifestyle. Jesus inaugurates this reign by announcing: 'The time has come, the kingdom of God is close at hand. Repent, and believe the Good News' (Mk 1:15 and parallels). Repentance and faith in Jesus' preaching become twin dimensions of the same response that signals a person's entire acceptance of God's invitation, extended through the person and ministry of Jesus. It confronts people with a decision to turn away from evil and wrongdoing in order to turn towards the living God, one that demands both an inner transformation and a visible outward reformation of one's entire manner of living. It comprises a change in thinking, attitudes and behaviour that continues throughout life, in other words, a lifelong striving for holiness. Furthermore, it entails acceptance of Jesus as one's personal Saviour; the insertion into a community where that commitment is lived out in worship and ethical living; and participation in the community's mission to extend the reign of God outside its boundaries. It also involves the development and deepening of one's relationship to the Triune God through faith, hope and love.

In the writings of the New Testament, apart from the Gospels and mostly pre-dating them, a technical vocabulary is found that suggests stages or moments in the process of

Christian formation and maturation. There are 'catechumens' (cf. Gal 6:6), those who are being initiated at the pre-baptismal stage; 'disciples' (Ac 11:26), those who are learning to follow the path of Jesus after Baptism;[3] the 'enlightened' (cf. Heb 6:4; 10:32), those who have been illuminated by the Spirit to see life differently; and 'perfect' (cf. 1 Co 2:6; 14:20), mature Christians who live out a life of love on a daily basis, following the example of Jesus. It is clear then that in the early Church there was a pre- and post-baptismal instruction, as well as ongoing formation throughout the Christian life until one became a mature Christian, having traversed all the preliminary stages. The formation of the Christian was regarded as an important matter and one that took time to accomplish.

From the very beginning of the Church, therefore, there was a certain itinerary of initiation that comprised different stages. This was also the period when the Gospels were taking shape, and it may be asked what function each one performed in this process of Christian initiation. Even a superficial reading of the four Gospels reveals a remarkable diversity. This diversity is usually attributed to the different motives, sources and audiences for whom they were written, as well as to the particular viewpoints of the evangelists themselves. But it may also be asked if there existed a specific usage of each of the four Gospels at certain moments in the Christian initiation process that can also account for their specific characteristics. C. M. Martini has suggested that, in their completed stage, the four Gospels were appropriated for four distinct moments or stages in Christian initiation.[4] In light of this process of initiation into full Christian discipleship, the four Gospels served as pedagogical tools for articulating the full meaning of Christian conversion and maturation. The gift of God's love so clearly manifested in the life of Jesus Christ and 'poured into our hearts by the Spirit which has been given to us' (Rm 5:5) is seen in a dynamic way in four stages of Christian maturation that correspond to the four Gospels. These, as a matter of historical fact, derive from the lived experience of these stages and can now function to lead others to the goal of each progressive stage.

In the early centuries of its existence, the Church felt the need for four Gospels[5] and appropriated them as 'manuals' in an ongoing process in response to God's love. Historically the Church employed the four Gospels as guides, both for the initiation of baptismal candidates into the foundational experience of God's love for us, and for their post-baptismal maturation. The initiation into the Good News and its integration into a lifestyle could not be accomplished all at once. Like any process of organic growth, it needed a longer period of time punctuated by successive stages of growth.

If we accept Mark as the earliest of the written Gospels, it is easy to see that it is a particularly fitting Gospel for the instruction of catechumens to introduce them to the person and activity of Jesus. The Gospel of Matthew, with its community orientation and lengthy discourses, is well suited to those who, already having been baptised, must now be initiated into the duties of communal Christian living. In the two-volume narrative of Luke-Acts,[6] the Gospel of Luke situates the life of Jesus in the world and in history. Its companion volume, Acts of the Apostles, narrates the early Church mission extending beyond cultural, linguistic and political boundaries. Both serve the baptised Christian, who has already been initiated into community life, to proclaim to those outside the community the Good News of Jesus Christ. The Gospel of John, the last to be written, represents the fruit of mature reflection on the mystery of revelation in the light of Christian experience. It is particularly suited to those who, having completed the previous successive phases, wish to contemplate the Christian life in its unity of faith, hope and love.

We have at hand, then, four manuals for four successive moments in the Christian maturation process – catechumenate, Christian community living, preparation for mission and contemplative maturity. In this way the Christian is equipped to give 'the reason for the hope that you all have' (1 P 3:15), and is readied for every good work. The four Gospels fulfil the need to explain in depth both to oneself and to others the Christian experience and how it is solidly founded. The four canonical versions of the Gospel story are authentic expressions of the God-given response of human beings to the gift of God's love in Jesus Christ. It was the same Spirit who inspired the evangelists and who enabled community leaders to recognise which Gospels were to be accepted by the Church. In recognising the four Gospels as inspired by the Spirit, the Christian community proposes them as a rule of faith, as the standard of revealed truth, and as the norm of Christian authenticity, development and maturity.

Christian conversion is a gift, a grace, and also an insight by which one comes to understand that the promise made by God in Christ concerns one *personally*: 'This is the love I mean: not our love for God, but God's love for us when he sent his Son to be the sacrifice that takes our sins away' (1 Jn 4:10). When one realises this, a person passes from a notional, or theoretical, to a real assent and is forced to take a stand. When we understand, judge and respond to the fact that God is talking through Jesus about us, we pass from a notional idea of God to a real one and may be said to be undergoing a conversion experience. Christian conversion is God's gift that enables us to hear the story of

Jesus. The inborn human drive to seek self-transcendence is fulfilled in the gift of the Spirit who fills our hearts with love. The story told in the Gospels now becomes *our* story; not only do we hear that story, but we also want to tell it to others.

The Gospel story calls its hearers to personal conversion and conversion to God. This may be likened to a true homecoming. The prophets of the exile saw their return to the land of their ancestors as a homeward journey to God. This sense of homecoming is well illustrated in the Gospel parable of the Prodigal Son (Lk 15:11-32). Having demanded his share of the estate from his father, the younger son leaves home for a foreign land, thus severing connections with his family and roots in the Promised Land. He cuts himself off from the source of life, identity and security. He squanders his capital to enhance a life divorced from its true source, and when he has spent it all, he finds himself cut off, not only from home and country, but also from his true self. Sitting among the pigs he feels the alienation and estrangement from his true self — he has lost his identity for he is no longer a son. To regain that identity he must return home to his father who, when he catches sight of him, casts aside his dignity and rushes to embrace him. The father refuses to treat his son as a paid servant, bereft of the status of sonship. In returning home the son discovers that he has returned to his true self, something he himself could scarcely have hoped for. This is the result of his father's forgiveness and generosity in gratuitously restoring him to his former status.

The story of the Prodigal Son is one of unconditional love on the part of the father, a love that frees us to accept ourselves in spite of our failings. It is the love of a patient, forbearing father who yearns for his son's return. The elder son, on the other hand, enjoys neither the fellowship of his father nor that of his brother. He seems incapable of grasping what it means to be a father or a son. His mentality is that of a servant or slave (v. 29). He works for this father out of obligation rather than out of love and expects payment for services rendered. His attitude towards his returned brother is one of contempt, and he regards his father as someone who has been duped and taken advantage of. The father, however, only sees himself as having lost and gratefully regained a son and the feast he orders for his returned child is an expression of his heartfelt joy. Because the elder brother is unable or unwilling to understand the father's unconditional love for his wayward son, he is also unable to relate to his brother in a fraternal way, dismissing him as 'this son of yours' (v. 30). But the father pointedly reminds him that it is 'your brother' (v. 32) who has returned, while also being patient and understanding. After all, everything the father possesses belongs to his children. The elder brother is not paid like a hired hand, much less is he expected to work like a slave. He ought to have understood how his father's heart goes out to his younger son, who, in any case, is his own brother as well. The father's unconditional love is a creative love that enables the younger son to accept himself and his father in the fellowship of those with whom he shares his newfound life. Jesus told this story and the Church communicates it through the Gospel so that we too might return to our true selves. Our conversion is a homecoming to the true God, our Father, and, at the same time, to our true selves and to the community of those who acknowledge God as Father: 'Lord, you have made us for yourself and our hearts are restless until they rest in you' (St Augustine).

Outward and visible membership of the Church is by itself no guarantee that a person has been converted, and members of the Christian community benefit from the story of Jesus only to the extent that they allow themselves to be shaped by it. The grace of conversion is a spirit of openness to change that allows one to be open to hearing the story of Jesus and to be transformed as a result. It is a willingness to accept that God loves us no matter what. The story of Jesus in the four Gospels is presented as an invitation to become his followers and to find in his story the meaning of our lives. Although all the dimensions of authentic discipleship are present to a greater or lesser extent in each of the four Gospels, certain *traits* stand out in each one. We will concentrate on these distinctive traits as we study each of the four Gospels in turn to highlight the Christological, ecclesiological, missionary and contemplative dimensions of discipleship.

NOTES

1. The catechumenate is the pre-baptismal instruction for candidates for the Sacrament of Baptism.

2. The Kingdom of God may be understood as a world in which everything that God stands for becomes a reality in the lives of people – a world built on truth, love, compassion, justice, freedom, human dignity and peace. This is what God wills for the human race, but it depends on our free response and cooperation. With the help of God, we work with him to make the kingdom a reality in our world.

3. Following Peter's speech in Acts 2:14-36, the hearers repent and undergo Baptism to receive the Spirit (2:38, 41). Immediately afterwards they continued to remain faithful 'to the teaching of the apostles, to the brotherhood, to the breaking of bread and to the prayers' (2:42). After the reception of Baptism there was a period of instruction, together with participation in community life.

4. C. M. Martini, 'The Stages of the Formation of the Christian in the Primitive Community in the Light of the Four Gospels', *Pontificium Consilium Pro Laicis Documentation Service* 5 (February 1979), pp. 1–10.

5. Tatian's *Diatessaron* (c. AD 150), a continuous narrative of the four Gospels, although used in the Syrian Church until the fifth century, never caught on in the universal Church.

6. Luke-Acts was composed by the same author as one narrative and was intended to be read as such. We will see this when we come to study the third stage of Christian maturation.

≈

CHAPTER TWO

FIRST MOMENT: CONVERSION TO CHRIST – THE GOSPEL OF MARK

Introduction

The Gospel of Mark, generally considered the earliest of the written Gospels, is particularly suited to presenting the catechumen with the essence of the Christian message. It is centred on the person of Christ, on his activity more than on his teaching, and reveals to aspiring Christians the difference between their sense of God imbibed from their upbringing and environment, and the true God revealed by Jesus Christ, his Son. This Gospel, however, is not only for catechumens. It is also for Christians who have been baptised, usually in infancy, but who have never really grasped the implications of what their Baptism entails as far as their personal lives are concerned. They are still 'outsiders' in the sense of never having received the Good News as a *personal* gift that transforms their lives. Consequently, the Gospel of Mark is also for those Christians who have yet to personally receive the mystery of Christ and his relevance for their lives.

The God revealed in Mark is one who acts with power in Jesus Christ to heal all kinds of human brokenness, examples and summaries of which are found in the first half of his Gospel. In the second half, the Passion story gradually comes to dominate. It shows how costly it can be to become a follower of this God who seems to have abandoned Jesus on the cross (15:34). This is hardly the kind of God one would have expected to find; it may even shock those who regard themselves as religious, but who, in reality, do not know the God of Jesus Christ. Nevertheless, at the end of the Gospel the resurrection of Jesus assures us that the God who seems to abandon human beings in their hour of need is still with them.

The Gospel of Mark also helps us to appreciate what is happening in our lives when it puts a person who is still on the 'outside' in contact with the mystery of Christ – his life, death and resurrection – as an invitation to change or to undergo conversion. Like Bartimaeus (10:46-52) the person who has experienced the reading of Mark may wish to cry out: 'Son of David, have pity on me.' When Jesus asks what he can do for him, the blind man, conscious of his need for healing, makes the request: 'Master, let me see again.' To those with eyes to see, the Gospel of Mark leads readers to receive the mystery of the Kingdom of God by coming into contact with Jesus who calls them to conversion: 'The time has come,' he said, 'and the kingdom of God is close at hand. Repent and believe the Good News' (1:15). Conversion comes about through an encounter with Jesus Christ, the Son of God (1:1). As portrayed by Mark, Jesus, by his manner of living and dying, reveals the authentic face of the true God and the attentive reader is led to exclaim with the centurion at the foot of the cross: 'In truth, this man was a son of God' (15:39). Jesus reveals a new and strange God, while his Passion points to a particular understanding of God's reconciling love: 'For the Son of Man himself did not come to be served, but to serve, and to give his life as a ransom for many' (10:45). For those who accept this self-transcending love, the first steps towards authentic discipleship are already being taken.

Outline of Mark

1. **Jesus' Ministry of Preaching and Teaching in Galilee (1:1–8:30)**

   a. Preparation for Jesus' public ministry by John the Baptist; a day in the ministry of Jesus; controversy at Capernaum (1:1–3:6).

   b. Jesus chooses the Twelve and trains them to become his disciples by teaching and miracles; he is rejected at Nazareth (3:7–6:6).

   c. Jesus sends the Twelve on a trial mission; feeds five thousand people; walks on the water; engages in controversy over Jewish traditions; performs healings in Gentile territory; feeds four thousand; is misunderstood by the disciples; heals a blind man (6:7–8:26).

   d. *Peter identifies Jesus as the Messiah* (8:27-30).

2. **Jesus, the Suffering Son of Man, Death and Resurrection (8:31–16:8, 9-20)**

   a. Three Passion predictions; transfiguration; instruction of disciples (8:31–10:52).

   b. Jesus' Jerusalem ministry: entry; cleansing of the Temple; teaching; eschatological discourse (11:1–13:37).

   c. Anointing of Jesus; betrayal by Judas; Last Supper; agony; trial; crucifixion; death; *centurion's recognition of Jesus as Son of God*; empty tomb (14:1–16:8).

   d. Resurrection appearances, added later as part of the canonical Gospel (16:9-20).

Storyline

The opening section of Mark (1:1-13) serves as an overture to the entire Gospel. It introduces the main character, Jesus, by identifying him as Messiah and God's Son through a quotation from Scripture, through the Baptist's witness, and finally through a voice from heaven after his Baptism by John. Jesus is the Son whom God has sent to rescue humanity through the service and sacrifice of his life. After the presentation of who Jesus really is, there is a brief reference to testing by Satan in the desert and how Satan's attack fails. In the Old Testament, the desert was regarded as a place of new beginnings and was also a place of testing. John is dressed after the manner of Elijah, the prophet expected to return at the end of the ages. So a new age is about to begin with the outpouring of the Spirit. This is the reason for the urgent message of repentance that John preaches. The Spirit of God then descends on Jesus to empower him for his mission as God's anointed to rescue human beings from the grip of brokenness and disability.

After a brief reference to John's arrest, the beginning of the Galilean ministry (1:14–3:6) opens with the first words spoken by Jesus in the Gospel. He proclaims not himself, but the Good News that the reign of God, already in process in the Old Testament, has now reached its time of fulfilment. God's reign as undisputed King over creation and over all peoples in justice and peace has already definitively begun and calls for repentance and faith. Followers of Jesus are asked to see reality with the new eyes of faith and transform their lives accordingly. The Gospel portrays Jesus as inaugurating God's rule through healings, teachings and the giving of his life for others. After choosing his first disciples, the remainder of the chapter describes a day in the life of Jesus as he begins his teaching and healing ministry.

Jesus calls disciples to follow him in order to share in his ministry (1:16-20). The essence of discipleship is the following of Jesus so as to participate in his mission, expressed in the metaphor of 'fishing' for people. On a Sabbath day in

Capernaum, Jesus combines teaching with miracles. His teaching with authority and the casting out of a devil fill his audience with astonishment and his reputation spreads rapidly. Jesus then heals Simon's mother-in-law and many others in the town before escaping to a lonely place to pray, after which he continues his ministry throughout Galilee. Feeling sorry for a leper who approached him, Jesus touches and heals him. Despite his injunction to silence, his fame spreads.

As Jesus continues his ministry, he meets with strong opposition from Jewish leaders. Capernaum now becomes the place where Mark centres five incidents in which objections to his mission are raised by opponents (2:1–3:6). His forgiving of sins leads to a charge of blasphemy. Opponents also object to his eating with sinners, to the failure of his disciples to fast, and to their doing what is not lawful on the Sabbath. Even during a ritual as important as the Sabbath observance, Jesus subordinates it to the needs of people by curing the man with a withered hand. Moreover, Jesus also claims to be master of the Sabbath. Clearly Jesus does not fit into the religious expectations of his contemporaries. He seems to be saying that new situations demand new rituals, and that the old cannot contain the new phenomenon that is occurring. The five conflict stories in this section reach their climax in a plot by his enemies to destroy him. The proclamation of God's kingdom is being opposed and that opposition is aimed at Jesus, the proclaimer. All these stories revolve around central values in Jesus' ministry – his power to forgive sins, his association with sinners and outcasts, and his compassionate interpretation of the law. Readers are reminded that fidelity to the Gospel will encounter opposition and conflict from those whose values are challenged by the justice and compassion of Jesus.

The following section (3:7–6:6) begins with an overview of the Galilean ministry, revealing the extraordinary success of the power of Jesus to draw people through his teaching and deeds of power. From his many followers, Jesus chooses twelve to be with him, to preach and to cast out demons. They are to share fully in his ministry. The story concerning Jesus' relatives coming to apprehend him is intertwined with a controversy with scribes from Jerusalem who interpret his behaviour as proof of demonic possession. To refute their contention, Jesus cites two comparisons – that of a kingdom divided against itself, and that of a house similarly divided. Satan's house is being plundered by Jesus, and far from being perceived as an ally of Satan, he has succeeded in permanently tying him up. With the appearance of Jesus, two kingdoms are locked in a struggle and Jesus emerges victorious. Blasphemy against the Holy Spirit is particularly serious in that it blinds people to their own need of forgiveness. Rather, those inspired by the Spirit are maligned as being in league with evil forces. Membership of Jesus' new spiritual family is maintained through a life in conformity to God's will.

The first extended teaching (4:1-34) consists of several parables used by Jesus to reveal the mystery of his mission to those who believe and embrace his message, while they conceal his message from the merely curious and those who oppose him. In the parable of the sower, Jesus is the sower whose message elicits diverse responses depending on the condition of the soil, yet the harvest is beyond what could reasonably be expected. This is followed by an allegorical explanation, with some additional interpretative material. It ends with an admonition for those with ears to hear, to listen. Hearing and the quality of one's response will determine the quality of one's life. In the parable of the seed growing by itself, the good soil of the kingdom produces its fruit by its own internal power, one that even the sower does not fully comprehend. Like the tiny mustard seed, God's kingdom will grow to become a great bush offering protection to birds of the air. While Jesus speaks publicly only in parables, he explains everything privately to the disciples.

Four miracle stories follow the teaching in parables (4:35– 5:43); the first is a nature miracle, the others are healing miracles. They occur on the same day as his teaching. Jesus manifests his power by exercising his authority over nature in the calming of the storm. The perplexed response of the disciples gripped by fear makes them wonder who this Jesus could be. The healing of the demoniac in Gentile territory is told in great detail. The presence of a legion of devils accentuates the intensity of the spiritual combat between Jesus and the forces of evil. Jesus reverses the direction of evil by sending the demon-possessed swine back into the sea, the abode of God's enemies, while the cured man announces to his own people what the Lord has done for him. The two following miracle stories highlight Jesus' power over sickness and death as his favourable response to faith. The importance of faith for Jesus' acts of healing is further emphasised in the episode involving his hometown of Nazareth (6:1-6). Although the people are astounded by his teaching and deeds of power, they are blinded by his ordinariness and refuse to accept him. Their lack of faith hinders Jesus' ability to do deeds of power among them.

In the following section (6:7–8:26), Jesus sends out the twelve disciples to share in his mission of healing and casting out devils. Inserted between the sending out and their return is the story of the death of John the Baptist in Herod's court that casts a shadow over the disciples' success. The feeding of the five thousand occurs in a place of wilderness. Jesus satisfies their spiritual hunger by teaching them many things, thus gradually showing himself as the shepherd of the new people of God. The miracle recalls the manna in the desert (cf. Ex 16) and points forward to the Eucharist. That so little food fed so many to the point of satisfaction demonstrates the miraculous nature of the event. In the second miracle, the walking on the water, the divine identity of Jesus is suggested when he speaks the divine name 'I am' (cf. Ex 3:14) and controls the destructive forces of nature – a prerogative of God in the Old Testament. However, the significance of the two miracles seems to have completely escaped the disciples. Their hardness of heart prevents them from comprehending Jesus' self-revelation. Following this is a Markan summary of Jesus' many healings.

Against the Pharisees' external practices of piety in matters of purification and worship (7:1-23), Jesus sets in contrast the true moral intention of God's Law and even sets aside elements of the law itself with regard to clean and unclean food. Purity comes from within, from the state of the heart, not from ritual behaviour. Defilement originates from within and fans out from there; nothing from the outside that comes in can defile a person. The state of the heart is central to Jesus' understanding of ethics and obedience to God. In sharp contrast to the hostility of the Jewish authorities is the faith of the pagan woman of Tyre who comes spontaneously to Jesus. He accedes to her clever and determined plea for the cure of her afflicted daughter. The healing of the deaf-mute recalls the messianic blessings prophesied in Isaiah 35:4-6, and marks Jesus as an agent of God's healing. The people's enthusiasm about Jesus' power overrides his command to secrecy. A second miracle of loaves, this time in pagan territory, shows that Jesus has also extended his saving mission to Gentiles. After all that Jesus has performed, the Pharisees still seek a sign to test him. On the other hand, the disciples in the boat are portrayed as not having grasped anything at all, thereby highlighting the unlikelihood that Jesus will ever be fully accepted or properly understood by them. The healing of the blind man that follows serves as a Markan commentary on the situation. The man regains his sight in stages, only when Jesus acts a second time does the man see clearly. The second half of the Gospel will describe what Jesus must still do to make his disciples see clearly, namely, to suffer, be put to death and rise again.

Peter's confession (8:27-30) is the climax of the first part of Mark's narrative presentation. As spokesman for the disciples, Peter proclaims Jesus as the 'Messiah'. The Gospel has been answering the question of the identity of Jesus for the reader up until now through its portrayal of Jesus' powerful words and deeds. But even his disciples are unable to grasp their significance. However, Jesus greets this profession with a command to silence since the title 'Messiah', although correct in itself, has been spoken without including the necessary component of suffering. To counteract expectations that the Messiah would be a political or military figure, Jesus immediately sets about instructing his disciples on the necessity of suffering and the humiliation he will have to endure in order to accomplish his mission, as well as the corresponding demands of discipleship. The cross, as a sign of Jesus' total commitment to his Father's will and of his selfless love for others, becomes the touchstone for understanding who Jesus really is and what discipleship entails.

The first section of the second half of Mark's presentation (8:31–10:52) is dominated by three predictions of Jesus' Passion, death and resurrection. The first prediction, misunderstood by the disciples, provokes Jesus' sharp rebuke of Peter who tempted him to abandon his Father's will. Jesus calls together the crowds and the disciples to teach them what following a suffering Messiah involves. The disciples must follow this same path if they are to be faithful to Jesus and his message. These utterances of Jesus challenge all authentic disciples to total commitment to himself through self-renunciation, acceptance of the cross of suffering, and even death itself. Life regarded as mere self-centred earthly existence ends in destruction. Whereas lived in loyalty to Christ, despite physical death, it attains its fullness.

In the following scene – the transfiguration – Jesus manifests his divinity before three of his disciples and converses with Elijah and Moses to counteract the growing disbelief surrounding him as he moves towards Jerusalem. Afterwards, he discusses the coming of Elijah in the presence of his uncomprehending disciples who are unable to perform an exorcism on a sick boy, despite being given the power to do so. Jesus exposes their lack of trust in God and highlights the importance of prayer. In response to their lack of understanding of his second prediction, Jesus gives them more intense instruction on the meaning of discipleship. Their role in Jesus' work is to be one of service, not power, symbolised by a little child, and he warns against jealousy and intolerance towards others. Even the smallest courtesies shown to disciples will not go unrewarded. Jesus uses hyperbole to emphasise the drastic measures needed to protect against causing others to sin. The Twelve are challenged to be like fire and salt – the refinement effected through the former, and the purifying and preservative qualities of the latter.

A question raised by the Pharisees is the context for Jesus' teaching on marriage and divorce (10:1-12). Jesus proclaims permanence to be the divine intention from the beginning concerning marriage. He returns to the issue of those entering the kingdom by stating that human receptivity, of which the child is a symbol, is necessary. The episode of the rich young man depicts wealth as a formidable obstacle to entering God's kingdom because of the false security it generates. This is demonstrated by the young man's refusal to part with his riches and embrace the Gospel. Only by cooperating with God can the demands of discipleship be fulfilled, but with his help all things are possible. Renunciation for Jesus' sake creates the proper dispositions for receiving the salvation offered freely by God.

After the third prediction of the Passion (10:32-34), the request of James and John for a share in the glory of Jesus must involve a share in his sufferings and the endurance of tribulation for the sake of the Gospel. However, the assigning of places of honour in the kingdom is reserved to God alone. Whatever authority is to be exercised by the disciples must, like that of Jesus, be rendered as service to others rather than as a means of self-aggrandisement or power seeking. The service of Jesus is his Passion and death for the sake of sinners. His death is to be regarded not as a tragic failure, but as the ultimate expression of his entire mission – an act of love for others. The disciples, likewise, must make the giving of their life for others the focus of their discipleship. In the story of Bartimaeus the emphasis is on the blind man's own determination to reach Jesus. His humble trust and honest expression of need not only brings about his cure, but also prompts him to follow Jesus on the journey of discipleship. Clearly Mark has interpreted this healing story as one of discipleship.

Jesus' Jerusalem ministry (11:1–13:37) begins with his triumphant entry into the city of David as Messiah-king coming to claim his kingdom. Nevertheless, he will face opposition and eventually death itself before final victory is achieved. The cursing of the fruitless fig tree becomes a sign of the Jerusalem Temple's failure to receive Jesus. It is not only cleansed of abuses, but also declared invalid. Mark foresees a new Temple and a new community emerging around Jesus. He regards the Temple as symbolic of a religious practice that has become empty. This also emerges in the conflict stories in this section as Jesus does battle with the chief priests, the elders, the scribes, the Herodians, the Pharisees and the Sadducees. Jesus' authority to act as he does has been a problem for the religious leaders right from the beginning. Only if they tell him the source of John's Baptism, will Jesus reveal to them the source of his authority. By their rejection of God's messengers they have incurred divine judgement and this is confirmed in the parable of the vineyard's tenants. The punishment of the tenants refers to the religious leaders, and the transfer of the vineyard to others points to the new community formed around Jesus.

In the ensuing conflict (12:13-37) the Jewish leaders continue to challenge Jesus' authority. Jesus vanquishes his adversaries by his responses to their questions regarding tribute to Caesar, the resurrection of the dead, and the greatest commandment, reducing them to silence. He questions the claim of the scribes about the Davidic descent of the Messiah, only to imply that he is much more than this. The denunciation of the public display of the scribes provides a background for an account of genuine religious behaviour in the incident of the widow's mite (12:38-44).

On the Mount of Olives, Jesus delivers the last discourse of his ministry that looks forward to the end times (13:1-37). Its focus is on the future of the Christian community as it carries out its mission in history. The content of the discourse is a collection of prophetic warnings (destruction of the Temple, persecution of the disciples, the need to be watchful) and apocalyptic signs (deceivers, wars, sacrilege, phenomena in the sky). Jesus' followers are not to be misled by speculations and claims that the end is near, but are to remain watchful instead. God's ultimate action is a saving one when Jesus, the Son of Man, will return to gather his disciples and lead them to God. This is the meaning of history, one that is ultimately full of hope.

Two lengthy chapters (14:1–15:47) form the longest narrative in the whole Gospel. It reveals how important the Passion is for Mark. Jesus' death for others sums up his entire mission and is the ultimate revelation of his identity as God's Son. The opening scenes set the mood as the leaders and Judas plot Jesus' death, while a faithful woman anoints his body for death. The Passover meal of Jesus with his disciples includes preparation and the dialogue of betrayal. The breaking of bread and the sharing of the cup become signs of Jesus' impending death for the sake of others, after which Jesus predicts the disciples' upcoming failures. While Jesus prays in Gethsemane for the strength to follow God's will, three of his disciples sleep. Judas leads an armed band into the garden to arrest Jesus, while the other disciples flee in panic.

The trials before the Sanhedrin and Pilate dominate the rest of the Passion narrative. Meanwhile, Peter denies his Master. False witnesses misconstrue Jesus' predictions regarding the Temple. Jesus unambiguously accepts that he is the Son of God and Messiah of Israel, after which he is condemned for blasphemy. In his arraignment before Pilate, Pilate remains unconvinced of Jesus' guilt, but lacks the integrity to release him. The soldiers' and the people's mockery of Jesus is surrounded by paradox and irony. The crucifixion, death and burial bring the great drama to its conclusion. It begins with the soldiers mocking Jesus as King of the Jews and ends with the pagan centurion confessing Jesus as God's Son (15:39). The rending of the veil symbolises the destruction of the Temple. Jesus is buried in an empty tomb by a stranger. A final episode (16:1-8) proclaims that the crucified Jesus is victorious over death. The scene also picks up the story of the absent disciples. The risen Christ does not abandon them; they are to go to Galilee where they will see him as he had promised. The Gospel ends on a note of awe as the women leave the tomb bewildered and struck silent. In Jesus' victory over death, the world has been transformed forever. The longer canonical ending (16:9-20) seems to have been added by a later hand. It is composed of elements from the other Gospels.

Literary Characteristics[1]

Mark has succeeded in shaping Christian preaching into a moving narrative about Jesus by weaving together his sayings and stories about his ministry into a single dynamic narrative that traces the ministry of Jesus from his Baptism by John in the Jordan River, through his preaching tour in Galilee, his journey to Jerusalem, to his death and resurrection. It is an engrossing story that grasps the reader right from the beginning. The story is fast-paced as Jesus moves rapidly from place to place, giving the impression that his mission is an urgent one to which a response must be given without delay. It is also a story filled with conflicts between Jesus and his opponents. Because the message of Jesus called for a radical change in lifestyle and challenged the reigning powers, it is hardly surprising that conflict and suffering have such a prominent place in the narrative. The Passion story at the end dominates the whole when Jesus is arrested, condemned and executed.

The central character in Mark's narrative is Jesus of Nazareth; understanding his identity and responding to it with faith becomes a major concern of his. Mark believes that Jesus is the Messiah, the Son of God (cf. 1:1), but he proclaims it for the most part in narrative form. Jesus' sayings and his activity – his healings, parables, instructions, his encounters with demons and the forces of nature, his conflicts with opponents, but above all his Passion, death and resurrection – reveal who Jesus really is. His power-filled ministry in Galilee, with its healings and exorcisms, demonstrates that God's liberating reign is already breaking into history to free people from the realm of sickness, brokenness, evil and death. Nevertheless, for Mark the most important revelation of Jesus' identity is in his Passion, death and resurrection, which were freely embraced by Jesus on behalf of others.

Another concern of Mark's is explaining what it means to follow Jesus, and so the disciples also play a prominent role in the story. The interaction between Jesus and his disciples, with whom the reader is inclined to identify, gives Mark the opportunity to instruct his readers. Called by Jesus early on in his ministry, they are present in almost every scene. But as the story progresses, the disciples find it more and more difficult to understand what Jesus is about, and as the Passion approaches, they misunderstand and eventually fail him. The narrative, however, ends in a note of reconciliation when the heavenly messenger instructs the women at the empty tomb to tell the disciples to go to Galilee where they will again encounter Jesus. The instructions Jesus had given them, the difficulties they encountered in understanding and following him, and the unbreakable bond despite their failures and abandonment, are both a challenge and a consolation to the reader of the Gospel. The narrative, however, abruptly ends in a note of awe as the women flee the empty tomb in silence.[2] It is clear that the Gospel of Mark is no dispassionate, objective report of the life of Jesus, but is more concerned with the identity of Jesus and the meaning of his person and ministry against the background of the story of Israel. Jesus 'proclaimed the Good News from God' (1:14),[3] which indicates that the story of Jesus is more a story of God's activity already at work in the history of Israel. God now intervenes in the person of Jesus to fulfil promises made to Israel and to inaugurate his definitive rule or reign. A divine perspective is therefore provided on Jesus' public ministry, which is set within the horizons of the Old Testament and the history of the Israelite people. Mark chose the medium of narrative to encourage the reader's sense of identification with the central character, Jesus of Nazareth, and, in a somewhat different way, with the disciples. He shaped the lives of the people within the narrative as well as the outcome of the story. Jesus is both the powerful miracle-worker and the suffering servant who is abandoned on the cross. Together these two apparently contradictory images disclose a fully integrated portrait of Jesus and his mission.

Two motifs of conflict and discipleship continue to revolve around Jesus' identity. Mark, however, did not compose his narrative out of nothing, but appropriated sources and traditions available to him that were grounded in actual events in the life of Jesus. Yet for all that, the final product is a literary creation of the author who made decisions about the literary genre, such as where to begin his work; how the narrative was to be structured so that its movement conveyed the meaning he wished to evoke; from what point of view the story was to be told; who the characters would be and how they would be developed; and what kind of reader he envisaged. It seems then that a literary approach to the Gospel is called for. The effectiveness of Mark's story stems from his presentation of Jesus in a long, unified narrative — one that is based on what Jesus actually said and did during his ministry. Jesus of Nazareth was a historical person, a first-century Palestinian Jew who carried out a God-given ministry to his people. But he was rejected by them, condemned to death and executed. The 'character' of Jesus portrayed in the Markan narrative is the same Jesus, only now he is viewed through Christian eyes and seen through the prism of resurrection faith. The literary genre of 'Gospel' is a distinctive one in that it expresses in narrative form the Christological convictions of the early Christian community and their implications for the living out of discipleship of a crucified and risen Lord. Mark narrates the earthly career of a recent historical figure, Jesus of Nazareth, who is now the exalted Lord. Consequently, he is portrayed in the Gospel as both Lord and a truly human servant who suffered and died and who now, as risen Lord, continues to be present in the community of believers. Faith in the resurrection is crucial to appreciate this double perspective. A literary approach provides valuable insights because meaning is found in the encounter between text and reader in the very act of reading.[4]

In spite of gaps and inconsistencies, the Gospel of Mark is a coherent narrative capable of having a powerful impact on readers who allow themselves to be caught up in the drama of the story, experience the tensions and conflicts, identify with certain characters and feel the suspense leading up to the outcome. To readers who 'get lost' in the story by reading it in its entirety, a new way of looking at the world around them is opened up. Readers imaginatively enter the story world depicted by Mark as they endeavour to understand it on its own terms, albeit one based on historical events and people. Readers look to Mark's portrayal of Jesus and the disciples, who are now actors in the story, and to the events as they appear in the narrative. The plot, characters, settings, etc., represent Mark's view of life – including beliefs and values, and possibilities and limitations within which ordinary people live their lives – while the characters reveal the human condition. For these reasons, Mark deserves to be read on its own terms as an independent story apart from the other Gospels.

The Reign of God[5]

God's definitive reign is inaugurated with the ministry of Jesus. In Galilee, Jesus gathers disciples and establishes a family-like relationship among all who respond positively, regardless of their status. Jesus heals people with various ailments, expels unclean spirits, welcomes tax collectors and sinners, and feeds hungry people in the desert. In this way the rule of God is demonstrated so that people can respond, revealing by their response whether they accept it or not. For those who respond positively, the blessings and joys are real. But given the opposition generated by the rule of God, it is clear that it has not yet come in power and glory. In fact, the rule of God remains hidden for the most part, yet it makes its appearance in unexpected places outside expected channels. Jesus speaks in parables and refuses to explain them to outsiders or give signs to those who demand them. People must decide for themselves. Some are deaf and blind to what is going on; others perceive in the healings and exorcisms the beginning of the disclosure of God's rule. Another factor is that Jesus does not announce his identity, and when others publicly proclaim it he orders them to keep silent. Even when he finally reveals his identity before the High Priest and the Sanhedrin, God's rule remains hidden to those who are blind. In the narrative it is not apparent to most people that the Jesus who is sentenced to death is the agent of God's definitive rule.

At this inaugural stage of God's rule during the public life of Jesus, power is limited. While Jesus and his followers have power over demons, the destructive forces of nature, and all kinds of sickness, they do not impose God's rule on people. They use power in the service of others, not to coerce or dominate them. Although Jesus denounces opposition, he has no power to stop the oppressors by force and ends up becoming a victim instead. This first stage lasts during the entire public life of Jesus, even beyond his death and resurrection, when the disciples and others will proclaim God's rule to Israel and the nations. Nevertheless, as agent of God's rule, Jesus has power over forces that threaten and oppress people – Satan, demons, all kinds of illnesses, even nature itself. He is victorious over Satan in the desert after his Baptism in the Jordan and this victory is subsequently seen in the exorcisms he performs. Jesus breaks the stranglehold of Satan over the world; by expelling demons he demonstrates that God's rule is a tangible reality. He cures the demoniac in the synagogue at Capernaum, the man possessed by a legion of devils, the daughter of the Syrophoenician woman, the boy with a deaf-mute spirit and many more besides. The demons survive by dominating and destroying people; they embody the evil that controls people. The conflict with demons is often dramatic and violent as they try to gain power over Jesus by naming him, but Jesus demonstrates that he is the more powerful one.

Jesus exercises similar power over illness and various disabilities that oppress and diminish people. In that particular culture, sickness was generally viewed as a consequence of sin. Jesus cures a leper; heals sickness, afflictions and paralysis; restores sight, hearing and speech; pardons sin and restores a withered hand. He gives the disciples power to do likewise. Jesus also has power over nature as a force that can deprive and destroy people. He commands the wind, calms the sea, walks on the water; twice he multiplies food for hungry people. All these exercises of power occur mainly during his ministry in Galilee. As he moves towards Jerusalem they become less frequent. The cures of the blind man at Bethsaida and Bartimaeus are more in the nature of stories that symbolise the disciples' failure to 'see' what Jesus is teaching them, while the exorcism of the epileptic demoniac illustrates the necessity of faith and prayer on the part of the disciples. The cursing of the fig tree near Jerusalem is an enacted parable that points to the failure of Jewish leadership. Conflict predominates in the second half of Mark's narrative, but Jesus has no power to dominate people, to compel them to obey, or even to have faith in him.

Centrality of the Cross

Jesus carried out his mission, Mark informs us, not only by what he did and said, but most of all by what was done to him and by what he suffered. But Jesus didn't just put up with what was done to him – he willingly embraced it. He offered his life freely out of love for human beings (cf. 10:45). The Passion as told by Mark shows how Jesus responded to what was done to him. His story of the Passion and crucifixion is one of stark abandonment of Jesus. He is betrayed by Judas, one of the Twelve, forsaken by his disciples and denied by Peter. He is accused of blasphemy by the High Priest and passed over in favour of a murderer by the crowds. He is condemned by Pilate, mocked by the soldiers and jeered by the crowds at the foot of the cross. Jesus dies in darkness and seemingly also forsaken by God. As Mark relates it, in his sufferings and death, Jesus plumbs the depths of abandonment only to be vindicated by God on Easter Sunday morning.

It is not his sufferings as such that saves us, it is the love with which he embraced his suffering that is the important thing. Mark does not play down the scandal of the cross, or the terrible suffering involved, but portrays Jesus as a man of courage who freely embraces what is being done to him. Although innocent of the charges that were falsely brought against him, he confronts suffering and death with determination and dignity. His self-forgetfulness allows him the opportunity to encourage his disciples to pray, to fearlessly confront his captors, to boldly proclaim who he is, and to suffer humiliation at the hands of the soldiers in silence. He dies in excruciating agony on the cross amid the mockery of passers-by and the taunts of the religious authorities. Jesus didn't suffer and die to save us from pain, but to set an example for us to follow. He invites us to take up our cross and follow in his footsteps.

The life of human beings is also determined more by what is done to them rather than what they do themselves. As we journey through life, things happen to us that are completely outside of our control. There is, for example, illness, suffering and anguish; failure, disappointment and tragedy; loss of friends; relationship breakdown; and the death of those nearest to us. As we grow older, there is the onset of old age and eventually death. These painful experiences are largely outside our control, though they are part of what it means to be human. The real cross in life is not the one people choose for themselves, but the things that life throws at them. These are part of the human condition and nobody escapes them. Still, there is no point in being sentimental about suffering. It can make people angry, bitter or depressed, or it can make them better people. The value of suffering lies not in the pain of it, but in what people choose to make of it. Though the road of suffering is never an easy one, it is not the same since Jesus traversed it. The Passion story as told by Mark shows how Jesus responded to what was done to him. He absorbed the violence, the injustice and the abuse and transformed them by means of the love with which he embraced them. Those who follow his example can become, like him, a source of encouragement, comfort and blessing for others. They can give hope to all who suffer in the conviction that they too will share in Christ's Easter glory.

Human beings hope for and expect 'good news' from God concerning suffering and the cross, for suffering is the lot of every human being. There is pain and agony hidden behind every human face. In fact, human beings do not know how to deal with suffering and so they try to resist and struggle against it. They have a similar difficulty in reconciling suffering with a good and compassionate God. Mark tells us that whenever Jesus spoke about his Passion, his disciples neither understood nor accepted it. And yet, there can be 'good news' only if people take suffering seriously and somehow endeavour to move beyond it. This is what Jesus did. He assumed suffering, went beyond it and gave it meaning by triumphing over it. The risen Lord is someone who suffered and died. Suffering and death are overcome, not eliminated. When people fix their gaze on the cross of Jesus, they can be healed of the pain and anxiety they experience in the face of the mystery of suffering and death. It is not an answer that can totally satisfy rational human beings. Nevertheless, it is a consolation to know that Jesus has gone down the road of suffering ahead of us and can accompany us in our suffering as well. For those who link their sufferings with those of Christ, Mark assures us that they too, like him, will share in his victory over suffering and death and partake of his Easter glory.

Portrait of Jesus

Jesus is the central character in Mark's story. A scriptural prophecy announces his appearance and John the Baptist prepares the way. As Jesus is baptised, the heavens are opened, the Spirit descends and God's voice declares him as his Son. By the time Jesus speaks, the reader already knows his true identity and is willing to trust whatever he says or does. The unfolding story demonstrates Jesus as God's anointed (Messiah),[6] sent to inaugurate God's definitive rule. But he occupies no position of power or status in society. He gathers a group of disciples around him, goes about the countryside healing, exorcising demons, preaching and eating with sinners. He assumes that his authority is from God, yet works outside the official channels of authority to inaugurate God's rule. What Jesus does reveals the nature and extent of his authority from God; what he says discloses his self-understanding as God's agent. His words and actions express his values. What others say and how they react reveal the controversial aspects of his character. These reactions include amazement, fear, offence, opposition, as well as loyalty and attachment. No human being recognises him as God's Son during his public ministry; Peter identifies him as the Messiah at the halfway point of the narrative. It is only the pagan centurion who 'had seen how he had died' who identifies him as the Son of God (cf. 15:39).

The evangelist shows Jesus healing people, his popularity with the crowds, the opposition of the authorities, and the hardheadedness of the disciples. He maintains a favourable view of Jesus throughout the narrative and this leads readers to align themselves with him. Readers are overawed by the mysterious and demanding aspects of Jesus' character; the difficulty they recognise in following him helps readers identify with the different reactions of the other characters. Jesus issues an invitation to all to enter the rule of God. He is empowered to confront and heal oppressive forces in human life as well as offering a new teaching with authority behind it, often speaking in parables and paradoxical sayings. Because his authority comes directly from God, Jesus can act independently. He is not prevented from teaching and carrying out the ways of God by tradition, laws, political pressure or fear of indictment. He is even prepared to face execution and to be abandoned by all. On the other hand, he summons others into a family-like relationship in a loose community of people that will form the nucleus of the expanding rule of God until it reaches its fullness. Because this rule represents unconventional values, Jesus must resist any pressures that would deflect him from his commitment. He is tested by Satan, by the authorities, even by the disciples who object to his having to face rejection and execution in Jerusalem. He struggles to submit to God's will in Gethsemane and dies apparently abandoned by God.

With authority from God and empowered by the Spirit, Jesus exorcises demons, heals the sick, forgives sinners, interprets laws, appoints twelve disciples to share his authority, commands nature, makes prophecies, enters Jerusalem as triumphant king and cleanses the Temple. He exercises power over unclean spirits, cures lepers and a woman with a haemorrhage, expels a legion of demons, raises a dead girl, and eats with Gentiles. All of these involved contact with people who were regarded as unclean by the religious authorities. Jesus refers to himself as a prophet, and the crowds associate him with one of the Old Testament prophetic figures. He prophesies the circumstances of his death and the events that will take place afterwards until the final establishment of God's rule. Jesus challenges hallowed institutions and customs, knows what God's will is in legal matters, condemns human traditions and disregards ritual practices. His interpretation of the law favours serving people, rather than vice versa. Although he has power over demons, illness and nature, he does not have authority to determine who will sit at his right or left hand in glory, nor does he know when the exact time of the end will come. Since he has no earthly position of power, he has to evade the authorities' efforts to pressure and silence him. Furthermore, since he has no power from God to lord it over others, he remains vulnerable in his confrontations with authorities. He cannot force people to have faith, or make authorities change their minds. Yet despite all this, Jesus is the one whom God will establish in power in the future when he comes in glory.

Jesus shows great trust in God and is dependent on him for all things. He becomes a model of faith. He is also portrayed as a person of prayer and gives himself wholeheartedly to God's rule in trust and obedience: 'Let it be as you, not I, would have it' (14:36). Jesus relates to people by way of service and the disciples are to follow his example, not lording it over others but using their power to benefit them instead. Jesus uses his power to liberate people as concrete expressions of his compassion to bring God's rule to others. He interprets even the desire for healing as an indication of turning to God. He serves the disciples by teaching them without controlling their responses: 'If anyone wants to be a follower of mine ...' (8:34). He leads the disciples primarily by example, especially in the face of persecution and death. He dies as a result of his total obedience to the will of God.

Jesus does not set out to please or to oppose the authorities but names and condemns their failures, leaving them free to choose their response. Jesus is not a political or military Messiah, nor is he a demagogue; he makes no attempt even to defend himself. He renounces all claims to status, wealth and power, even his very life. He never uses power for his own advantage. He acknowledges his true identity only when confronted by the High Priest, being usually content to refer to himself as the Son of Man, a title that embraces the power to forgive sins, authority over the Sabbath, his rejection and execution, his rising from the dead and his future coming. His final renunciation comes when he is executed for the sake of God's rule, crucifixion being the ultimate price of a life of service and his refusal to save himself.

During the course of the Markan narrative, Jesus moves from being a powerful healer and provider to a vulnerable one who is rejected and executed. In the first half of the narrative, the breaking in of God's rule is shown in Jesus' words and deeds; in the second half the authorities persecute and seek to destroy the one who would inaugurate that rule. Jesus senses the inevitability of his death and sets his face towards it. He invites the hostility of the authorities by his triumphant entry into Jerusalem and his attack on the Temple system. Rather than passively accepting death, he protests and condemns the actions of the authorities. He accepts his execution as an inevitable consequence of being faithful to the rule of God, despite experiencing fear and anguish at the prospect. He faces his captors without resistance, gives truthful evidence to the authorities, endures ridicule in silence and experiences the full pain of crucifixion. God does not rescue Jesus from his ordeal and he faces death alone, abandoned by his friends and seemingly by God as well. In the midst of this abandonment and pain, he faces humiliation, shame and ridicule by soldiers, high priests and scribes. He is buried by a member of the Sanhedrin. But the Jesus who is executed and dies is also raised and will return in power and glory at the end of the ages.

It is the commitment to be faithful, at whatever cost, that Mark emphasises both for Jesus and his followers. Jesus' death is the result of human actions, but it is also in accordance with God's will. He believes that his death has meaning as an act of service for others, 'a ransom for many' (10:45) by which people are liberated for a life of service in God's rule. They are freed from their own fears of rejection, persecution and execution so that they can have the courage to spread the rule of God to the ends of the earth. At the Last Supper Jesus portrays his upcoming death as the sealing of a covenant:[7] 'This is my blood, the blood of the covenant, which is to be poured out for many' (14:24) as a covenant sacrifice. His death will seal the covenant of God's rule with all in the new community of Jews and Gentiles who will follow the way of service in God's rule.

The Markan narrative also recounts events associated with Jesus' death. The Temple veil is rent in two, symbolising the destruction of the Temple as the locus of God's presence among his people, and with it the end of Jewish spiritual leadership. The evangelist wishes the reader to see that Jesus is indeed God's Messiah: at Calvary everything Jesus' opponents say in mockery is true; the charge placed over his head reads: 'The King of the Jews'; the ridicule and jeering of the bystanders is ironic testimony to the true kingship of Jesus as agent of God's rule. The Anointed One is King because he is willing to live for others even at the cost of dying. Only when Jesus dies in this manner does a character acknowledge Jesus as 'Son of God'. But the death of Jesus is not the end. Jesus is raised to life; the grave is empty. Although there are no resurrection appearances in Mark, the fate of Jesus is clear – he has been raised from the dead and will return in glory and power (cf. 13:26). The absence of resurrection appearances serves to highlight the life that Jesus lived: he was one who served others, who encountered opposition and was crucified in the service of God's rule.

Portrait of Disciples

Jesus chose twelve to follow him, each of whom is identified by name. They form a group of companions around him. There are others who also follow Jesus – women and minor characters who carry out discipleship functions. Jesus chose twelve from the crowd to be with him so that he could send them out to participate in his mission. They have no connection with any authority groupings. Mark's characterisation of the Twelve reveals a continuous struggle between living on God's terms and living on human terms. Initially they strive to live on God's terms when they leave everything to follow Jesus, yet they continue to be preoccupied with their own security, status and power. What they actually do reveals their loyalty to Jesus; what they say exposes their difficulties in following through. They are on Jesus' side but fail to live up fully to the expectations set for them. They possess conflicting traits and much of their portrayal is built on their deficient understanding, fears and lack of faith. Unlike the authorities, they want to understand but are prevented by false expectations and fears. Their traits unfold in response to changing developments in the story. The disciples serve as a contrast to Jesus in their failure to properly respond to the rule of God, and much of Jesus' teaching is given in the context of correcting their attitudes and behaviour.

From the beginning they attach themselves to Jesus as disciples to a master, having left behind everything to enter into a family-like relationship with him. They are devoted to Jesus and stay with him despite corrections, storms or hunger, with little or no praise or assurance of immediate reward. Yet they are beset by difficulties because of their fears and lack of understanding. They do not understand Jesus' parables; they fail to see the full possibilities of the rule of God. They are also frightened by the storm, overawed by Jesus' power over it, perplexed by his walking on the water, and anxious about their lack of provisions. Fear for their well-being prevents them from understanding, and their inability to understand leaves them terrified. It is not that they lack intelligence, rather they are thinking more on human terms and have not grasped the mindset of faith necessary to embrace the rule of God. At the heart of it all is lack of trust in the rule of God: 'Are you still without perception?' (8:21) Jesus asks in exasperation.

Midway through the narrative, Peter as spokesperson for the disciples identifies Jesus as the Messiah, but he mistakes him for a triumphant Messiah who will reward his followers with positions of power and honour. The disciples, with their human mindset, reject the idea that persecution and death may be a consequence of service in God's rule. They are fearful at the prospect of persecution and suffering, and are hesitant in asking Jesus the meaning of the predictions of his suffering, death and resurrection: 'They did not understand and were afraid to ask him' (9:32). Their way of coping with the prospect of Jesus' death is to cling to their personal hopes and values – their desire for honour and power (9:34; 10:37). But God's rule involves becoming the least of all and a servant of all, not a means to gain favour or be rewarded. In their culture, serving was the task of slaves and women. Their human and cultural mindset prevents them from carrying out their mission. Yet, as a result of their experiences on their journey with Jesus, they do gradually begin to change. They follow Jesus to Jerusalem and are determined to be loyal to him until death. However, they have overestimated their ability to be faithful by failing to take into account their human limitations and frailty in the face of death. At the Last Supper, when Jesus predicts that they will all fail him, they vehemently object. Yet when the time comes, fear takes over and they flee for their lives. Only Peter follows Jesus at a distance, but in response to the servant girl's questions, he renounces Jesus three times, swearing that he never knew him. But then he remembers Jesus' prediction and breaks down weeping. It is this acknowledgement of failure that opens up new possibilities of a turnabout, but at this point in the narrative the disciples disappear.

Unlike the authorities, the disciples are not against Jesus, but they fail to be *for* him. The final scene at the empty tomb evokes a similar ambivalent attitude. The women witness the crucifixion, burial and empty tomb, yet fail to deliver the young man's joyful message to the disciples. So the fate of the disciples in the narrative hangs in the balance; their restoration depends on their willingness to return to Galilee. Readers also must face the disciples' terrible failures and can't help wondering how they will fare in the future of the story world. Mark has characterised the disciples as fearful, with little or no understanding, overly concerned with self-protection and preoccupied with their own self-importance. Although, despite obstacles, they left everything to follow Jesus, they failed to prepare themselves for the prospect of persecution and death. Readers have a lot to learn from their failures. Nevertheless, Jesus still promises to go ahead of them to Galilee after his resurrection where they are invited to follow. Readers can do the same – even when they fail, they can always begin again.

The Reader

What have readers been experiencing as they read the Markan narrative and how have they been affected by that experience? Readers have come with different expectations, perspectives, reactions and prejudices. By the way he tells the story, the evangelist has led readers to experience the powerful blessings of God's rule step by step. They are able to enter into new life, understand and embrace the expectations and cost of the rule of God, and be empowered to live for the Good News with courage and perseverance. These correspond to the main development of the narrative: the experiencing of the power-filled rule of God in Galilee; overcoming resistance to it on the journey to Jerusalem; and facing persecution and death in its service in Jerusalem. The evangelist guides his readers and leads them to follow Jesus through the way he tells the story. Readers identify with the disciples and learn both from their positive and negative examples; they side with Jesus against the authorities and learn from his teaching and example the full cost of following him. They also witness the empty grave.

What Mark has described is nothing less than momentous. The long-awaited rule of God has finally arrived; throughout the first half of the narrative readers see the effects in healings, exorcisms, cleansings, forgiveness of sin, feeding the hungry and overcoming the onslaughts of nature. They also witness hope for the outcasts and marginalised and the challenge to all forms of human oppression and abuse of power. Readers are invited to embrace this new reality in joy and amazement, to be converted, and to put their faith in the Good News. Mark has guided readers in following Jesus, nudged them to identify with the disciples who, despite their failures, have an ongoing relationship with Jesus. Readers have already been given inside information about Jesus' identity as Messiah and Son of God and are privy to explanations given privately to the disciples.

After Peter's initial recognition of Jesus as the Messiah, readers experience startling and difficult developments when Jesus predicts his sufferings, death and resurrection and teaches the disciples the demands and cost of following him. They are forced to grapple with these challenges, they must revise their expectations and, like Jesus, be prepared to face persecution and death. The rule of God demands relinquishing the quest for status, power and wealth to instead embrace lowliness, service and self-giving. The evangelist teaches through the negative example and misunderstandings of the disciples in such a way that readers are inclined to sympathise with their struggles. They are invited to work through their own struggles and resistance and to strengthen their allegiance to Jesus. Mark invites his readers to follow Jesus to Golgotha and leads them to see revealed in the cross God's idea of what true greatness is – the willingness to risk security, status, power and even life itself in the service of God's rule. They are encouraged to face their own fears of persecution and death – fears that might otherwise overwhelm and paralyse them. In the end, readers are left with Jesus and identify with him. The example of a life given for others in the face of death helps to free readers from the grip of self-centredness and self-preservation so that they can live for others even in the face of persecution and death. The narrative invites readers to become faithful followers of Jesus through the very act of reading, by allowing their imagination to visualise the characters, what they say and what they do, and to express what they themselves feel or think.

At the grave comes the announcement readers are hoping to expect: 'He has risen, he is not here' (16:6). God has had the last word that can now become the first word for readers who wish to follow in the footsteps of Jesus. It is Jesus who has been raised from the dead and God will also raise those who associate with him and follow him. He will also raise those who live the rule of God and are willing to face persecution and death in order to be raised, and those who live a life without end when the rule of God comes in power and glory. As the women are told to invite the disciples to follow Jesus to Galilee in spite of their flight and denial, readers are assured that no matter what their own fears or failures may be, Jesus is still calling them to follow him. The abrupt ending of the narrative, in a final ironic twist, points readers to a new beginning. The women fled in fear and silence and 'said nothing to a soul, for they were afraid' (16:8). At this point the story confounds readers for there is no satisfying or happy ending, no sense of closure. Readers themselves are left to complete the story. They can see their own lives and their own society reflected in the story world of Mark. Having experienced the story, they are invited to think anew about the meaning of life, its purpose, its possibilities and its outcome. As they struggle to live lives that are more authentically human, they encourage others to share this new life as well.

Repent and Believe

Mark, the Gospel of catechumens, leads baptismal candidates to break with former images of God in order to accept a new type of experience of God and his love in obedience to the demands of the crucified and risen Christ. Catechumens must learn a new lifestyle, a new way of living and relating the way of Jesus by first of all abandoning images of God made to the measure of their own self-interests and suited to their personal tastes and comforts. Human beings, it seems, cannot survive for long without placing reliance on something or someone outside of themselves. We humans quickly realise that we are not self-sufficient and we experience the precariousness of our lives rooted in the tension between desires and limits, in the threats posed by the hazards of life and by the prospect of death. As created beings we experience life in two different and dissimilar ways with contrasting and divergent characteristics. On the one hand, there is the desire for something above and beyond our present experience in order to enhance the quality of life and to acquire knowledge that leads to its mastery and control. There is no limit to what one may desire, imagine or inquire about, and this is entirely natural and so God-given. On the other hand, there are limits to the realisation of our potential with the result that we also experience inescapable shortcomings that tend to encroach more and more with the passing of years until the narrowing comes to a point in the experience of illness, tragedy, old age and eventually death. Desires and limits interact and influence each other in such a way that a necessary tension exists between them. Since this tension is powerful and can be the cause of suffering, there is the understandable temptation to short-circuit it in an attempt to resolve it. Precisely because there is in human beings a strong desire for enhancement of life and immortality, as well as for knowledge to master one's existence, there is the ever-present temptation to overstep human limitation by using, contrary to the Creator's intention, creaturely objects of desire as 'immortality symbols'.[8] These are used to assuage the tension between desires and limits as a means of escaping the experience of insignificance and the dread of extinction, but also to give the illusion of being the guarantor of one's own well-being. Ultimately, we cannot be indifferent to our fate and so we search for some ground for our faith and hope, either in God or some idol of our own making.

Immortality symbols can take many forms, reflecting the temptation to self-sufficiency by making an idol that can be manipulated by us. For example, money, pleasure, drugs, domination, physical comfort to be master of one's own well-being, or consumerism. Human relationships may also be sought for affection, recognition or self-esteem; even 'religious experience' may become a means to satisfy one's desires by making God into an instrument in the fulfilment of one's wishes. Moral self-righteousness also may express itself in legalism as a means of self-justification rather than of self-transcendence. Knowledge too may become an idol when it is sought to enable one to be master of one's destiny by searching for an intelligible pattern in history that will eliminate risks and so help predict and control the course of history. All of these function to make oneself the guarantor of one's present and future well-being, as a means to overcome failure, suffering and death.

All idolatry is ultimately self-idolatry, making ourselves into a god by refusing to transcend ourselves. The human tendency to idolatry and the use of immortality symbols reflect the drive to self-sufficiency and self-fulfilment – the divinisation of created things in the service of self-divinisation. It is a maladaptive attempt to cope with creatureliness and the problem of evil in the world, a self-protective attempt to evade the powerful tension between desires and limits. In the end, imprisoned by our own quest for self-fulfilment, we are trapped and prevented from achieving the fulfilment that comes from self-transcendence, through a proper relationship with God and other people. Conversion means a turning away from the self-destruction that is a consequence of seeking self-fulfilment, which in turn is self-idolatry, self-gratification, self-indulgence and self-satisfaction. Abandonment to our cravings becomes a way of life that ultimately leads to death, for no human being can fulfil what God alone can fulfil. That is why self-fulfilment is an illusion, because we are made for something greater.

Human beings cannot satisfy their boundless desires by themselves, yet there remains a radical hunger and thirst for something or Someone that transcends their own finite reality. That is why transcendence of self is at the heart of the Christian tradition, for human authenticity is achieved in self-transcendence, not in self-absorption. Human beings need to be rescued from their self-centredness – they cannot save themselves. Therefore, what we call sin is primarily the exaltation and the deification of the self above all else. If the human thrust to self-transcendence, beginning with the desire to know and extending to the desire to live responsibly and happily, is to be brought to fulfilment, there must be the hope of Someone who transcends ourselves. Christians believe that a way out of the prison of the self involves a process of transformation, of self-transcendence, of conversion to the loving God. This is revealed by Jesus as the ultimate fulfilment of the human capacity for self-transcendence that liberates people from the chains of self-absorption and the illusion of a merely human fulfilment.

In religious conversion, one no longer stands at the centre of one's world, but surrenders oneself to God in faith, hope and love, and leaves it to God to bring about the ultimate solution to life and death. Faith is a knowledge born of love in the light of which all other values are relativised. With hope, one is liberated from the despair regarding the fulfilment of one's deepest desires and from the presumption of wishing to be the guarantor of one's own fulfilment. God's love floods our hearts and calls for a response. And so, authentic religious experience is the experience of the God of Jesus Christ that comes to us when we pay attention to the story of Jesus. The way Jesus lived and died reveals the meaning of authentic love and gives us a vision of the true God. The life story of the crucified and risen Christ is that of the Word of God made flesh, so that in his human nature we encounter the true God.

Conclusion

The story told by Mark prepares catechumens for the first moment of conversion by inviting them to break with former images of God and to accept the God revealed in Jesus Christ. It leads them to reject all idols and to accept the rule of God who demands total self-abandonment to his will in the service of others. The suffering Messiah portrayed by Mark reveals how costly it can become to make God a priority in their lives. The way of the cross, the pattern of Jesus' self-transcendent love, is, according to Mark, the only way to authentic human existence and becomes an implicit condemnation of all forms of idolatry. Mark summons us to a life of following the way of the crucified Lord: 'If anyone wants to be a follower of mine, let him renounce himself and take up his cross and follow me. For anyone who wants to save his life will lose it; but anyone who loses his life for my sake, and for the sake of the gospel, will save it' (8:34-35). Commitment to the Father's will necessitates the suffering of overcoming self-will: 'Let it be as you, not I, would have it' (14:37), and the pain of utter self-abandonment: 'My God, my God, why have you deserted me?' (15:34). If catechumens are to enter into the fullness of life that belongs to the risen Lord, they must also experience the suffering of self-denial that is entailed in seeking and doing the Father's will by embracing the Christian vision of a life that is Spirit-filled, love-filled and God-centred. The process of conversion may be symbolised as a journey away from the self to become centred on God. Mark's Gospel is 'the beginning' (cf. 1:1), with the implication that the story is still in progress and has yet to reach its culmination in the fullness of the kingdom. The Good News is that this way of living – God's way of living and loving – can be ours if we accept the invitation to repent and believe the Good News brought by Jesus.

The newly converted Christian then must reckon with the cost of living a life so radically God-oriented 'in this adulterous and sinful generation' (8:38). This gives an active meaning to the cross as the ultimate symbol of a life's commitment for the sake of others. The cross is to be willingly 'taken up' – not merely endured – in a lifelong process of conversion. The disciple, who has begun to live as Christ lived, very quickly comes to realise the power of the Good News to arouse opposition, having seen the large place that conflict occupies in Mark's narrative. So it would be surprising if Jesus' followers were never called upon to suffer in a similar manner. True service is authenticated by voluntary self-sacrifice on behalf of others, otherwise there is the danger of self-deception. Mark presents the *via crucis* (way of the cross) as Good News, as the inevitable growing pains that attend the process of self-transcendence, and as the gateway to glory. His whole narrative is structured as a way of the cross to underscore the truth that the path of love is not the way to easy popularity, but the road to true glory that can be achieved only by suffering.

The numerous conflict stories in Mark demonstrate the various forms that human resistance can take when faced with the grace and demand of God's rule. Jesus' adversaries represent the mindset of those who oppose the event and process of Christian conversion that brings about personal and social transformation, the result of surrendering to the rule of God. This surrender will inevitably entail conflict, both at intrapersonal and interpersonal levels. Consequently, we might well question the tendency to believe that conflict at both levels is always an indication that something is wrong. Perhaps, rather, we should be concerned about the authenticity of a Christian life that does not encounter resistance or opposition. These conflict stories, however, must not be read outside the context of the Good News that enables self-sacrifice in the belief that God is love; where there is true love there will always be struggle. Nevertheless, Mark's Gospel ends with a promise of a return to Galilee to encounter the risen Lord. In this way he presents the full spectrum of the conversion process – from the call in Galilee to the purification of false values in the course of the journey to Jerusalem, through suffering abandonment and death of the old self, to reconciliation and renewal. The death of Jesus is not the last word in Mark. The empty tomb gives meaning to Jesus' crucifixion as a movement from death to fullness of life that is at the heart of the Christian message. Mark chose to emphasise the suffering aspect by ending his narrative with the empty tomb rather than recount resurrection appearances. Triumph over death is assured in Mark, though it is not narrated.

Jesus preached the Good News of the reign of God. He not only announced the reign of God, his whole public ministry was shot through with 'deeds of power' (*dynameis*, 6:2, 5; 9:39) that we call miracles. Miracle stories occupy one-third of Mark's narrative. They present in dramatic and symbolic form the ultimate purpose of his ministry to destroy the power of evil and death in all its forms and manifestations in order to free human beings for fullness of life. Jesus' main activities involved teaching and tending to the sick, the possessed, the outcasts and the socially isolated. Mark relates twelve healings and exorcisms, and other miracles such as the stilling of the storm, raising Jairus's daughter, the two miracles of the loaves, walking on the lake, as well as five summaries. When Jesus heals sick people, drives out demons, calms the waters and raises the dead, he is confronting the powers of chaos, healing a damaged and distorted world so that the reign of God may become visible. The world in which Jesus lived attributed many physical and psychic ailments to the power of evil spirits, and Mark shows Jesus' commitment to freeing people from all kinds of oppressive powers by giving specific examples as well as summaries of cures.

Miracles, though, occur only in response to faith. Jesus says to the woman with the haemorrhage: 'Daughter, *your* faith has restored you to health; go in peace and be free from your complaint' (5:34). It was belief in Jesus as Saviour that healed her. If faith is not present, miracles cannot happen. In Nazareth, Jesus could not work miracles because of their unbelief (cf. 6:5-6). During his ministry, Jesus healed only individuals; he did not perform any group healing because God's action is tied to the faith of concrete people. Exorcisms are Jesus' confrontations with the powers of evil and everything in the world that stands in opposition to God. His miracles are always worked for other people; they are acts of concern for persons in need. Jesus rejected any kind of authenticating miracle and any wonder performed for show (cf. 8:11-13; 15:31-32). His miracles are signs of the beginning of the new world, the breaking in of the reign of God.

Mark uses miracle stories to give instruction, to exhort and to point to the person and action of Jesus. He is telling us that Jesus not only made the paralytic walk, but invites us to believe that Jesus has authority on earth to forgive sins — that he not only healed the sick, cleansed lepers, cast out devils, but also demonstrated his ability to overcome the powers of evil and sin so that people can be whole again. He not only opened the eyes of the blind and enabled the dumb to speak, but has the power to make people see and proclaim the truth of God. He not only fed hungry people in the desert, but also dispenses spiritual food to nourish followers in their pilgrimage through a barren land to their destination. He not only calmed the storm and walked on the waves, but also restrained the destructive forces inherent in nature and in society. He not only raised a child to life, but he himself is the resurrection and the life. It is the resurrection of

Jesus that authenticates all these signs, the full implications of which are seen only in the light of the resurrection. All of them witness to the truth that in Jesus, God's rule and with it God's salvation begins to draw near. These are realities grounded in concrete events and people, fulfilling and surpassing Israel's hopes when viewed through the eyes of faith. The life of Jesus then becomes an apocalypse – an unveiling of the truth of God, his power and his purpose for people of faith that fulfils the promise of Jesus to his disciples: 'I tell you solemnly, there is no one who has left house, brothers, sisters, father, children or land for my sake and for the sake of the gospel, who will not be repaid a hundred times over ... now in this present time, and in the world to come, eternal life' (10:29-31).

NOTES

1. Mark was probably the first to connect the notion of the Good News (i.e. what God accomplished in the life, death and resurrection of Jesus, the Messiah) to a narrative of what Jesus himself said and did and called it a Gospel, or Good News (1:1). By shaping Jesus' ministry in a way that reaches its climax in the Passion account, Mark invites his readers to understand Jesus' words and deeds to be inextricably linked with it. Because Mark set out the traditions about Jesus in narrative form, the term 'Gospel' henceforth will have the connotation of a literary medium as well as a message.

2. In the most ancient and reliable manuscripts, the Gospel ends at 16:8. Verses 9-20, which now form part of the canonical Gospel of Mark, seem to have been added later. They contain a general summary of appearances of the risen Christ, reflecting traditions found in Luke and John.

3. The prophet of the exile announced the good news of Israel's liberation from captivity in Babylon and the return to the Promised Land (cf. Is 40:9; 41:27; 52:7). In the New Testament it refers to the Good News preached by Jesus that God's rule, foretold by the prophets in the Old Testament, is now being definitively inaugurated.

4. An excellent example of a narrative approach to Mark is D. Rhoads, J. Dewey, D. Michie, *Mark as Story*, second edition (Minneapolis: Augsburg Fortress, 1999), to which this section is much indebted.

5. The kingdom, reign or rule of God expressed Israel's hopes and longings for a time when God would rule over Israel and the nations in justice and peace, unlike Israel's kings who failed the people and instead became agents of oppression. Mark portrays Jesus not only announcing that coming kingdom, but as actually inaugurating it in word and deed. Jesus' preaching and healing ministry is carried out within the framework of the rule of God which is now close at hand (cf. 1:15). Future manifestations of God's sovereignty are both expected and promised when God's reign will be definitively established and Jesus returns in glory at the end of the ages. Jesus takes up the Old Testament symbol of God's sovereignty and redefines it. Rather than a visible kingdom dominating earthly realms, Jesus speaks of a kingdom that is real, but hidden at the present time and only discernable to the eyes of faith. Yet it is not simply a 'spiritual' reality, as though it had no implications regarding how people live their lives both individually and corporately in the here and now. It is a gift of God made present in Jesus and calls for a radical reorientation of life's priorities and loyalties by following Jesus as a disciple.

6. In the Old Testament, the word 'Messiah' usually referred to the reigning Davidic king. With the exile and the end of the Davidic rule, the hope persisted that a future descendant of David would restore Israel's fortunes. By the time of Christ, the hope for liberation was expressed in a variety of ways. One was the expectation of a Davidic descendant who would defeat Israel's enemies, gather the dispersed Jews and settle the tribes in the land (*Psalms of Solomon*, first century BC). Jesus reinterprets this symbol. He is not a powerful king sent to deliver Israel, but the shepherd of Israel foretold by the prophets who would seek out the lost. His own lifestyle, preaching and actions point to a messianic vocation, but it is now redefined as a suffering Messiah, one who offers his life for the sake of others.

7. Covenant was a central symbol, used in the Old Testament, of God's special relationship with Israel as God's people and sealed by the covenant at Sinai. It was borrowed from the political and social world of the ancient Near East to symbolise the initiative taken by God, and was understood as containing both promise and demand. It was ratified in a solemn religious ceremony (cf. Ex 19–24). Israel's historians present the history of Israel (cf. Jos–2 K, the Deuteronomic history comprising Joshua, Judges, 1 & 2 Samuel and 1 & 2 Kings) as a flagrant betrayal of that covenant leading to the exile. The prophets also denounced Israel's infidelities but looked beyond inevitable catastrophe to a time when God would establish a new covenant (cf. Jr 31:31-34) and bestow on his people a new heart and a new spirit (cf. Ezk 36:26-27). This would be effected by the Servant who will justify 'many' through his sufferings

(cf. Is 53), and who will bring Israel and the nations into full covenant relationship with God. The covenant that Jesus enacted by his suffering and death will realise the one promised by the prophets. It was ritually anticipated at the Last Supper and continues in the Eucharistic liturgy of the Church to this day.

8. Cf. E. Becker, *The Denial of Death* (New York: The Free Press, 1975).

CHAPTER THREE

SECOND MOMENT: COMMUNITY LIFE – THE GOSPEL OF MATTHEW

Introduction

The second stage of Christian formation is represented by the Gospel of Matthew – a catechist's Gospel – and so is suitable for post-baptismal instruction. Matthew provides a manual to help the newly baptised mature in their experience of God's love within the community of believers. Authentic commitment to the gift of God's love in Jesus Christ is possible only within the community of Christian believers where the risen Christ is now present (cf. 28:20). Having broken the chains that bound them to themselves, Matthew leads the baptised to the new experience of living out their relationship to Christ in the company of other believers. That is why the Gospel contains a considerable amount of details concerning Jesus' teaching, moral precepts and ethical instructions, absent from Mark, to instruct newly formed Christians in all aspects of living, in particular social involvement *within* the community. The baptised now become disciples, for they have taken upon themselves the yoke of Jesus to learn from him (cf. 11:29), and the Church becomes the discipleship of Jesus' family (cf. 12:49-50).

The Gospel of Matthew is a well-structured, highly articulate and deeply theological narrative. This is evident especially in Matthew's arrangement, adaptation and structuring of the material available to him from various sources. His Gospel is a combination of alternating narratives and discourses. Five lengthy discourses are inserted into the narrative of the Gospel at strategic points. The obvious care with which he has woven them together helps us to discern where his main interest lies. Many important sayings of Jesus are included in the discourses, clustered around basic motifs that help to bring the newly baptised into vital contact with Jesus' teaching. Nevertheless, this discourse material is inserted into the narrative of a living person, and so Matthew manages to keep his focus on the person of Jesus and his kingdom as the Good News of God's salvation. The subject matter of Matthew's narrative is God's saving actions in Jesus Christ, addressed to the Church of his time to help it understand, clarify and live out its faith in the risen Jesus. The five discourses, though, add an important structuring element to the Gospel; each one is preceded by a narrative section and ends with a concluding formula. No other evangelist gives the teaching of Jesus such prominence, so much so that in time the Gospel of Matthew came to be regarded as a catechist's or teacher's manual. The following outline will highlight where Matthew's emphasis lay.

Outline of Matthew

1. **Introduction: Origin and Infancy of Jesus (1:1–2:23)**
   a. Identity of Jesus: genealogy and conception (1:1-25).
   b. Birth and destiny of Jesus: magi, flight to Egypt, massacre, return to Galilee (2:1-23).
2. **Preaching of the Kingdom in Deed and Word (3:1–7:29)**
   a. Narrative: John's preaching, Baptism of Jesus, temptations, Galilean ministry (3:1–4:25).
   b. Discourse: Sermon on the Mount, beatitudes, fulfilling the law, almsgiving, prayer, fasting, judging others, the *Golden Rule*, true discipleship (5:1–7:29).

3. **Ministry in Galilee (8:1–10:42)**
   a. Narrative: miracle stories intermingled with discipleship stories (8:1–9:38).
   b. Discourse: sending out of the Twelve, hardships and conditions of discipleship (10:1-42).
4. **Opposition and Teaching on the Kingdom (11:1–13:52)**
   a. Narrative: Jesus and John, reproaches on unrepentant towns, Jesus interprets the law and overcomes Satan, Jesus' true family (11:1–12:50).
   b. Discourse: parables of the kingdom (13:1-52).
5. **Community, Peter, Discipleship (13:53–18:35)**
   a. Narrative: rejection at Nazareth, death of John, miracles of loaves, Jesus walks on the water, disputes with Pharisees, healings, Peter's profession of faith, prophecies of Passion, transfiguration, prominence of Peter (13:53-17:27).
   b. Discourse: greatest in the kingdom, scandal, care for the lost, fraternal correction, prayer, forgiveness (18:1-35).
6. **Journey to Jerusalem and Ministry There (19:1–25:46)**
   a. Narrative: teaching, parables, healings, entry to Jerusalem, cleansing of Temple, controversies with authorities (19:1–23:39).
   b. Discourse: eschatological discourse, seven parables ending with Last Judgement scene (24:1-25:46).
7. **Passion, Death and Resurrection (26:1-28:20)**
   a. Conspiracy against Jesus, Last Supper, agony in garden (26:1-46).
   b. Arrest, trials before the Sanhedrin and Pilate, mockery, crucifixion, death, burial, guard at tomb (26:47–27:66).
   c. Empty tomb, bribery of guards, resurrection appearances (28:1-20).

Storyline

Since the storyline of Matthew extends from Jesus' birth to his resurrection, but, unlike Luke-Acts, does not continue into the post-Easter period, his characterisation of Church life is communicated indirectly in the narrative. The story of Jesus and of the disciples is narrated on two levels simultaneously, so that the pre-Easter narrative framework becomes transparent for the post-Easter Church and its faith in Jesus as risen Lord. Accordingly, the disciples are often addressed as the post-Easter community (e.g. chapters 10 and 18). The Twelve represent the larger body of disciples, at times representing all the post-Easter Christians, so that the reader can easily identify with them.

The Infancy Narrative (1:1–2:23) forms the prologue of the Gospel and sounds major themes that will reverberate throughout the entire narrative. It consists of a genealogy and five stories that present the birth of Jesus as the climax of Israel's history and the events surrounding his birth as the fulfilment of Old Testament prophecy. Beginning with a genealogy that inserts Jesus within the community of his people, the first story describes the virginal conception of Jesus as the work of the Holy Spirit. Through Joseph's adoption, the child belongs to the family of David, thereby fulfilling the prophecy of Isaiah 7:14. The birth of Jesus elicits two responses. The powerful Jerusalem elite rejects and tries to murder him. In contrast, Gentile wise men led by an astral phenomenon pay homage to him. God thwarts Herod's murderous intent by a warning dream and Jesus finds refuge in Egypt, thereby reliving the exodus experience of Israel. After Herod's death, the family returns and resides at Nazareth.

In the following section (3:1–4:25), Matthew takes up the order of Jesus' ministry found in Mark, beginning with the preaching of John the Baptist who urges the people to repent in the light of God's coming reign by producing the appropriate fruit. John testifies to Jesus' superior role in manifesting God's saving presence in both judgement and salvation. The Baptism of Jesus is the occasion on which he is equipped for his ministry and proclaimed Son of God. He is then subjected to a triple temptation reminiscent of those of Israel in the desert. Obedience is a characteristic of true Sonship, and Jesus is tempted by the devil to rebel against God overtly in the third temptation, more indirectly in the first two. Each refusal of Jesus is expressed in the language of Deuteronomy (cf. 8:3; 6:13, 16). The victory of Jesus, the true Israel and the true Son, contrasts with the failure of disobedient Israel. The beginning of his preaching fulfils the prophecy of Isaiah 8:23-9:1. In his proclamation, the Kingdom of Heaven has already begun with his calling of disciples and his preaching and healing ministry. The function of the narrative in chapters 1 to 4 is to establish Jesus as the Messiah of his community, a Moses-like figure, but greater than Moses, for he is Emmanuel, God-with-us. It also prepares the way for true discipleship in the stories about John the Baptist and Jesus at the beginning of his public ministry. Jesus is the one who does *all* righteousness (cf. 3:15) and lives by *every* word that comes from God (cf. 4:11). Together with the calling of the first disciples, they prepare for further teaching on discipleship in the Sermon on the Mount.

The first discourse (5:1–7:29), a Matthean composition, begins with the Beatitudes, which express the essential spiritual profile of the true disciple modelled on Jesus himself, and is characterised by a spirit of trust and dependence on God. The mission of the disciples is compared to that of salt and light. What follows is Jesus' interpretation of the Old Law as the completion and perfection of the Mosaic Torah so that disciples are enabled to become perfect like their heavenly Father (cf. 5:48). Jesus also reshapes the traditional Jewish expressions of piety by warning against ostentatiousness. He gives further practical instruction on attitudes towards other people and material things, culminating in the Golden Rule. The discourse concludes with a warning to those who say but do not practice.

The narrative in 8:1–9:37 highlights the authority of Jesus in deed, interspersed with stories on discipleship. It comprises nine miracles including healings, calming of a storm, an exorcism and six discipleship stories, with a comment on the severe requirements of discipleship that leads to dialogue about Jesus' followers and the nature of discipleship. Jesus is presented both as a worker of miracles and a teacher of the kingdom. His actions manifest God's powerful and merciful empire, especially towards the marginalised and outsiders. The narrative ends with a transition passage that leads into the mission discourse when Jesus sends out his disciples on a trial mission to continue his work of teaching and healing. Jesus recognises the need for leadership of a people 'who are like sheep without a shepherd' (9:36).

Jesus' prayer for more workers is answered. The second discourse (10:1-42) deals with the mission about to be undertaken by the disciples. It establishes their authority to participate in Jesus' ministry by giving them power to proclaim the kingdom, cast out devils and cure diseases, but their mission is restricted to Israel for the present. They are not to take with them money, provisions or unnecessary clothing; their lodging and food will be provided by those who receive them. The discourse, however, also becomes transparent for the instruction of the post-Easter Church. Any disciple who follows Jesus can expect indifference, hostility, rejection and persecution, reflecting the experience of the Church in Matthew's time. The secret coming of the kingdom is to be proclaimed by them, and no fear must be allowed to deter them. Disciples are encouraged not to be intimidated since, as participants in Jesus' mission, they are identified with him, and words of encouragement assures them of divine care and acknowledgement. Loss of earthly life for Jesus' sake will be rewarded with everlasting life in the kingdom. All who receive the disciples of Jesus receive both him and the God who sent him, and will be rewarded accordingly. Matthew's concern for mission will re-emerge at the end of his Gospel when the disciples will be fully equipped and commissioned to teach all nations.

The narrative in 11:1–12:50 deals with the growing opposition to Jesus. It is largely devoted to disputes and attacks relating to faith and discipleship, including Jesus' relationship to John the Baptist; woes uttered against unbelievers; thanksgiving for revelation to the simple; the gentle mastery of Jesus; Sabbath controversies and Jesus' power vis-à-vis the powers of evil; and the issue of Jesus' family. John's pre-eminent greatness lies in his announcing the imminence of the kingdom, while opponents of Jesus are trying to prevent people from accepting it. Reception of the kingdom depends on the Father who grants it to those open to receive it. In place of the yoke of the law, Jesus invites the burdened to take the yoke of obedience to his word and they will find rest. Jesus' attitude towards Sabbath observance demonstrates his claim to authority over Israel's God-given institutions. Besides pointing to the absurdity of the charge of the Pharisees that he is doing the work of Satan, Jesus asks how the work of their own exorcists is to be interpreted. Blasphemy against the Spirit is the sin of attributing to Satan what is the work of God's Spirit, for a tree is known by its fruit.

In this narrative section there is also considerable teaching that highlights the failure of the Jewish leaders to recognise Jesus who is greater than John the Baptist, the Temple, Solomon and Jonah. Now that the kingdom is being proclaimed, disciples who do the will of their heavenly Father become members of the family of Jesus.

The parable discourse (13:1-52) sheds light on the mystery of the kingdom that emerges suddenly and inexplicably in the world. Seven parables identify the salient characteristics of this kingdom. Already there is a discernable rift between those who accept and those who reject Jesus. The first part of the discourse takes place outside the house to Jews who do not understand him; the second half takes place inside the house (cf. 13:36) to disciples who do. The parable of the sower and its interpretation identify the different kinds of obstacles and failures encountered by the proclamation of the kingdom. And yet, despite these, a bumper harvest is the result. The parable of the weeds among the wheat and its explanation highlights the fact that adherents of the kingdom continue to be a mixture of good and bad until the final judgement comes. The two parables of the mustard seed and the leaven illustrate the present small beginnings of the kingdom and its glorious future. The parables of the hidden treasure and the pearl of great price stress the great value of the kingdom and the necessity of seizing the present opportunity to gain access to it at any cost. The parable of the dragnet and its interpretation, like that of the weeds, postpones the separation of the good and the bad until the end of the age. From now on Jesus will concentrate on instructing his disciples who see, hear and understand him.

The narrative in 13:53–17:27 generally follows the Markan sequence (chapters 6–9) and is mainly concerned with the community of true disciples from which the Church will develop. It is a three-part narrative, each ending with an episode concerning Peter that highlights his pre-eminence among the other disciples. The narrative includes rejection at Nazareth; the fate of John the Baptist; two miracles of the loaves; controversies with the Pharisees; healings and cures; Peter's confession; the transfiguration; and two Passion predictions. The most significant addition is the scene where Jesus invites Peter to come to him on the water, and when Peter begins to sink, Jesus comes to his rescue (cf. 14:22-33). This is the first of three episodes of special Petrine material. Yet in spite of his 'little faith' at Caesarea Philippi, Peter confesses that Jesus is the Messiah, the Son of the living God (cf. 16:13-20). This confession is the result of a revelation, not a matter of human reasoning. Peter now becomes the rock on which Jesus will build his Church, a Church against which not even the destructive demonic powers will be able to prevail. He is given the power of the keys, symbolising his authority to teach what must be observed. This exaltation of Peter does not eliminate Jesus' subsequent chastisement of Peter as one who thinks on a human level because he finds the idea of Jesus' suffering repugnant. This sobering correction leads into directives for disciples about the suffering required for discipleship, contrasted with the prospect of future glory (16:21-28). Following the transfiguration scene, the question about Elijah, the cure of the epileptic demoniac, and the second prophecy of the Passion are related. The narrative ends with a third Petrine scene centred on the Temple tax that Peter is to pay 'for me and for you' (17:27).

The discourse on the Church in 18:1-35 is a collection of ethical teachings originally addressed to the disciples but with a perspective that is suited to the later Church (cf. 16:18). Its purpose is to ensure that the values taught by Jesus are not obscured by worldly ones. It begins with a dispute about greatness in the kingdom that is concerned with the rightful use of authority in the community where ambition for the highest positions inevitably arises. In Jesus' scale of values, the humble are more important than the powerful, for they are more likely to be open to God's rule, symbolised by the trustful, open attitude of a child. What follows are condemnations of scandals and temptations that can cause believers to sin. The parable of the lost sheep shows that Jesus' set of values differs from worldly prudence. Instructions on procedures for reproving an erring community member and community prayer follow the parable. The necessity of frequent forgiveness is illustrated by a parable that shows the unlimited range of God's forgiveness.

The following narrative (19:1–23:39) is mixed with much dialogue and follows Mark 10–12 with some Matthean additions. It begins with an example of Jesus' standards for the kingdom, the question about divorce and an uncompromising assertion of the indissolubility of marriage. This gives rise to the possibility of continence for the sake of the kingdom as a sign anticipating the fulfilment of the kingdom. The story of the rich young man and its aftermath adds to the commandments of the Decalogue the demand to love one's neighbour as oneself. A warning on the danger of riches and the rewards of renunciation follow. The parable of the workers in the vineyard highlights God's sovereignty and a graciousness that is not based on what is earned. The third prophecy of the Passion contrasts with the mother of the sons of Zebedee's request for places in the kingdom that leads Jesus to emphasise the necessary attitude of service (20:17-28). After the healing of the two blind men, Jesus enters Jerusalem. The quotation from Zechariah stresses the meekness and peacefulness of the messianic kingship of Jesus. The cleansing of the Temple and the cursing of the fig tree that failed to bear fruit lead to the necessity of faith and prayer. To the challenge to Jesus' authority, Matthew joins the parable of the two sons. The sharpness of Jesus' judgement continues in the parable of the wicked tenants and the authorities understand themselves to be the target. The parable of the marriage feast is another instance of the rejection of the leaders. Three leading questions by them – taxes for Caesar, the resurrection and the great commandment – ends with Jesus proposing a question about the Messiah as David's son that his opponents are unable to answer. The narrative ends with a denunciation of the scribes and Pharisees for their proud behaviour and love of titles. It includes seven woes against their casuistry. They are criticised for their talk or pretence that is not accompanied by action, as well as acting from base motives. The tone is that of a polemic that employs typical language to highlight major differences between two groups. These woes also serve as negative examples for disciples and Christian leadership as well. The section concludes with a warning to Jerusalem.

The eschatological discourse (24:1–25:46) operates on two levels: the destruction of Jerusalem in AD 70, and the end of the world, with no sharp distinction drawn between them. The former is a forerunner and a prefiguration of the latter. The destruction of the city and the Temple marks the end of the old era. Such a decisive intervention will not occur again until the end of time when God will judge the human race. Conventional images of war, famine, earthquake, unprecedented distress and cosmic catastrophes are to be understood symbolically. They refer both to the destruction of Jerusalem and to the end of the world that follows and is prefigured by it. The end of the world is linked to Christ's final coming and to the power he will display when he comes to definitively establish the Kingdom of Heaven. Since there is no precise timetable for these final events, seven parables underline the need for vigilance, prudence and the faithful use of one's gifts or talents. The discourse ends by describing the judgement that will take place at Jesus' return. The scene shows the reason for the vindication and condemnation that will take place. It depicts the judgement of all the nations based on deeds of mercy performed for the benefit of the least of Jesus' followers. The righteous will be astonished to learn that in caring for the needy they were ministering to the Lord himself. The accursed will likewise be astounded that their neglect of the needy was neglect of the Lord and will receive from him a fitting answer. A concluding verse summarises their respective destinies.

Matthew's narrative (26:1–28:20) of the Passion, death and resurrection of Jesus follows the Markan account closely with some omissions and additions. These latter include the fate of Judas (27:3-10), the placing of guards at the tomb (27:62-66) and the precautions taken by leaders of the people (28:11-15). There is a brief account of the conspiracy against Jesus, his anointing at Bethany, the betrayal of Judas, the Passover meal and institution of the Eucharist, together with the foretelling of Peter's denial. The scene at Gethsemane precedes the arrest, arraignment before the Sanhedrin, and Peter's denials. Following the scene before Pilate where Jesus' innocence is declared by a Gentile woman (27:19), Jesus is scourged, crowned with thorns and mocked as King of the Jews. He is crucified and reviled by passers-by, chief priests, scribes and elders. He cries out in the words of Psalm 22 before giving up his spirit. Jesus' death brings judgement on the Temple, but also the resurrection of the saints of Israel. The resurrection appearances of Jesus culminate in the mountain scene that recapitulates all the major themes of the Gospel. The risen Jesus has received power, dominion and authority over all the nations. Endowed with these, Jesus commissions his disciples and sends them out with authority to baptise and teach all that Jesus taught them with the promise that he will be with them until the end of time. They are now ready for mission in the in-between time, a theme that will become a central concern in Luke-Acts.

Literary Characteristics

Matthew lacks dramatic force because of the way he has arranged the sayings of Jesus into lengthy discourses and inserted them in block fashion into the Markan narrative that seems to have been one of his sources. The result is a slower, less dramatic plot development. Furthermore, the evangelist's distinctive understanding of Jesus as Teacher affects his presentation of the parables. In contrast to Mark, parables are intelligible to insiders, while the prophecy of Isaiah applies only to outsiders (cf. 13:10-15). The disciples are those who 'see', 'hear' and 'understand'. It is their commitment to Jesus in faith that enables them to grasp the significance of Jesus' teaching. Since Jesus' presence in his Church is now mediated through his words, it is essential that those who hear them grasp their meaning so that they can pass them on to others, for the disciples in turn perform a teaching function within the Church. Parables, therefore, are genuine tools for teaching and Matthew includes seventeen of them in his Gospel. Believers now hear the words of Jesus as those of the risen Lord, for Jesus the Teacher is now Lord of his Church.

Another feature of Matthew's presentation is the balance between the first and second half of his Gospel. Up until

13:35 Jesus speaks to all Jews; afterwards the major focus is on the disciples who, in contrast to the Jews, both hear and understand him and so become the true Israel. In addition, the Gospel gravitates towards the authority of Jesus in word and deed (chapters 1–9), and that of the disciples (chapters 10–28). By the end of the Gospel the disciples are properly instructed to go out from the community and make disciples of all the nations. Only at the end-time judgement will the definitive demarcation occur between those who do and do not belong to the kingdom. Matthew's concern for the identity and integrity of the Christian community explains his hostility towards the Jewish leaders who in turn provide negative examples for disciples. Although he treats the disciples more favourably than Mark, since they will be commissioned to pass on the Good News, he does not downplay the fact that they all abandon Jesus at the Passion and even in the presence of the risen Christ 'some hesitated' (28:17). Matthew characterises their problem as one of 'little faith'. He invites future generations of disciples to identify with the first followers so that the latter's successes and failures become examples for them as well.

Portrait of Jesus

Matthew does not simply repeat Mark's Christology; he edits, expands and adds new insights. His distinctive contribution is evident in the narrative accounts of Jesus' birth and resurrection appearances. These serve to connect Jesus to the story of Israel and to the life of the Church respectively. In this way the life of Jesus is stretched over a larger canvas. Matthew adds the appearance of the risen Jesus to the disciples on the mountain in Galilee, where they are commissioned to preach all that Jesus taught them to the whole world. They are given the assurance that the risen Jesus will be with them and so the Church becomes the locus of Jesus' activity as risen Lord. The ongoing work of Christ is especially evident in the community discourse (chapter 18), which is shaped with the post-Easter community in mind. In it the presence of Christ, who exercises authority in and through the Church, is easily recognised: 'For where two or three meet in my name, I shall be there with them' (18:20). The risen Christ, by his presence, guides his community, the Church, until the end of the age (cf. 28:20) when he will come again to judge the nations (25:31-46). 'Thus the picture of Jesus Christ encompasses the Jesus who was at work on earth, was installed in power at the resurrection, and continues his salvific work in the Church.'[1]

In focusing on Jesus' ancestry, birth, Baptism and temptation scenes, Matthew presents a clear portrait of Jesus' identity for the reader. His birth is the fulfilment of prophesy, his mission is to save his people from their sins as the name 'Jesus' indicates. Jesus is the presence of God (Emmanuel) with his people. He is the messianic son of David, the legitimate King of the Jews who will shepherd God's people. Conceived through the power of the Spirit, he is the beloved Son of God who embodies the history of his people and fulfils the Scriptures. The appearance of Jesus is therefore in accordance with God's plan. In the temptation scenes, Jesus demonstrates that he is God's Son by his obedience to God's will. The Sermon on the Mount presents Jesus as an authoritative interpreter of the will of God, the Teacher of righteousness par excellence who fulfils the Law and the Prophets. The mighty deeds of Jesus are the works of the Messiah (cf. 11:2-5). The apocalyptic events surrounding his death and resurrection open up a new stage in the establishment of the kingdom since the exalted Christ already possesses total power over the cosmos (28:18). His return at the end of time will mean the final and definitive establishment of God's kingdom (16:27). In the meantime, making disciples of all the nations is the mission of the Church as it journeys through history towards the consummation of the kingdom.

Jesus' most prominent activity in Matthew is that of teaching. The very structure of the Gospel makes it clear that Jesus is *the* Teacher. His whole public ministry is divided into narratives, followed by five lengthy discourses addressed primarily to the disciples. What Jesus teaches is the content of the five discourses and it is to this teaching that the risen Jesus refers in 28:20. From the beginning of his public ministry, Matthew focuses on the teaching of Jesus. After the parable discourse in chapter 13, Jesus devotes himself more and more to the instruction of his disciples, the nucleus of the future Church. In addition to the five discourses, the teaching of Jesus is evident from different periscopes scattered throughout the narrative sections. Jesus is also the one who presents the love and mercy of God in his person and in his words and deeds. In turn, he requires works of love as the concrete expression of the new and greater righteousness. The love of neighbour is placed on the same level as the love of God (cf. 22:37-40).

Matthew also regards Jesus as Lord of the Church, whose whole public ministry is aimed at gathering disciples into the embryonic Church (cf. 21:43). It is made up of those who heed Jesus' call to follow him and whose ultimate norm of morality is Jesus himself both in word and example. Matthew has juxtaposed the sending of the disciples to the lost sheep of the house of Israel with the commission of the risen Christ to all the nations. Here the historical situation in the time of Jesus becomes transparent for future mission (cf. 10:1-42). Jesus' instructions given to the disciples whom he sent to Israel retain their validity for the post-Easter Church. All Jesus' activity is regarded as being under the guidance of God, a compassionate healer whose unobtrusive work brings about the salvation of the human race. What is remarkable is that the bringer of salvation achieves his goal, not through political conquest or military rule, but through his death — a vicarious atonement for sinners interpreted in the light of the Suffering Servant of Isaiah (52:11–53:12). The Kingdom of Heaven that was first offered to Israel but rejected by its leaders, passes to a new people and so the history of salvation lives on in the person of the risen Jesus present in the community called together by him. He is Emmanuel, God-with-us, who will abide with his community until the end of time, when he will lead his people out of history into eternity.

Community and Discipleship

Matthew regards the Christian community composed of both Jews and Gentiles as the continuation of the Old Testament people of God that has now come to full realisation. He does this by frequent use of Old Testament fulfilment quotations. The new community is represented by the twelve apostles, since the Jewish people led by the scribes and Pharisees have forfeited their claim to be God's people. The issue for Matthew is not racial prejudice (anti-Judaism) but religious conflict, i.e., internal strife among rival Jewish groups. His negative attitude towards Jewish leadership (cf. chapter 23) is part of this polemic. The true Israel is now to be found in the Christian community founded by Jesus on Peter, and led by the apostles who are invested with Christ's authority to go and make disciples of all the nations. What is important for Matthew is the ecclesial aspect of the

Jewish rejection of Jesus, so that new leaders must be designated to guide the people who are 'like sheep without a shepherd' (9:36). The rejection of Jewish leadership is foreshadowed in chapters 1–10, made explicit in chapters 11–13 and taken for granted throughout the rest of the Gospel, culminating in their condemnation in chapter 23, the prediction of the destruction of the Temple, and their self-condemnation in 27:25: 'His blood be on us and on our children.' The Gospel of Matthew is not anti-Jewish, for his community is predominantly made up of Jewish Christians who have accepted Jesus as their Messiah and his messianic Torah together with Peter, a Jew, as the rock or foundation of that community. Moreover, the evangelist sees the Christian community in continuity with the faithful 'remnant of Israel'. The true Israel, comprising both Jew and Gentile, is defined in contrast to the Jews who are led by the scribes and Pharisees. It is characterised by faith in Jesus, the Messiah, and by a 'justice' that exceeds that of the scribes and Pharisees by putting into practice the messianic Torah as taught by Jesus.

Matthew has been called the 'ecclesial Gospel' since it is the only Gospel in which the word 'church' (*ekklesia*) occurs (cf. 16:18; 18:17). The post-Easter community quickly came to understand itself as the *qehal Yahweh*, the assembly of God gathered in worship, the true Israel, in continuity with the Israel of old. This is expressed throughout the Gospel by means of abundant fulfilment quotations, by portraying Jesus as a Moses-like figure, and by Jesus' reinterpretation of the Mosaic Torah. The disciples of Jesus form a distinct community apart from their contemporaries that is founded on the rock of Peter who is to exercise authority to bind and loose. In chapter 23, Jewish leadership is held up as an example of what Christian leadership should never become. Although the phrase 'institutional Church' evokes hostility today even from elements within the Church itself, the institutional element is nevertheless important to preserve the initial experience and to keep alive the memories, traditions and wisdom acquired through the centuries. The institution offers a historical perspective for our self-interpretations. Jesus evidently wanted his Church to be a human community with all its attendant flaws and imperfections. It is naive to suppose that the original experience could have survived in its integrity without institutional support. Jesus clearly teaches that God calls us, not just as individuals, but also as part of a community, and how we relate to one other within that community has important implications for living and witnessing to the Christian life. For Jesus, the love of God and neighbour, while distinct, can never be separated (cf. 22:35-40). For the Christian, then, concrete involvement in the community of faith is an important aspect of discipleship. The individual quest for God, however sincere, risks becoming more of a private fantasy rather than real faith, without the corrective of community involvement.

Matthew concentrates on post-baptismal instruction of the disciples to teach them the messianic Torah of Jesus. He goes out of his way to emphasise that the apostles, who will later teach what they have learned from Jesus, have 'understood' (13:52) all that Jesus taught them. This is in contradistinction to Mark who represents the disciples as consistently failing to understand Jesus. Disciples in Matthew, in contrast, are being prepared for their future teaching apostolate: 'teach them to observe all the commands I gave you' (28:20). It is therefore important that the disciples understand what Jesus taught them. Matthew paints a more sympathetic picture of the disciples than Mark. He underlines the bonds between them and their Master. They are the privileged companions of Jesus. Although still capable of failure, they are able to penetrate more deeply the mystery of Jesus' identity. The disciples must leave everything and follow Jesus, yet they have to remain in the world to continue his mission, to preach and instruct the newly baptised regarding the day-to-day living of the Christian life. The lifestyle of the disciples, therefore, involves both separation and participation. They have to live in a certain tension between detachment from society because of their commitment to Christ, and a continuing participation in the affairs of the world through involvement in mission.

Besides developing their 'little faith' (8:26), disciples must profess their allegiance to Christ by the kind of lifestyle they lead. The followers of Jesus are called to be perfect as the heavenly Father is perfect (cf. 5:48). Throughout his Gospel, Matthew emphasises the necessity of 'doing' or observing God's Law as opposed to simply knowing and talking about it. There is the positive example of Jesus who does the will of God perfectly. The first words of Jesus characterise him as a 'doer' of God's will: 'It is fitting that we should, in this way, do all that righteousness demands' (3:15). Jesus is not only a teacher but a doer, and he tells his disciples: 'Your light must shine in the sight of men, so that, seeing your good works, they may give praise to your Father in heaven' (5:16). The scribes and the Pharisees are condemned: 'since they do not practice what they preach' (23:3) and become negative examples for disciples. Matthew's insistence on 'doing all' that Jesus commanded is regarded as the primary characteristic of true disciples. It is summed up in the love commandment, the importance of which is highlighted in the Last Judgement scene (25:31-46). When disciples stand before Jesus in judgement, they will be judged according to their observance or non-observance of only one commandment – the law of love. The scene as situated in Matthew's Gospel constitutes the final teaching of Jesus. It is surely significant that the last thing Jesus says is that in the final judgement the only thing that will count is the observance of the law of love as the norm of Christian conduct: 'You must love the Lord your God with all your heart, with all your soul, and with all your mind. This is the greatest and the first commandment. The second resembles it: You must love your neighbour as yourself. On these two commandments hang the whole Law and the Prophets also' (22:37-40).

Love in itself, however, is not a sufficiently articulated ethical norm for guiding disciples in the manifold and often complex circumstances of daily living. The extensive moral teaching proffered by Matthew provides love with an articulation that remains indispensable if love is to be translated into the language of concrete Christian living. This teaching derives its validity and meaning from its vital connection with the law of love. External moral teaching protects love from the subjectivism and self-deception to which disciples are constantly exposed, not because they are bad people, but simply because they are human. Moral teaching has a role in relation to Christian love, even when the connection is not obvious. It fulfils a positive function in informing and illuminating Christian conscience and strengthening the will, as well as playing a positive part in the practical living out of the Christian life. For the disciple exists in the community we call Church; the Church in turn is for humankind, to the extent that it already exists as a loving community. This reflects the Church's self-understanding as the holy people of God, the instrument of God's glory in the world, and also the tangible beginning of a transformed humanity.

Leadership

The figure of Peter already occupies a position of prominence in Mark. Matthew also portrays Peter as a leading figure among the disciples. He is among the first to be called by Jesus (cf. 4:18) and ranks first in the list of apostles (cf. 10:2). Jesus works a miracle for him (cf. 8:14-15), he is present at Tabor and Gethsemane (cf. 17:1; 26:37) and becomes the spokesperson for the Twelve (cf. 16:16; 17:4; 19:27; 26:33-35). He follows Jesus to his trial (cf. 26:69). Matthew already found these in his Markan source, but adds two further references (cf. 15:15; 18:21) where Peter asks Jesus to explain the parable regarding clean and unclean, and the extent of forgiveness respectively. In addition, Matthew has three further incidents that concern Peter: walking on the water (cf. 14:28-32); conferral of authority (cf. 16:16-19); and the paying of the Temple tax 'for me and for you' (17:27). Yet Matthew does not gloss over Peter's negative features – he is fearful, weak in faith, chastised by Jesus and denies Jesus three times. In all this, Peter is a representative figure exemplifying both the positive and negative features of Christian discipleship. Nevertheless, on Peter alone is the Church built and to him alone the keys are given (16:18-19). His role is not limited to Jesus' public life, but extends into the post-Easter period as a symbol of the developing functions of pastoral leadership in the Church and the founding model for the later emergence of the papal office. Yet leaders are and must remain disciples. Matthew refuses to idealise Peter or place him above the demands of the Gospel.

In the second episode peculiar to Matthew (16:16-20) it is difficult to avoid the conclusion that Jesus founded his Church on Peter as the 'rock', against which not even Satan's destructive power will prevail. He is given 'the keys of the kingdom of heaven', symbolising Peter's authority with regard to the regulation of Church teaching and discipline. This is one of the most discussed texts in the New Testament. The heavily Semitic background of the phraseology, with its indirect reference to Isaiah 22:22, makes it likely that the evangelist is preserving an original passage as evidence of the Petrine function in the post-Easter Church. His primacy is asserted despite his lack of faith and subsequent denial of Jesus.

Kingdom and Church

The Kingdom of God (of heaven, in Matthew) and the Church overlap to some extent in the Gospel. The kingdom is the sovereign reign of God, realised fully only at the end of the ages, but inaugurated by Jesus during his public ministry. The kingdom is then both otherworldly (eternal life with God) and this-worldly (human liberation and growth here on earth). The Church is the door through which people enter the kingdom. The kingdom is 'at hand' in the ministry of Jesus and the parables in chapter 13 explain some fundamental aspects of it. Jesus inaugurates the kingdom, a task that is continued by the Church, so that the Church and the early stages of the kingdom overlap. The disciples are 'citizens of the kingdom' (cf. 21:43) who produce the fruits of righteousness, yet the kingdom remains an object of hope for the future in the Lord's prayer 'your kingdom come' (6:10). Matthew associates the Church with the kingdom, but the Church is not totally identical with the kingdom, for disciples are still being 'called' (cf. 22:14); while 'elect' or 'blessed' is reserved for those to whom the Son of Man will grant eternal life (25:34, 46) when the kingdom is brought to fulfilment. Matthew directs the attention of the Church to the 'end of the age' so that disciples live their lives in the light of the approaching kingdom in all its fullness. There is an evident tension in the Gospel between present/future; already/not yet; ethics/eschatology. The disciples are to ensure that their lives are being shaped by God's future promises in the beatitudes (5:3-12) by following Jesus in taking up their cross, and by losing their life in order to find it. The Church already lives within the sphere of God's gracious rule and is commissioned to preach the Good News of the kingdom to all the nations. At present it is exposed to the forces of evil that will not, however, prevail against it. We will now turn to the teaching of Jesus in Matthew, concentrating on the first of the five great discourses to keep the discussion within manageable limits – the Sermon on the Mount (chapters 5–7).

The Sermon on the Mount

INTRODUCTION

The Sermon on the Mount is the first of the five discourses placed within the narrative framework of Matthew's Gospel. It is not a system of clear-cut laws, nor is it a collection of impossible abstract ideals, but offers instead a practical guidance to those wishing to be faithful to the Gospel in the community of Jesus' disciples. The Sermon illustrates the *spirit* of Jesus' teaching, one that all disciples must embody in their own situations. It is a *sketch*, not a system of laws, and functions to shape the identity and way of life of disciples who represent the Christian community in responding to Jesus' gift and call. The Sermon is pictorial and abounds in vivid, concrete speech. Its teaching is illustrated directly from common life. The style resembles the proverbial kind found in the Old Testament where truths are stated in a vivid, extreme and hyperbolic manner so that it is the principle, not the literal meaning, that matters. Principles are laid down and illustrations of that principle are given, e.g. the principle of non-vindictiveness is illustrated by five examples (5:38-42). In 5:33-37 it is sincerity and truthfulness in speech, not the prohibition of oaths as such that is advocated. The Sermon is concerned with principles of morality that are to be internalised and applied by the disciples who are likened to a fruit tree; if one is looking for good fruit, the tree itself must be good. It is what a person *is* rather than what one *does* that is important. The Sermon is addressed primarily to followers to instruct them on the implications of discipleship, in particular, what they are to become and how they are to behave. For faith in Jesus to be real, it must first be demonstrated in a way of life inside the Christian community.

The Sermon is delivered on the mountain, the place of revelation in the Old Testament, and recalls the experience of Moses at Sinai (cf. Ex 19). It is the charter of the kingdom — an orientation in view of the future fulfilment of God's reign, a future that is already impacting on the present in Jesus' preaching and activity. It is offered to instruct those who have responded positively to the preaching of the Good News by repentance and Baptism. Jesus sits as a sign of his authority and dignity as Teacher and the solemnity of the occasion is noted: 'Then he began to speak. This is what he taught them ...'. His teaching provides paradigms of attitudes, character and actions required of disciples to shape their identity and lifestyle within the Christian community. It delineates a distinctive way of life, often in tension with the values and norms of contemporary Jewish society, and is guided by the principle of love. In it Jesus exhorts rather than commands by giving guiding principles and examples for which the disciples are called upon to find analogies in their own lives. It is not intended to be a complete rule of life, but pointers and examples of what it means to live out the life of faith. The real hearers are the readers who now listen to the address of Jesus, the Lord of the Church, who continues to be present among his disciples to the end of the age.

The Sermon on the Mount, therefore, is not a law code, but a collection of beatitudes, precepts, exhortations and prayers that describe the life of disciples. The following outline will highlight the content of the Sermon:

Setting (4:25–5:2) – crowds gather with the disciples to listen to Jesus.

Beatitudes and Role of Disciples (5:3-16) – the beatitudes delineate the personal characteristics (values, attitudes, actions) that are to be cultivated in the present and that will be rewarded in the fullness of the kingdom. The disciples' service to the world is described in images (salt, light).

Fulfilment of the Old Testament (5:17-48) – Jesus came not to abolish but to fulfil the Old Testament. His intensification of the law is illustrated by six antitheses regarding murder and anger; adultery and lust; marriage and divorce; oaths and truthfulness; retaliation and non-violence; and love of enemies.

True Piety (6:1-18) – almsgiving, prayer and fasting are to be performed for God alone; brevity in prayer, how to pray (Our Father), forgiveness.

Material Possessions (6:19-34) – topics: treasures, eyes, masters, anxiety.

True Wisdom (7:1-12) – no judging, discernment, prayer for wisdom, the Golden Rule.

Exhortation, Warnings (7:13-27) – parables about gates and ways, trees and fruits, saying and doing, houses and foundations. All highlight the necessity of doing.

Conclusion (7:28-8:1) – Jesus' authority impresses the people who follow him.

The theme of the Sermon is given in the key word 'righteousness' (doing the will of God) that reaches its climax in the Golden Rule. It signifies both God's saving activity (5:6; 6:33) and human beings' response to it by way of acting in accordance with God's will. Jesus has already been described as fulfilling all righteousness (cf. 3:15) before he teaches it, and so is the authoritative teacher who practises what he preaches. The Sermon, then, is concerned with character formation and decision-making on how to behave in the new community of disciples.[2] It includes general principles, attitudes, parables, exhortations, examples, declarations and actions as things to be put into practice that tell who disciples *are*. Decision-making and the resultant behaviour are concerned with what disciples *do*. Who we are conditions what we do, and so the Sermon is proposing an ethics of Christian character, since becoming a disciple involves first of all formation of character. It is concerned with vertical relationships (instruction on worship and prayer) as well as horizontal (how to behave towards others), the result of a properly formed Christian character. This is how disciples are to prepare themselves to enjoy the fullness of the kingdom by acting appropriately in the present. The Sermon is not a comprehensive ethic, much less a New Testament Decalogue. It is, rather, emblematic of the *kinds* of things disciples should be and do. It ends with a warning to build one's life on solid rock, i.e. on the words of Jesus who already embodies what he teaches.

THE BEATITUDES

The Beatitudes begin on a joyous note that may be translated as 'Oh the blessedness (happiness) of ...'. It is a blessedness that *God* bestows, not one we ourselves can achieve or earn. They respond to the desire for happiness that is natural to the human heart, though not in the way one would expect. The desire for happiness put into the human heart by God finds its response in God's sharing of his own happiness with us, if only we would allow ourselves to be led by him. 'Beatitude' declares that certain persons are in a privileged, blessed state. It is a prophetic declaration made on the conviction that the Kingdom of God is already present. Beatitudes are not advice for successful living, or a declaration of a subjective state of happiness, but an objective reality, the result of divine intervention. They are a declaration of blessedness for those already oriented to the future consummation of the kingdom. They bring with them an indirect ethical imperative in calling members of the community to act in accordance with the coming kingdom. The first and last beatitude refer directly to the coming kingdom, the others to some future aspect of it. The Beatitudes do not have different kinds of good people in view; they are rather a declaration of the blessedness of the end-time community living in anticipation of the consummation of God's reign. They are oriented to people living together in community.

The Beatitudes call into question modern assumptions that money, power and possessions can produce happiness. They question much contemporary wisdom concerning fulfilment – blessed are the poor in spirit, not the rich; those who mourn rather than those who laugh; the gentle not the bully; the merciful rather than the hard-hearted; the pure in heart rather than the pragmatists and compromisers; the peacemakers rather than the warriors; the persecuted and reviled on Jesus' account, not those praised and honoured by the world. The future reward is expressed in various ways. All of them are variations of the same theme when God's definitive kingdom will be fully established.

The Beatitudes underline the future-oriented perspective of Jesus' mission and highlight those virtues, attitudes and characteristic actions that define authentic discipleship living in the in-between time, between the already/not yet. Disciples are blessed precisely because their present circumstances will be reversed at the end of time. They are those people who, because of their experience, commitment and virtuous living, will fully participate in the Kingdom of God. They enjoy blessedness even now, although its perfection belongs to the heavenly world. The Beatitudes outline the moral ideal of the Christian personality seen from different angles, which is in reality the character of Jesus himself who is poor in spirit, meek and humble, mourns, hungers for righteousness, is merciful, pure, single-minded, brings about peace and suffers for righteousness' sake – all of which are illustrated in the Gospel of Matthew. They all blend in his character and express the spirit of self-giving love. These characteristics will be brought to perfection in the Kingdom of Heaven, described under various aspects of dominion, comfort, vindication, mercy, vision of God and divine sonship. They recall the messianic promises in the Old Testament, especially those of Second Isaiah (chapters 40–55).

Taken together, the Beatitudes form a character portrait of the Christian: three of them deal with the beginning of the Christian life (poverty of spirit, mourning, hunger and thirst for righteousness); four deal with what a Christian is (gentle, pure in heart, merciful, a peacemaker), and one concerns the result of the Christian life (persecution, cf. Ws 1:16-2:24). The first four deal with the disciple's vertical relationships, the last five with the horizontal ones. Eight of them are in the third person; the ninth is in the second person so as to draw the reader into identification with the portrait given, as well as serving as a transition to the next section in the second person.

Poor in Spirit: Poverty, first of all, refers to those deprived of earthly goods, those who have nothing to rely on. This original sense is interpreted here in a spiritual and ethical fashion by the addition of 'in spirit'. They are now the humble as opposed to the proud and self-sufficient. In the Psalms the 'poor' (*'anawim*) are the true people of God who know that their lives are totally dependent on him. The spirituality characteristic of the poor evolved and developed over the centuries preceding the coming of Christ. Even those who were no longer materially poor adopted it as a way of life and outlook on the world. They regarded God as their only support.[3] This beatitude speaks of those who are content, who accept their creaturely limitations and the truth about themselves, and so becomes an ethical demand to behave accordingly. Poverty of spirit can take many forms – material, ill-health, loneliness, failure, ageing, trials, tragedy, guilt, emptiness – the realisation of which can also lead to rebellion in the form of anger, resentment, envy or rage, which can harden us, or to acceptance in humility, which then opens people up by freeing them from the bonds of possession and riches that can imprison when they become idols. Poverty of spirit is the admission of not being self-sufficient, that human beings are dependent on God and need his help, and so it becomes a religious rather than an economic designation. Those who live with these attitudes and dispositions will receive the ultimate blessings.

Those Who Mourn: In the Old Testament, those who mourn are those who lament the eclipse of God's people and God's cause and who long for the salvation promised (cf. Is 40:1ff; 61:2ff; Si 48:24; Lk 2:25). They include disciples who lament the fact that God's kingdom is not yet established in its fullness, and that his will is not done on earth as it is in heaven. Their yearnings will be fulfilled when sin and death are finally overcome and God will wipe away every tear from their eyes (cf. Rv 7:17). Those who mourn are also people who are sorry for the wrongs they have committed, who mourn for the sins and wrongdoings of others and for evil in the world. The book of Revelation 21:4 associates mourning, crying and pain with the experience of the evils of the present age. This attitude leads to repentance and reparation, accepting the crosses of life and trials in this valley of tears because suffering and affliction are part of the human condition.

> All kinds of mourning are covered in the reference to those who mourn. People mourn their own and others' oppression, poverty, dislocation, and every kind of mental and physical suffering. They mourn the loss of innocence and the presence of sin in the world. They mourn their own mortality and the mortality of those around them.[4]

We need courage to face and accept these limitations. For this we have the example of the Passion of Christ who saved us by what he underwent, rather than what he did, and which was borne out of love. Suffering and authentic love go hand in hand; without it, love tends to become selfish and egocentric, and suffering without love is meaningless. Those who mourn will be comforted (cf. Is 61:2-3). To be comforted is to experience God's saving help.

The Meek/Gentle: The meek or the gentle in the Old Testament are those who are conscious of their status as an oppressed people but who have renounced violence as a means to regain their freedom. It is the gentleness that goes with strength of character. They shall inherit the land. Originally this referred to the Promised Land, but already in Isaiah (cf. 57:13; 60:21) it had acquired a figurative and messianic meaning and now becomes a metaphor for participation in end-time salvation. Psalm 37:11 says that the meek shall inherit the land, and Zephaniah 3:12-13 speaks of a people meek and lowly, i.e. poor. Matthew uses this designation with reference to Jesus as the meek king who enters Jerusalem riding on an ass, rather than on a horse, the symbol of power (21:5, cf. Zc 9:9). Jesus is also portrayed as one who is 'gentle and humble in heart' (11:29). He has already realised in his person that gentleness and meekness, and so he becomes our model. This beatitude is a summons to deeds not determined solely by anger or revenge, but by goodness. However, meekness is not resignation, or allowing others to dominate us, but refers to courage born out of suffering and self-control. Meekness is opposed to aggression, rage and violence, but also to withdrawal, non-involvement, giving in, not standing up for oneself. It is not suppression of feelings, but their proper ordering through self-control that channels our anger and leads to forgiveness. Jesus who is meek and humble of heart shows control, strength of character and mastery over his passions. Such people in the Old Testament were promised the land of Israel, which is now spiritualised to refer to participation when the kingdom comes in all its fullness.

Hunger and Thirst for Righteousness: This beatitude refers to those who have an active, energetic longing and make a decisive effort towards the realisation of righteousness, i.e. ethical conduct in keeping with God's will. People long for God's saving justice just as a starving person longs for food, or a thirsty person for water. They want goodness and justice to prevail and are prepared to act to realise them. They long for the coming of the kingdom in its fullness and the vindication of right that accompanies it. On the basis of this hope, they carry out God's will now and that hope of theirs will be satisfied. 'Righteousness' is also an attribute of God that is shown in his faithfulness to his covenant. For the Old Testament people of God it meant fidelity to the covenant relationship that involves God and other people. What emerges from the wider biblical context is the concept of saving or restorative justice beyond retaliation that seeks to bring healing and reconciliation with God and the community.

The Merciful: This beatitude is an exhortation to be merciful in order to receive mercy when the kingdom is fully established. It is, first of all, an attribute of God that is seen especially in his forgiveness (cf. 18:23-35). God forgives and expects the recipients of his forgiveness to forgive others in return (cf. 6:12). Mercy also finds expression in kindness towards the poor. It comprises both an attitude and an act, exemplified many times by Jesus during his ministry (cf. 18:33; 9:13; 12:7; 17:15; 20:30-31). It connotes compassionate action, not just a feeling. The doers of mercy are the true followers of Jesus and they will be vindicated at the last judgement (cf. 25:31-46). Merciful actions realise the demand for unlimited love; it refers to those who can enter the minds and hearts of others to empathise with them.

Pure in Heart: In Psalm 24:3-6, 'he whose hands are clean, whose heart is pure' is said to 'seek your presence, God of Jacob' — to experience God and receive his blessing when they visit the Jerusalem Temple on pilgrimage. The beatitude resembles this psalm with its reference to the pure in heart, the promise of seeing God and receiving his blessing. In biblical anthropology, the heart is the core of the personality, the true self. The pure in heart refers to people of integrity who desire to please God by doing his will. It is not just a passive attitude, but manifests itself in right conduct towards God and one's neighbour. There is a correspondence between inner thoughts and desires and external actions (cf. 7:13-27). Single-hearted persons are focused entirely on God's will and so qualify as members of God's family. They are people with a good conscience who harbour no evil intentions. Such persons 'shall see God'. In the Old Testament, worshippers went to the Temple to seek the face of God through participation in its liturgy. The pure in heart will see God face to face in the kingdom — the promised gift of communion with God. So blessed are those whose motives are unmixed, who always act for the right reasons with a clear conscience, and whose actions and intentions correspond.

Peacemakers: This beatitude does not refer to peace lovers or those who let things be 'for the sake of peace'. True peace comes from facing up to, not running away from, problems. *Shalom* in Hebrew is a relational concept. Blessed are those who help restore relationships as they ought to be, the fruit of justice and charity. These include relationships with God, with others, with God's creation and with oneself. The duty of reconciliation, of peacemaking, is a central Christian commandment (cf. 5:23-24). To such people membership in God's family is granted. They prove themselves to be children of a God who causes his sun to rise on good and bad alike, and his rain to fall on the just and unjust alike (cf. 5:45).

The Persecuted: The reason for the persecution of Christians is that they are practising righteousness, i.e. acting in accordance with God's will as revealed by Jesus. Since Christians belong to the community of faith, they are out of step with the value systems of the world and will be persecuted for that reason just like the prophets of old. Suffering for righteousness' sake is frequently found in the Old Testament (e.g. Ps 22; 34; Ws 2:10-20). Disciples have the opportunity to demonstrate their convictions when they are reproached, persecuted and slandered. They must, therefore, be prepared to suffer for their beliefs. They should not be ashamed to be different, but insist on doing certain things and refraining from other things out of personal conviction. This will inevitably provoke insults, calumnies, lies, condemnations, animosity, mockery, ridicule, cruelty and gossip, as it did for Christ. Persecution occurs because they belong to Christ 'on my account'. 'The beatitude, however, speaks more of suspicion, calumny and false accusations as though the active persecution is past and ripples continue in society.'[5] Reward in heaven suggests that the endurance of suffering is meaningful and hence the reason for the joy and exultation.

The present tense used throughout the Beatitudes indicates that they are expressions of what is already true of the Christian community, a sign of God's blessing and an invitation to all Christians to conform their common life more and more to these values. The future passive tense reminds Christians that they will have to await ultimate vindication by God in the future when his kingdom will be definitively established. Christian discipleship, then, is a particular way of living in community, based on the sure hope that such a manner of living will be finally rewarded as the inevitable issue of goodness in a world ruled by a good and loving God.

Every person encounters situations depicted in the Beatitudes — creaturely limitations, poverty, violence, injustice, weeping and mourning, difficulties in forgiving and showing mercy, struggle for purity of heart, problems of peace in families, communities, nations, enduring calumny, insults, injustice because of fidelity to Christ, and the prospect of suffering and martyrdom. Today there is a tendency to minimise the differences that distinguish Christians from other groups as regards beliefs, morals, lifestyle and future hopes. Without the hope that comes from God, in contrast to the optimism that stems from what we can achieve ourselves, Christianity becomes just another utopia. The Beatitudes promise new life to those immersed in daily tasks and invite us to build *now* the foundations of another world which God in Christ has already inaugurated. The content of the Beatitudes is twofold: promises of present and future blessings, and a portrait of the recipient of those blessings. They are concerned with shaping character by offering a sketch of a person of piety towards God and of right behaviour towards others, and they draw the reader into identification with them. It is a new way of looking at themselves and the world. This is the way Jesus sees his followers.

MISSION OF DISCIPLES

It is people imbued with such traits that are called to mission in the world in which they live. The role of disciples is seen both in terms of being (salt and light — metaphors that are evocative and contain multiple layers of meaning) and doing (good works). Disciples are to act in accord with their nature and the scope of their mission is universal (earth, world, everyone), the goal of which is to glorify God, not themselves. They are challenged to stay salty and not become so mixed with impurities as to become savourless and useless. They are to the world what salt is for eating – a necessary and indispensable component. Disciples can make a real contribution to society. As salt adds flavour to food, so also Christians add flavour to life by being content with their lot, thereby showing where true happiness lies. Salt also has preservative qualities, keeping food fresh and pure. Likewise, Christians in society by their positive example can be a force for good, inspiring and influencing others in numerous ways.

The light of the world is used to designate their role as well. Just as the natural function of light is to shine, so also an essential part of being a disciple is to radiate light. Disciples are meant to be seen and to be a beacon for others. Two other images drive home the point. A city on a hilltop cannot be hidden. Nor is an oil lamp placed under a bushel where it becomes extinguished, but placed on a stand to give light throughout the house. Christians help others to find their way through life to their final destiny, but to do that they have to be seen, to be an example, not for self-aggrandisement, rather that others 'may see your good works and give glory to your Father in heaven'. Christians are called to responsible action in and on behalf of the world. These metaphors also warn community members not to fail in their mission by becoming introverted, shielding themselves from the world around them. Just as it is the property of light to illumine, salt to season and preserve, a city on a hilltop to be seen, and a lamp to give light, so also the disciples' good works ought to allow the world to recognise and praise God. It is an exhortation for disciples to become what they really are, for the lifestyle of fully committed disciples constitutes an important witness in the world.

NEW RIGHTEOUSNESS

Disciples of Jesus are to obey the Torah, the revealed will of God that includes the Law and the Prophets. Jesus affirms the Old Testament and 'fulfils' it, i.e. brings it to full measure by virtue of his authority as divine Teacher. Four sayings in 5:17-20 function as a control on the manner in which 5:21-48 is to be understood. The 'righteousness' of Christians is to be considerably different from that of the scribes and Pharisees; it is marked by 'more' and thus realises the will of God more fully. Righteousness here is a relational term that means faithfulness to a covenant relationship. God acts with righteousness when he saves his people as covenant partner. Humans act with righteousness when they worship God alone and behave properly towards others. What follows are pointers and illustrations of this righteousness that proposes a distinctive lifestyle.

The Old Law summed up in the Decalogue has less to do with rules and regulations than with relationships among people and with God. The Decalogue may be summed up in one word – reverence or respect.[6] Reverence for God and for the name of God; reverence for the Lord's Day. Respect for parents, respect for life, respect for persons, respect for property, respect for truth and for another's good name, respect for oneself so that covetous desires may never overpower one. It is this respect that Jesus came to draw out and he gives three examples to illustrate what he meant.

In 5:21-48 Jesus properly interprets the Law by means of antitheses. The scribes and Pharisees by their casuistry evade the true meaning of the Law, whereas Jesus focuses on God's original intention. In none of the six antitheses is Jesus annulling the Law, rather he is interpreting it through the commandment of love and the Golden Rule. He fulfils the Law and the Prophets, not only in outward acts, but also in inner feelings, thoughts and desires. His aim is the purification of the heart. Three commandments of the Decalogue are expounded – the fifth (killing), the sixth (adultery), the eighth (false witness). Jesus illumines the depths of these demands by showing that we also share in these sins through anger, hatred, failure to forgive, envy and covetousness.

Jesus says that in God's sight it is not only the person who commits murder who is guilty. Relationships among God's family can also be destroyed by holding on to anger, and publicly humiliating another person. He gives two examples where this deep-seated anger turns into insulting words. A person shows contempt for another by calling him a fool, or by casting aspersions on his moral character, thereby taking away his good name and reputation. Those who are slaves of anger, Jesus says, who speak with the accents of contempt or destroy another's good name, may not have actually killed anybody, but have done so in their heart. God's will is that there be no destruction of relationships by any means, and Jesus goes on to illustrate how to take the initiative to restore broken relationships before taking part in worship (cf. 5:23-26), for it is not possible to be right with God without at the same time being reconciled with others. Jesus not only condemns the evil deed, but evil thoughts, feelings and desires as well.

Not only is adultery forbidden, anyone who fixes his gaze on another man's wife for the purpose of coveting her has already committed adultery with her in his heart. Jesus has in mind the deliberate harbouring of desire for an illicit relationship. The divine intention behind the commandment is that one does not violate another's spouse whether by means of the eye (intention) or of the hand (act). Not only the sinful act, but also the sinful look and the perverted will ('in his heart') is forbidden. Linked to it is the question of divorce that was allowed in the Old Testament. But Jesus expounds the original divine will that marriage is indissoluble.[7] Lifelong fidelity is the ideal in marriage as willed by the Creator. The kingdom inaugurated by Jesus represents a return to the order of creation as God originally planned it (cf. Gn 1–2). Positively, it encourages married couples to work at lifelong fidelity and to do everything possible to contribute to mutual flourishing within marriage.

In the Old Testament, God was regarded as the defender of oaths, so vows made in his name had to be kept and perjury was punished. Jesus' prohibition of oaths and other means of evading the truth (cf. 5:34-36) is an ethical demand for truthfulness in relationships. Ideally, Christians should never have to take an oath to guarantee the truth of anything they say. The character of the person speaking should make oaths unnecessary. Christians should be so *trustworthy* that everyone will know that when they speak, they speak the truth. For disciples, a simple Yes or No should be sufficient to guarantee the truth of what they say. Jesus does not prohibit oaths as such, nor does he forbid making statements under oath, but reminds disciples to always tell the truth so that they can be trusted to keep their word or promises. Lying and evasion of truth are wrong precisely because they undermine that *trust* necessary to foster relationships. Jesus is dealing not with rules and regulations, but with character formation and the decision-making that flows from it.

Jesus next cites the *lex talionis* ('eye for eye and tooth for tooth') that attempted to curb a revenge that was blinded by rage and consequently one would be tempted to take the law into one's own hands. The Old Testament command was intended to end vendettas and blood feuds that permitted unlimited retaliation. Jesus says that the true intention behind the command is best realised by non-retaliation in personal relationships. It is followed by four illustrations of a hyperbolic nature. The intention behind these exaggerated examples is that the disciple should practise compliance, humility and self-denial as examples of the greater righteousness that the followers of Jesus will try to realise. These examples appeal to the imagination to see situations in a new way so as to be able to contemplate new possibilities of action. This type of language functions to form character, rather than being rules of conduct to be literally obeyed. Disciples then become those who do not retaliate.

Love of neighbour in the Old Testament was confined to relations among fellow-Israelites and was not usually extended to outsiders. Jesus says that God's intention requires love of one's enemies as well as interceding for one's persecutors whoever they may be. God's unrestricted love towards all alike should serve as motivation. Christians are to imitate God and be as inclusive in their love in the same way that God is. Loving the enemy, however, does not mean affirming their behaviour, or that one does not demand change of conduct. Neither does it mean passivity in the face of evil. However people may feel towards us, we treat them with goodwill, kindness and benevolence. Love seeks the ultimate good of the other person, and so may at times involve correction and punishment as well.

The six antitheses serve as examples or illustrations that help clarify the meaning of fulfilling the Law and the Prophets, i.e. doing the will of God. It means first of all affirming the original divine intention over against interpretations that seek to cloud, minimise or evade it. The higher righteousness has to do primarily with character formation – becoming the kind of person who neither breaks nor fails to restore a relationship; who does not violate another's marriage partner by act, thought or desire, or the indissoluble marriage-bond; being truthful and non-retaliatory and not excluding enemies from loving concern. A character so formed will have an effect on individual decisions about ethical behaviour. What Jesus is doing is interpreting the Old Law through the commandment of love and the Golden Rule of treating others like we would like them to treat us. Jesus completes the Law not only in outward acts, but also in thoughts and words, feelings and desires. His aim is to purify the heart, the seat of motivation. Love of neighbour needs external direction if it is to be translated into concrete behaviour. The reason is that the Christian life is lived out in the context of community relationships that are meant to form disciples for mission in the world.

ACTS OF PIETY

In the Jewish religion, prayer, fasting and almsgiving belonged to the essence of religion – alms to the poor, prayer to foster a relationship with God, and fasting for self-discipline. In identically structured pieces, each one castigates the example of hypocrites and the long-winded prayers of Gentiles before giving the Our Father as a model of prayer with an added saying on forgiveness. Appropriate piety is done before God to be seen and rewarded by him alone. The aim or intention should be directed towards God, not to the applause and adulation of others. The focus is on the vertical relationship with God. Inner attitudes should be congruent with outer appearance and behaviour. There is hyperbole and caricature to highlight a tendency in human nature to which people are usually blind. Earlier in 5:16 there was the concern about the visibility of the good deeds of disciples because otherwise people will not be moved to praise God. Here the emphasis is that almsgiving be done in such a way that premature praise by others is avoided. The aim is the purification of motives in relating to God. Whether public or private, all forms of piety are to be done for God alone.

In praying, there is no need to imitate the garrulous prayers of the pagans in an effort to control God, since God already knows our needs and wants only our good. The prayer of Jesus consists of an address to God, three Thou-petitions and three Us-petitions. It is addressed to 'Our Father in heaven', which gives prayer an upward, transcendent direction. Addressing God as Father shows that a deep trust characterises the relationship between Christians and their God who is also the Father of Jesus. We speak of God as Father, not to say that God is male, but to maintain the otherness and transcendence of God from his creation and, at the same time, to show that God is related to his creation in a personal way. This mode of relating has been revealed to us by Jesus.

The three Thou-petitions are virtually synonymous. They are a prayer for the speedy, definitive establishment of God's kingdom when God's name will be held in respect and his will is fully carried out. The Us-petitions concern both the present and the future. Daily bread can refer to a request for daily sustenance as well as for the hastening of the heavenly banquet already anticipated in the Eucharist. When Christians forgive others, they are assured of God's forgiveness by adopting an attitude that makes forgiveness possible (cf. 6:14-15). The petition not to be brought to the time of trial or testing is a prayer not to be led into a situation where faith will not be able to survive. It also includes a petition to be rescued from the evil one. A deep trust characterises the disciple's relationship with God.

For the Jews, fasting often accompanied prayer and took on a dismal aspect so as to be seen by others and win their admiration and applause. The person who is truly fasting for religious reasons will not be interested in others' praise. Nobody will know they are fasting except their heavenly Father who will reward them accordingly.

MATERIAL POSSESSIONS

In 6:19-34 there is a set of directives dealing with priorities in relation to God and possessions, and of trust in God to provide for our needs. It begins with a warning against greed and hoarding, for one's heart will be where one's treasure is. Rather than hoarding, it is far better to make a habit of storing up treasures in heaven by practising generosity towards others. In Jewish thinking, the eye was used metaphorically to indicate one's disposition towards others. A sound eye reflects a generous disposition, while an evil eye indicates greed and selfishness. On the spiritual level, no one can serve two masters – it has to be either God or Mamon (wealth conceived as a rival to God). These three sayings are concerned with relationships, so it is important to get priorities right about possessions. Enslavement to possessions cannot easily be brought into harmony with service to God and others.

At the root of hoarding, greed or stinginess is anxiety that is now dealt with by advocating trust in God to provide for one's needs: 'You are not to worry.' Although food, drink and clothing are regarded as necessities of life, the focus here is reassuring disciples of God's trustworthiness. If God provides for the birds of the air, here held up as an example of freedom from anxiety, how much more will God provide for human beings? Since God is a loving Father, disciples should give priority to God's kingdom and its righteousness and leave the future in God's hands. A life free from undue anxiety about the necessities of existence opens up new possibilities for living and decision-making.

TRUE WISDOM

Taken in context, 'Do not judge' (7:1) does not mean abstaining from discernment that evaluates the difference between good and evil. There is a legitimate judging in which disciples should be engaged. Jesus' teaching is opposed to pharisaic judgementalism, not discernment. It refers to the condemnation of another by one who has not judged oneself. This is brought home by the use of vivid metaphors and grotesque contrasts to make the point. Insight into one's own imperfection should lead to a loving interaction with others, for attempting to correct the faults of another without first attending to one's own is surely hypocritical. On the other hand, disciples should not fail to discern between what is holy and what is unclean and act accordingly. God will supply the wisdom to enable this discernment when we ask, seek and knock for it in prayer with confidence and perseverance. Judging and evaluating are to be done in the light of the Golden Rule – to do the good that one would wish done for oneself. The commandment of love practised towards others lays the foundation for the new community of disciples. If we can see differently then we can become different people, and so character is formed.

EXHORTATIONS AND WARNINGS

There are three units, each built around a contrast: two gates/ ways; two trees; two houses that are concerned with the theme of judgement and expectation of the end. The command to enter the narrow gate makes the choice between the two ways clear-cut. The basis of the choice is explained by contrast: the wide gate and spacious way lead to perdition, whereas the narrow gate and difficult road lead to life. The images set before the disciple an either-or choice. The assertion that only few find it establishes the urgency of the admonition rather than the significance of the number involved. The second image of two trees is preceded by a warning against false prophets and the basis of their recognition is their fruits or deeds. The nature of a tree is revealed by its fruit, i.e. deeds emerge out of and reveal one's character. The destiny of a tree is also revealed by its fruit. Accordingly, the criterion for distinguishing between true and false prophets is their deeds. The basis for entry to the kingdom is *doing* God's will and so a scene is described where various groups come before the Judge who is Jesus. But he refuses to acknowledge them because the crucial test is bearing good fruit, not merely profession of faith, exorcisms or miracles alone. These are subordinated to the ethical demands of doing God's will as interpreted and proclaimed by Jesus.

The Sermon begins with blessings and ends with warnings. There is a contrast between two houses with an emphasis on their fate – will they be standing when the storm is over? It all depends on their foundations. The parable puts before the disciples two possibilities of wise and foolish builders. One builds on rocky foundations and so the house is able to withstand the storms with their attendant floods and gales; the other builds on sandy foundations and the house collapses when the storm comes. The forces of nature symbolise the verdict of the final judgement. Jesus and his teaching, spoken with authority and conviction, is the true foundation on which disciples are to build their lives.

The Reader

The Sermon on the Mount is not a set of rules or exhaustive guidance for every situation. Rather it is emblematic of the kind of persons disciples are and the kinds of things they do. The essence of the Christian life, though, is the love of God poured into our hearts at Baptism by the Spirit, to which we respond by loving in return. How disciples are to love is the subject matter of the Sermon on the Mount. It is on the basis of this love that we will be judged (cf. 25:31-46). The Good News of the kingdom inaugurated by Jesus is both the inward power of the Spirit's activity and the response to it in a faith that works through charity. However, without external guidelines to form character and help decision-making, even disciples could easily become prey to self-deception. Love needs external direction if it is to be translated into concrete human actions, hence the Church's moral tradition. The Christian life is lived out in a community context – the Church – that is ruled by the Spirit and the external word of those placed over it by the same Spirit. Jesus is both teacher and guide who trains disciples throughout the Gospel of Matthew, and he also models who Christians are to become not only as individuals but also as a community of disciples for mission in the world.

Conclusion

The Gospel of Matthew presupposes the initial preaching of the Gospel (*kerygma*), conversion, faith, Baptism into the community and the experience of new life in Christ. The gift of God precedes the demand of God. The evangelist is concerned with post-baptismal catechesis (*Didache*) to enable the newly baptised to live out the Christian life in community – what believers are to do, how they are to behave as disciples of Jesus. Jesus himself provides the great example in doing 'all that righteousness demands' (3:15) right up to his Passion as an act of obedience to the Father (cf. 26:42). Those who love God and neighbour as taught by Jesus fulfil God's will.

Matthew serves to remind the Christian that authentic commitment to the gift of God's love given to us in Jesus Christ is possible only within the context of membership of his community where the risen Lord continues to be present. It is here that disciples will mature in their foundational experience of God's love in the company of those who have freely submitted to his rule in Jesus Christ. Matthew gives considerable teaching on discipleship, not only in the five discourses that characterise his work, but also throughout the many narrative sections. The teaching serves to specify what the acceptance of Christ and of his demands mean for an authentic experience of his love within the community. The wealth of precepts and examples of conduct for Christian living serve to instruct the newly baptised on the meaning of authentic communion with the risen Christ present in the midst of his Church. Adherence to Jesus Christ is gauged by fidelity to the demands of fraternal love within the community.

The newly baptised person is equipped with guidelines for the fostering of such love, for example, true greatness in the kingdom (18:1-4), on leading others astray (18:5-10), rescuing the lost (18:12-14), fraternal correction and authority within the community (18:15-18), prayer in common (18:19-20) and forgiveness of hurts (18:21-35). The disciple must cultivate that love which sees the presence of the risen Lord in one's brothers and sisters, in the poor, the needy and the weak. In this way, newcomers are introduced into the community where the risen Christ is experienced, and they are taught how to behave in a community setting. The Gospel of Matthew accordingly serves as a practical initiation into the life of the Christian community. He also tells us that this community is a structured one; Christ has placed leaders to guide disciples in the living out of their commitment so that they avoid the danger of self-deception. The Church, however, is not some kind of cosy, exclusive club that becomes an end in itself. It is meant to prepare disciples to go out and evangelise the world. This is the focus of the third moment of Christian initiation and a major theme in Luke-Acts.

NOTES

1. Rudolph Schnackenburg, *Jesus in the Gospels: A Biblical Christology* (Kentucky: Westminster John Knox Press, 1995), p. 83.

2. Charles H. Talbert, *Reading the Sermon on the Mount: Character Formation and Decision Making in Matthew 5-7* (Columbia, South Carolina: University of South Carolina Press, 2004).

3. Michael Mullins, *The Gospel of Matthew* (Dublin: The Columba Press, 2007), p. 152.

4. Ibid., p. 156.

5. Ibid., pp. 167–168.

6. William Barclay, *The Gospel of Matthew*, vol. 1 revised and updated (Louisville, KY: Westminster John Knox Press, 2001), p. 151.

7. Matthew alone has an 'exceptive' clause ('except for *porneia*' 5:32; 19:9). He is referring to incestuous unions, i.e. marriages within prohibited degrees of consanguinity and affinity that were already forbidden in the Old Testament (cf. Lv 18:6-18).

CHAPTER FOUR

THIRD MOMENT: CHRISTIAN MISSION – THE GOSPEL OF LUKE-ACTS

Introduction

Luke-Acts serves as a two-volume manual for meeting the needs of the third phase of Christian maturation. It was written for Christians who, already committed to Jesus Christ and living out that commitment in the community he formed, seek to grasp its meaning and significance for the world at large. Living the Christian life in a pagan world created the need for the early community to defend and explain itself to outsiders. Accordingly, Luke explains the roots of the Christian community in the Jewish world (Lk 1–2) and relates the salvation promised to Israel and accomplished by Jesus to the whole world (cf. Ac 1:8) through the prophetic witnesses of his disciples. Luke's narrative meets the need for a transcultural dialogue by compiling a new synthesis of the traditions. Disciples need to be intellectually equipped to confront the social, political, economic, cultural and religious complexities of life in the world outside the Christian community. They also need to be able to appreciate the values existing in secular society and other religious traditions, and to demonstrate that Christianity complements and brings them to fulfilment. Their situation called for a new presentation in a powerful, well-articulated literary narrative that demands a literary interpretation. William Barclay sees in Luke's Gospel 'Jesus at his most beautiful and the Gospel at its widest'.

The Gospel of Luke was originally joined to the Acts of the Apostles as part of a two-volume work and was intended to be read as such. It is a magnificent narrative that blends the story of Jesus with that of the early Church. Luke provides an account of Jesus' life and teaching, followed by a narrative of the disciples' missionary work and preaching to equip his readers for a universal mission in the world. Luke is engaging in intercultural dialogue when he retells the story of Jesus for predominantly Greek-speaking, non-Jewish converts who inhabited the eastern part of the Roman Empire. He places his story in the context of world history and connects it not only with Israel (cf. Lk 1:5), but also with the civilized world of the time (cf. Lk 2:1-2; 3:1-2; Ac 18:12) by identifying powerful figures in Palestine, Asia Minor and Europe. He shows that the Gospel message is not limited to any one culture, for the story of Jesus belongs to all people. Luke's original contribution was connecting events in the early Church to those of Jesus' ministry and to the whole story of God's people in the Old Testament. God first fulfilled his promises to Israel through the ministry of Jesus and later extended these blessings to the Gentiles. Acts continues the story of the Gospel and confirms it. The Christian community of Luke's time is now sufficiently equipped and mature enough to bring the Good News to the world outside that community.

Luke is positive towards the world that he sees not only as God's creation, but also as the arena of history and human activity. The Roman Empire provides for the safety and spread of the Gospel whose messengers are law-abiding and reasonable people. Luke also affirms the value of culture by taking care to shape his story using forms of Hellenistic literature creatively, thereby implying the compatibility of Christianity with culture.

To affirm the world does not mean approving all human conduct or structures. On the contrary, in God's drawing near to his people through Jesus, a great reversal is proclaimed and carried out – the powerful and the rich are cast down, while the lowly, the marginalised and the outcast are lifted up and accepted by God (cf. Lk 1:51-54). These become part of the restored people of God. God's 'visitation' is for the salvation of his people, especially of the lost. This theme of salvation is pronounced in the Lucan parables (cf. Lost Sheep, Lost Coin, Lost Son, Lk 15). God's salvation brought by Jesus is a revelation of his kindness above all to the poor and the outcast.

The apostles continue Jesus' outreach to all kinds of people – powerful and weak, wealthy and poor, men and women, poor widows and provincial governors, kings and philosophers, as well as Jews. A significant part of historical Judaism became part of the restored people of God in Jerusalem (cf. Ac 2:41; 4:4; 21:20). Even though Paul's preaching was largely rejected by diaspora Jews, he never gave up trying to convince fellow Jews. The story of Luke-Acts shows that God's will is still the seeking of a people that include both Jews and Gentiles.

Outline of Luke

1. **Prologue (1:1-4)**
2. **The Infancy Narrative (1:5–2:52)**
   a. The Annunciation of the births of John and Jesus (1:5-56)
   b. The births of John and Jesus (1:57-80)
3. **Preparation for Public Ministry (3:1–4:13)**
   a. John the Baptist (3:1-20)
   b. Baptism, genealogy, temptations of Jesus (3:21–4:13)
4. **The Ministry of Jesus in Galilee (4:14–9:50)**
   a. Nazareth and Capernaum (4:14-44)

b. First disciples, cures, discussions, choice of the Twelve (5:1–6:16)

c. Discourse on the plain (6:17-49)

d. Ministry of Jesus, mission of the Twelve, prophecies of Passion (7:1–9:50)

5. **The Journey Narrative (9:51–19:27)**

   a. First section of journey to Jerusalem (9:51–13:21)

      I. Refusal in Samaria, hardships of disciples, mission of 72 (9:51–10:24)

      II. Good Samaritan, Martha and Mary, prayer, discussion (10:25–11:54)

      III. Disciples in the world, call to repentance (12:1-13:9)

      IV. Healings, parables (13:10-21)

   b. Second Section (13:22–17:10)

      I. Rejection of Jews, call to Gentiles (13:22-35)

      II. Parable of the banquet, renunciation (14:1-35)

      III. Three parables of God's mercy (15:1-32)

      IV. Temporal possessions, correction, service (16:1–17:10)

   c. Third Section (17:11–19:29)

      I. Ten lepers, Day of the Son of Man, importunate widow (17:11–18:8)

      II. Pharisee and publican, children, danger of riches (18:9-30)

      III. Third Passion prophecy, blind man, Zacchaeus, the pounds (18:31–19:27)

6. **The Jerusalem Ministry (19:28–21:38)**

   a. Entry, debates, wicked husbandman, resurrection, widow's mite (19:28–21:4)

   b. Apocalyptic discourse – warnings, destruction of Jerusalem, disasters, coming of Son of Man, sobriety and vigilance (21:5-38).

7. **The Passion of Jesus (22:1–23:56)**
   a. Plot, Last Supper, arrest, trials (22:1–23:25)
   b. Crucifixion and burial (23:26-56)
8. **The Resurrection of Jesus (24:1-53)**
   a. Appearances to women, on Emmaus road, to disciples (24:1-43)
   b. Mission of apostles and Ascension (24:44-53)

Storyline

After Luke's distinctive Greek-style literary prologue (1:1-4), his account of the birth and childhood of Jesus begins with chronological, political and geographical notes (1:5) that parallel the beginning of the next section (3:1-2). In between is a carefully structured infancy narrative (1:5-2:52) in which the stories surrounding the births of John and Jesus correspond to each other. Divine promise and fulfilment have a central role but the evangelist makes it clear that the real beginning is in the ancient past, in God's plan to bless the nations through Israel (cf. 1:55, 73-75, 79). Accordingly, Luke highlights the piety of Israel exemplified in the parents of John, Mary, the shepherds, Simeon and Anna. He also notes the importance of the Mosaic Law, the centrality of the Temple, and expectations for the restoration of a scattered Israel. Luke sets the story of Jesus within the larger story of God's dealings with Israel and can properly be understood only from within that context. The story of God's plan for the salvation of the human race, beginning with Abraham (cf. Gn 12:1-3), properly understood, leads up to and includes the coming of Jesus.

In Luke's account of the announcement of John's birth, the spotlight falls on his parents who are introduced as exemplary Jews. It begins with Zechariah's service as priest in the Temple.

Attention is drawn to the good news he receives from Gabriel, for John will call his people back to God through repentance. Zechariah's unbelief contrasts sharply with Elizabeth's response of welcome. Gabriel's announcement to Mary highlights God's favour, for it is in partnership with her that God will intervene to redeem Israel. Jesus is presented as the actualisation of the promise made to David of an everlasting dynasty, and he is characterised as Son of God in a special sense. Mary is blessed both as mother and for her faith by Elizabeth, while John hails the coming one even prior to his birth. The birth of John is followed by rejoicing, and Zechariah is enabled by the Spirit to prophesy. The importance of John as prophet and forerunner is noted. The hymns emphasise God's redemptive purpose, his faithfulness, and the character of the coming deliverance and restoration of God's people. News of Jesus' birth, however, does not go to the privileged and powerful but to lowly shepherds (2:8-20). The angelic announcement makes it clear that the true source of peace lies with the Saviour, Messiah and Lord who has been born in the Davidic town of Bethlehem. The circumcision of Jesus incorporates him into the people of Israel. In the Temple, Jesus is recognised and acclaimed as God's agent of salvation by Simeon and the universal reach of God's redemptive project is briefly mentioned. Simeon and Anna represent pious, expectant Israel in their single-minded devotion to God. A final episode in the Temple presents Jesus in the role of a faithful Jewish boy, raised in the traditions of Israel and fulfilling all that the law requires. But his divine Sonship, his obedience to the will of his Father, takes precedence over his earthly family.

The next major section of the Gospel is focused on Jesus' preparation for public ministry (3:1–4:13). John in his prophetic role prepares the way for the coming of the Lord. The Baptism he performs ought to result in behaviour consistent with their status as Abraham's children. Jesus is readied for his Spirit-filled mission as Son of God, and his Baptism is interpreted as his anointing for divine service. His genealogy reaching back to Adam hints at the universal scope of his mission as Son of God. Finally, the temptation scene shows Jesus fully embracing his status and mission as Son of God in the face of testing.[1] As God's Son, Jesus knows the ways of God, and Luke in the Gospel will reveal them to others.

The first phase of Jesus' public ministry is centred in Galilee (4:14–9:50) and highlights the power of the Spirit active in the ministry of Jesus. This ministry includes teachings and healings that demonstrate the character of Jesus' programme in concrete terms. It invites discipleship, but it also attracts hostility. Jesus' presence provokes a crisis within Israel. The scene at Nazareth (4:16-30) defines the nature of his ministry and tells us how to interpret his subsequent acts of ministry. Jesus situates his mission within the prophetic hope for the restoration of Israel, and extends the nature of that hope. The sermon inaugurates the time of fulfilment of Old Testament prophecy by proclaiming a jubilee year. His interpretation of 'the poor' is understood in the light of the healing ministry of two of Israel's prophets. One recipient is a widow, a non-Jew; the other is also a non-Jew who is a leper. Mention of these pagans provokes hostility among the hearers. The rejection of Jesus in his own hometown hints at a greater rejection of him by the people of Israel later on.

To the portrait of Jesus as prophet is now added, in the episodes that follow (4:31-44), a presentation of him as teacher, exorcist, healer and proclaimer of God's kingdom. They illustrate the missionary programme set forth by Jesus in his Nazareth sermon. Disciples are present for the first time. Simon

Peter's call to follow Jesus is linked to the story of a miraculous catch of fish (5:1-11). Peter and the sons of Zebedee respond as exemplary disciples; they leave everything to follow him, thereby demonstrating the nature of an authentic response to Jesus' ministry. The restoration of Israel is furthered by the choice of the Twelve as apostles (6:12-16). They symbolise the new leadership for God's restored people chosen after a night of prayer, and will provide continuity between the historical Jesus and the Church of Luke's day. As the original eyewitnesses, they guarantee the fidelity of the Church's beliefs and practices to the teachings of Jesus. They are named 'apostles' because they will be sent out as missionaries to proclaim the Word of God. The Sermon on the Plain (6:20-49) serves to identify and develop a vision of the new world that Jesus proclaims and introduces. It begins with a carefully balanced series of blessings and woes. New attitudes and behaviours flow from Jesus' image of God as a merciful Father. At the core of the sermon is Jesus' teaching on the love of one's enemies motivated by God's graciousness and forgiveness for all humanity. Jesus brings his discourse to a close by urging his audience not only to listen but also to hear and obey his message. There is need for changed dispositions and commitments that manifest themselves in changed behaviour.

In the exemplary stories that follow, Jesus sets out the new values, commitments and behaviours to be shared by those who participate in the new community being formed around Jesus (7:1-8:21). They reflect some of Luke's particular interests: the faith of a Gentile centurion; Jesus' compassion for a widowed mother; his ministry to the afflicted and unfortunate; the role of John and Jesus in God's plan of salvation; a forgiven sinner's manifestation of love; and the association of women with the ministry of Jesus, something that was unusual at that time. They model Jesus' own graciousness and mirror his service towards others, exemplifying for others his message regarding faith and wealth. In the following parables (8:4-18), authentic hearing is demonstrated by producing fruit, because how one hears will eventually become manifest in one's behaviour. Threats to discipleship include those who will not believe the initial preaching; others will be deflected from discipleship by temptation, cares, riches or pleasure, while others still will lack the patient endurance necessary to bring forth a harvest in good deeds. Kinship with Jesus is determined not by ancestral ties, but through hearing and doing the Word of God. The following section (8:22-56) records four miracles that manifest Jesus' power and authority to save – the calming of the storm, the exorcism of a demoniac, the cure of a woman with a haemorrhage, and the raising to life of Jairus's daughter – with a focus on the faith of the recipients.

Jesus expands his mission (9:1-50) by sending out the Twelve to proclaim the kingdom, exorcise demons and heal the sick and, on their return, Jesus feeds five thousand, which represents feeding the hungry. Herod's perplexity raises the question of Jesus' identity. None of the popular opinions capture the truth that Jesus is the Messiah who must suffer, and his followers must be willing to take up their cross 'every day' and follow him (9:23). Jesus' sonship is affirmed at the transfiguration as Moses and Elijah converse with him about his departure from the world to his heavenly Father in Jerusalem. Following the cure of the epileptic demoniac, the disciples do not understand Jesus' prophecy of the Passion, instead their arguments and rivalry over greatness coupled with jealousy of an outsider, show that they are not yet ready to follow Jesus in suffering (9:43-50).

The Journey to Jerusalem (9:51-19:27) is, as Luke presents it, a time of preparation of the disciples for the formation of God's people. Jesus teaches his followers about the character of God as a gracious Father who bestows the blessings of salvation on all people. That is why his teachings, especially in the form of parables – many of them found only in Luke – dominate this section of the Gospel. Miracles underline Jesus' conflict with opponents over the merciful application of the Law. Although it is called a Journey Narrative, a reflection of Israel's exodus journey, it is more concerned with the ongoing transformation of the disciples given their obduracy up to this point. Still, the end of the journeying is important to the progress of the Gospel. It is in Jerusalem, the centre of the Jewish world, with its Temple and leaders, that the climax of God's salvific purpose will be accomplished. It is here that Jesus will undergo his 'exodus' from the world and be 'taken up', and it is from Jerusalem that the mission 'to the ends of the earth' will begin.

While the Samaritans reject a salvation history centred in Jerusalem, Jesus dissociates himself from the attitude expressed by the disciples (9:51-56). Luke underlines Jesus' resolve to embark on a journey that will end in Jerusalem. Also included is the radical call to join him in fully embracing God's will. All other commitments and considerations, even family ties and filial obligations, are secondary. The appointment of seventy-two missionaries, with the spotlight on their participation in Jesus' mission, also anticipates the universal mission in Acts (10:1-48). Because of the urgency of the mission and the single-mindedness required of missionaries, attachment to material possessions is to be avoided. The experience of mission results in mixed responses including conflict, division and even rejection. On their return, Jesus recognises that his own mission, now

THE FOUR GOSPELS: *Following in the Footsteps of Jesus*

shared with his followers, spells the defeat of all evil forces. As the Kingdom of God is gradually being established, the dominion of Satan over humanity is coming to an end. It is the privilege of the disciples to witness the presence of God's reign in the mission of Jesus.

In response to a question from a Jewish expert in the Mosaic Law about inheriting eternal life, Jesus illustrates the superiority of love over legalism in the story of the Good Samaritan (10:25-37). The religious representatives of Judaism who would have been expected to act in a neighbourly fashion towards the victim pass him by and continue their journey. Moreover, the identity of the 'neighbour' requested by the lawyer turns out to be a hated Samaritan. In this encounter, the emphasis falls on doing, while in the following story of Martha and Mary the focus is on hearing. Both are necessary. Luke now presents three episodes concerned with prayer (11:1-13). Jesus teaches the disciples a communal prayer, the importance of persistence in prayer, and the effectiveness of prayer. Jesus reveals the fatherhood of God in terms of generosity, compassion, care and faithful activity on behalf of his children, outstripping even the best of human fathers in his bestowing of the Spirit on those who ask him.

An exorcism (11:14ff) provokes a reply from Jesus that situates his ministry of exorcism within the struggle between two domains – that of Satan and that of God. There is no middle way. Hearing and doing God's Word are the basis of blessedness. The sign of Jonah is interpreted as the need for repentance in anticipation of the impending judgement. The Pharisees and legal experts with whom Jesus dines are adept at interpreting the Law, but their lack of proper inner dispositions, Jesus tells them, leads to self-aggrandisement that in turn gives rise to neglect of the poor and opposition to God's spokespersons

(11:37-54). Several topics are woven together under the theme of vigilance in the face of crisis (12:1-13:9). Disciples are to be aware of the influence of those who do not practise what they preach. This is followed by a collection of Jesus' sayings exhorting his followers to acknowledge him and his mission fearlessly, assuring them of the Spirit's protection even in times of persecution. Luke has joined sayings contrasting those whose focus and trust in life is on material possessions, symbolised by the parable of the rich fool, with those who recognise their complete dependence on God. Jesus' disciples are freed from the danger of possessions and are enabled to reorder their lives so as to care for the poor (12:13-34). All this is in view of the certainty of Jesus' return and the uncertainty of its timing (12:35ff). The present time is a time of readiness, vigilance and waiting that affords an opportunity for faithful service in view of future rewards and punishments. Jesus' message is like a purifying fire that meets with acceptance or rejection and will be a source of conflict and dissension even within families (12:51-53). The presence of God's reign in Jesus' person and ministry marks an epochal shift, confronting people with the need to embrace the new rather than clinging to the old. People who are able to interpret the present time will see it as a demand for a personal decision. They must judge what is the right thing to do (12:54-59).

The cure of the crippled woman, and later on of the man with dropsy healed on the Sabbath, and the controversies that result show Jesus' concern for both women and men. Two parables (13:18-21) are used to illustrate the future proportions of the kingdom that will result from deceptively small beginnings in the preaching and healing ministry of Jesus. Great effort is required for entry into this kingdom (13:22ff) and there is an urgency to accept the present opportunity to enter. Otherwise the places at table reserved for the people of God will be taken by Gentiles from the four corners of the world who will precede those to whom the invitation was first extended. Nobody, not even Herod, will prevent Jesus from carrying out God's will and establishing his kingdom. Only when Jesus reaches Jerusalem will his work be accomplished.

The banquet scene (14:7-14), found only in Luke, provides an opportunity for teaching that preoccupation with social status is less important than concern for others coupled with a modest estimation of oneself. The parable of the great dinner (14:15-24) is a further illustration of Israel's rejection of Jesus' invitation to share in the banquet of the kingdom and the extension to those who recognise their need of salvation, including Gentiles. Another collection of sayings focuses on the total dedication necessary for a disciple of Jesus — no attachment to family or possessions can stand in the way. The half-hearted disciple is like contaminated salt that cannot serve its intended purpose (14:34-35).

Pharisees and scribes present a challenge to Jesus concerning the maintenance of socio-religious boundaries. Jesus' reply takes the form of two brief parables and a lengthy parable-story (15:1-32). All three are focused on the recovery of what is lost, followed by celebration at the finding as illustrations of the joy of the heavenly jubilation accompanying the repentance of a sinner. God is not withdrawn from human affairs, but is actively seeking out those who are lost. The third parable in particular demonstrates the gravity of the situation of the lost son whose declining lifestyle is far removed from Jewish faithfulness. The character of the elder son mimics that of the Pharisees and scribes. The motif of celebration at the return of the lost son gives expression to the magnitude and persistence of God's graciousness and his boundless mercy towards those who recognise their errors and return to God.

The parable of the crafty steward illustrates the need to learn from the 'real world' about how the new age works (16:1-13). Just as the steward was astute enough to engage in business practices that guaranteed his future security, so also disciples should engage in prudent practices that guarantee their heavenly future. Wealth should be used to welcome outsiders, particularly those who are incapable of making a return. Serving God and being a slave to riches, like the Pharisees, are incompatible. John is presented as a transitional figure between the period of Israel, the time of promise, and the period of Jesus, the time of fulfilment. Marriage is presented as a lifelong commitment.

The parable of the rich man and Lazarus (16:19-31), found only in Luke, illustrates his concern with Jesus' attitude towards rich and poor. The rich man should have extended the compassion of hospitality to the beggar at his gate. Yet for all his worldly comforts, the rich man's total disregard for the poor plunged him into ruin, while Lazarus, despite his earthly hardships, is escorted to Abraham's side. The reversal of fates illustrates the teachings of Jesus' Beatitudes and Woes in the Sermon on the Plain. Jesus turns to his disciples to warn them against scandal, the necessity of fraternal correction and the power of faith. Disciples can make no claim on God's graciousness in fulfilling the demands of discipleship, for they are only doing their duty (17:1-10).

As the journey continues, a number of suitable examples regarding the nature of discipleship and the ongoing transformation of disciples are drawn from the margins of acceptable socio-religious society (17:11–18:14). They include a leper who is a Samaritan, a widow and a tax collector. In the episode of the healing of the lepers, at least one of them is a Samaritan who returns to thank him. It provides an instance of Jesus holding up a non-Jew as an example to follow in the faith manifested by this foreigner that brought him salvation. The kingdom is already present in Jesus' healing ministry. Further traditional sayings of Jesus about the unpredictable suddenness of the day of the Son of Man assures his audience that, in spite of the delay, it will bring judgement unexpectedly on those who fail to be vigilant (17:22-37). They underscore the need for a faithful response to the presence of God already at work in their midst.

The parable of the persistent widow (18:1-8) emphasises the importance of tenacious, hopeful faith. The widow should have accepted her fate, but by refusing to do so, acts so out of character that the judge is astonished. In this way she becomes a model of perseverance in prayer so that disciples do not fall victim to apostasy. The second parable condemns the critical, self-righteous attitude of the Pharisee and teaches that the fundamental attitude of the Christian disciple must be a recognition of sinfulness and complete dependence on God's graciousness like the tax collector (18:9-14). The sayings on children furnish a contrast to the attitude of the Pharisee and that of the wealthy aristocrat in the following story. They both assume that they can lay claim to God's favour by their own merit. The attitude of a disciple, on the other hand, should be one of receptivity and trustful dependence characteristic of children. Detachment from material possessions results in total dependence on God on the part of one who would inherit eternal life (18:15-30). Wealth is inextricably woven together with issues of power, status and social privilege and so can be a danger for disciples whose renunciation will be rewarded. The disciples, however, are still possessed by values that do not allow them to fully understand Jesus' prophecy of his coming sufferings. The blind beggar is an example of the 'poor' to whom Jesus' ministry is directed.

The episode of Zacchaeus (19:1-10) is marked by irony, since he goes to great lengths to see Jesus only to discover that Jesus is already seeking him. By his repentance and generosity towards the poor, he shows himself to be a true descendent of Abraham. Zacchaeus exemplifies the proper attitude towards wealth in giving half his possessions to the poor and consequently becomes the recipient of salvation. In the parable of the pounds, Luke combines two originally distinct parables – one about the conduct of faithful and productive servants, and a parable about a rejected king (19:11-27). Jesus stresses the need for diligence and responsibility. He expects the disciples to fulfil their Christian duty in his absence. His return is closely linked with the judgement on Israel seen in the downfall of Jerusalem, and of his Second Coming in glory to judge all nations at the end of time.

The Jerusalem ministry (19:28–21:38), characterised by Jesus' daily teaching in the Temple, begins with the triumphant entry of Jesus into the holy city and a reception appropriate to a royal figure. The peace that Jesus brings is associated with the salvation to be accomplished in Jerusalem. But by refusing to accept him, Jerusalem will not find peace; instead it will become the victim of devastation represented as God's judgement (19:28-44). Jesus' action in the Temple is highly symbolic. The Temple, intended as a house of prayer, has become instead a cave for bandits. Jesus seeks to reclaim its courts as the place to preach his 'good news to the poor'. His subsequent interaction with the Jewish authorities (20:1-19) revolves around the question of authority – who speaks for God? The result is a tug-of-war between Jesus and the Jewish authorities over the fundamentals of the faith of Israel. Luke underscores the fact that Jesus' authority comes from God, that he interprets the will of God faithfully, and that the Jerusalem leadership do not have divine approval. Jesus provides an answer to their question concerning his authority in the form of a parable that provides a shorthand summary of God's dealings with his people by locating the story of Jesus within the story of Israel (20:9-19). By distinguishing between the vineyard and the tenants, the parable foresees the vitality of Israel beyond the judgement that falls on Jerusalem and its leaders. In an attempt to incriminate Jesus with the Roman authorities and to discredit him with the people, the leaders pose a question regarding the payment of taxes. Jesus uses the trap question put to him on the issue of taxes to illustrate a higher duty towards God.

The Sadducees challenge Jesus about his teaching on the afterlife by ridiculing the idea (20:27-40). Jesus argues for belief in the resurrection of the dead on the basis of the written Torah that the Sadducees themselves accept. After successfully answering the questions put to him by his opponents, Jesus in turn asks them a question (20:41-44). Their inability to respond implies that they have forfeited their position and authority as religious leaders of the people because they are unable to explain the Scriptures. Jesus goes on to mention a series of public practices characteristic of those seeking honours. The widow is another example of the poor whose detachment from material possessions and dependence on God lead to blessedness. Her simple offering provides a striking contrast to the pride and pretentiousness of the leaders of the people.

In the eschatological discourse (21:5-38), Luke focuses on the importance of the day-to-day following of Jesus and reinterprets the meaning of some of the signs of the end to explain to the early Christian community what seems like a delay of the second coming. He separates the historical destruction of Jerusalem from the signs of the coming of the Son of Man by what he refers to as 'the times of the Gentiles' when the Good News will be proclaimed to them. In the meantime, the fall of Jerusalem inaugurates a new stage of salvation history during which God protects Christians who will face hostility and even death from both Jews and Gentiles. Christians who live in the world in the in-between time can remain confident that Jesus' words will not pass away. They are to remain watchful and pray for the strength to endure before appearing in the presence of the Son of Man, whose coming will be heralded by cosmic signs.

The Passion of Jesus (22:1–23:56) in Luke incorporates his own special traditions into the narrative: the tradition of the institution of the Eucharist; Jesus' farewell discourse; the mistreatment and interrogation of Jesus; Jesus before Herod and again before Pilate; words addressed to the women on the way to Calvary; words to the penitent thief; and the death of Jesus. Luke stresses the innocence of Jesus who is a victim of the powers of evil and who goes to his death in fulfilment of his Father's will. Throughout, Luke emphasises the compassion, mercy and healing power of Jesus who is accompanied by others on the way of the cross.

Judas provides a way for the Jewish leadership to apprehend Jesus by agreeing to betray him for money. At a deeper level, the conflict against Jesus and his ministry is the work of Satan and so takes on cosmic dimensions. Nevertheless, Jesus is no helpless victim in the events of his suffering and death. Instead he demonstrates foresight with regard to the preparations. Luke clearly identifies the last supper of Jesus with the apostles as a Passover meal that commemorated the deliverance to Israel from slavery in Egypt. Jesus reinterprets the significance of the feast by setting it in the context of the kingdom, in particular by regarding it as a covenant-making event grounded in the covenant sacrifice provided by Jesus' own death, and symbolised by the words spoken over the bread and the cup. Meals have already played a pivotal role in the Gospel of Luke, so a final meal's setting is again crucial. In the context of his approaching death, Jesus draws together important threads of his message, interpreting his death within the purposes of God and preparing those gathered around him for the future. Judas's betrayal is seen to serve a higher purpose without, however, excusing his culpability for his act of betrayal. Jesus forbids his followers from imitating the attitudes and practices of the kings of the Gentiles. The apostles are identified as empowered leaders who will govern the restored people of God. They must be ready for the opposition and violence that are sure to come in their missionary endeavours. The disciples misunderstand Jesus' teaching by taking literally the language of sword-bearing (22:35-38).

The scene at the Mount of Olives (22:39-46) is the critical moment in which Jesus' faithfulness to God's will is fully embraced in the context of prayer. Jesus is portrayed as an example to be followed by his disciples. In the arrest scene, Jesus appears as a person in control of circumstances that would otherwise seem overwhelming. This is because he discerns and willingly embraces God's will. Only Luke recounts the healing of the injured servant. After Peter has denied him three times, the Lord's expression leads to his weeping bitterly over his denial. Jesus is mocked as a prophet by the guards. Luke's version of the trial (22:66–23:25) underscores the wickedness of the Jewish leadership in having Jesus condemned to death. There are four scenes: the hearing before the Sanhedrin where false accusations and a verdict has already been decided; the hearing before Pilate; the hearing before Herod; and the sentencing of Jesus by Pilate. Luke's description of the trial before Pilate insists that Jesus is innocent of the charges of stirring up political rebellion. Even though Pilate persists in affirming Jesus' innocence, he is manipulated by an angry crowd into handing Jesus over for crucifixion, while the Jewish leaders ask for the release of a known murderer and rebel.

Throughout the Gospel, Luke has emphasised the need for the Christian disciple to follow in the footsteps of Jesus. This is highlighted in the incident of Simon of Cyrene who takes up the cross and follows after Jesus in the company of a large crowd of people. Even at his crucifixion, Jesus continues to take the initiative. In the shadow of death, he intercedes on behalf of his enemies, extends the hope and promise of salvation to the penitent thief, and offers up his life to God. Jesus' royal status and role as Saviour are confirmed on the cross. He is portrayed in the Old Testament language of the righteous sufferer (23:47) who opens up the way for Jew and Gentile alike to respond hopefully after his death. Joseph, a member of the Jewish elite, cares for Jesus' dead body and gives it a fitting burial.

Luke has rewritten traditional stories about the empty tomb and the resurrection appearances (24:1-53). In a well-crafted story (24:13-35), he emphasises that Jesus' suffering and death are not a contradiction of God's plan of salvation, rather they bring it to completion. Jesus' death, resurrection and ascension are grounded in Scripture, vindicating Jesus' life, identity and the nature of his mission. The Messiah has suffered, entered into glory, and at Emmaus renews his presence to two disciples at a meal that recalls the Eucharist. The Jesus who appears is the crucified one raised up by God to a glorious life. The Old Testament is best understood in the light of Jesus, whose followers must be enabled to interpret it and carry out the ministry of Jesus to the whole world. The mission of the disciples continues the work of Jesus' ministry and reflects a new stage of salvation history. Jesus ascends into heaven to exercise royal power. This constitutes the bridge between the ministry of Jesus and the mission of the Church, for it is as a consequence of his exaltation that Jesus sends the Spirit. The resurrection stories have introduced the reader to ways in which Jesus will now be present to the Church – through the Spirit and in the breaking of bread. The Gospel concludes with the disciples offering prayer and praise in the Temple while awaiting the Spirit to initiate the next stage of the drama of salvation – the spread of the Gospel from Jerusalem to the whole world that is recounted in Luke's companion volume, the Acts of the Apostles.

Literary Characteristics

Luke begins his narrative with a literary prologue that shows his sensitivity to the surrounding pagan culture by imitating the great historians of Greek antiquity. Together, the opening verses make up a formal periodic sentence, written in elegant Greek. Its purpose is to dispose the reader to appreciate the grandeur of the theme he is about to recount. The episodes in the Infancy Narrative are filled with joy and hope that Jesus will bring all the Old Testament promises to fulfilment. Luke anchors his Gospel in the traditions of the Old Testament by portraying Jesus as the Saviour of God's covenant people. This salvation extends also to Gentiles. His Gospel is an artistic and spiritual masterpiece and, together with Acts, gives a clear and convincing witness to the greatness of Jesus as he continues his worldwide mission of salvation through the Church. The author also wishes to make it attractive to the Hellenistic world in which he and other Christians lived. He instructs and equips his readers by narrating the teaching and example of both Jesus and his disciples. His Gospel already shows a Gentile provenance: Luke seldom quotes the Old Testament, omits Semitic words and Jesus' controversies with the Jews. He stresses instead episodes involving Samaritans and Gentiles and consciously relates his narrative to contemporary events (cf. Lk 1:5; 2:1; 3:1-2). Luke contains some of the best-known and best-loved stories in the Gospel. He is a superb and gifted storyteller; only in Luke do we find memorable stories like the Good Samaritan, the Prodigal Son, the Rich Fool, the Rich Man and Lazarus, and the Emmaus encounter. In Acts are recounted the wonderful stories of Ananias and Sapphira, Simon Magus, Peter's release from prison, and Paul's shipwreck.

The Infancy Narratives (Lk 1–2) portrays Jesus emerging from the best in Judaism, the *'anawim*, the poor, who prayerfully await the fulfilment of God's promises made to their ancestors. These Old Testament characters represent Israel: Zechariah and Elizabeth, the shepherds, Simeon and Anna encounter Mary and the infant Jesus. In this way, Luke shows that neither Jesus nor his proclamation contradicts Judaism. In the opening chapters of Acts, he tells of thousands of Jews who accepted the apostolic preaching. Luke emphasises that God's plan is being carried out by recapitulating the hopes of the faithful people of Israel. Nevertheless, the light that is to be a revelation for the

Gentiles and the glory of Israel is set for the fall as well as the rising of many in Israel (cf. Lk 2:34). The joyful expectation of Israel's awaited Messiah has become a reality in the birth of Jesus to bring salvation to all people. Through Jesus, God's peace and blessings will become a reality for both Jews and Gentiles (cf. Lk 2:29-32).

Luke relates the greater part of Jesus' ministry in the form of a journey from Galilee to Jerusalem (9:51–19:27), during which he instructs his disciples and includes traditions that are special to him. He then treats of the Jerusalem ministry, Passion, death, resurrection and ascension. In Acts, the risen Jesus instructs his disciples and prepares them for the coming of the Spirit who will establish the Church through their preaching and miracles. There is continuity in God's plan of salvation from beginning to end. The second volume, Acts, opens with a programmatic statement (Ac 1:8) before tracing the beginning of the Church in Jerusalem (chapters 1–5), its expansion in Palestine and the beginning of the Gentile mission (chapters 6–12). The author then recounts Paul's journeys in Asia Minor, Macedonia and Greece (chapters 13–20) and ends with Paul's imprisonment, his journey to Rome (chapters 21–28), the goal of Paul's journey and his preaching to the pagans who will listen (28:28).

A note of universality is struck early in the Gospel. Jesus is to be a light to enlighten the pagans (2:31-32); preparations for ministry begin in a world context (3:1-2); and *all* people will see the salvation of God (cf. 3:6). Luke traces Jesus' ancestry back to Adam, the forefather of the human race (3:23-38). In his preaching at Nazareth, Jesus singles out for mention the Sidonian widow and the Syrian Namaan, both non-Jews (4:26-27). Disciples are called 'apostles' who are sent out to preach and heal (9:2). Luke alone includes the mission of the seventy-two[2] who prepare the way for Jesus' coming (10:1-20). Jesus says that people will come from east and west, from north and south to take their places at the feast in the Kingdom of God (13:29). He envisages a worldwide horizon for his mission. The parables of the Good Samaritan (10:29-37) and the Samaritan leper (17:11-19) show Jesus' reaching out to outsiders. He declares that disciples will be hauled before pagan kings and governors (21:12) and repentance will be preached to all nations (24:47).

This worldwide mission is carried out in Acts (1:8) with missionary sensitivity under the guidance of the Spirit. The author traces the first thirty years from the Ascension of Jesus to the imprisonment of Paul in Rome. His intention is to continue the story of Jesus through the life and mission of the first disciples. It is not, however, a lifeless, historical account, but one filled with stories of inspiring heroes, moving speeches and daring adventures. Neither is it an exhaustive account of early Christian beginnings, for Luke is more interested in the activity of the Spirit who descends on the apostles at Pentecost and sends them out to evangelise first Israel and then Gentiles with the Good News. He gives us glimpses of the attractiveness of the early Christian community (chapters 2:42-47; 4:32-35). Thanks to the Spirit, the Good News meets with astounding success and the Church is quickly built up, but not without opposition, imprisonments and persecutions. Philip instructs the Ethiopian who asks for an explanation of the Jewish Scriptures (8:26-40), while Peter crosses barriers to accept pagans (10:1-48) and comes to the realisation that God has no favourites. The evangelist is at pains to show that Paul is no missionary maverick, but a chosen messenger sent by the risen Christ by recounting his conversion three times (cf. chapters 9,

22, 26). The same power that was working through Peter in the beginning is also at work in Paul who preaches to the Jewish diaspora and to the pagans. When he encounters opposition and non-acceptance for his message among the Jews, he turns to the pagans who prove to be more receptive.

Acts of the Apostles

What Jesus began in the Spirit during his ministry is now continued in the same Spirit working through the apostles. Their ministry is the legitimate continuation of Jesus' proclamation of the kingdom. Luke shows that the preaching and teaching of representatives of the early Church are grounded in Jesus who, during his historical ministry, prepared specially chosen followers and commissioned them to be witnesses to his resurrection and to all that he said and did. This unbroken sense of continuity is Luke's way of guaranteeing the fidelity of the Church's teaching to that of Jesus. Moreover, by presenting the era of the Church as a distinct phase of salvation history, Luke shifts the early expectation of the Second Coming to the day-to-day concerns of the Christian community in the world. He is more interested in presenting the words and deeds of Jesus and his disciples as guides for the conduct of Christians in the in-between period, and with presenting Jesus himself as a model of piety and of the Christian life.

Acts employs a geographical plan for the spread of the Gospel. Dramatic episodes are fitted into a pattern of journeys. Persecutions, trials, imprisonments, shipwrecks and journeying provide readers with instruction as well as entertainment. Great harmony existed in these early communities. Luke shows us how Christians ought to live together and how they should work through difficulties they face in their mission to the world. Whatever history Acts preserves is put at the service of theology and pastoral preaching to give believers assurance and to strengthen their convictions. There is a marked parallelism between the Gospel of Luke and Acts. There is also emphasis on the Spirit and on prayer, meals, concern for the poor and the use of riches, fulfilment of Scripture, and witnessing. The missionary activity of the disciples is parallel to that of Jesus.

Outline of Acts

1. **The Beginning of the Church (1:1–2:47)**
   a. Prologue, Ascension, election of Matthias (1:1-26)
   b. Coming of Spirit, Peter's sermon, early community (2:1-47)

2. **The Church and the Jewish Authorities (3:1–5:42)**
   a. Healing, Peter's sermon, arrest, prayer, early community (3:1–4:37)
   b. A case of fraud, growth of the Church, second arrest (5:1-42)

3. **The Expansion of the Church (6:1–9:31)**
   a. Seven deacons, Stephen's speech and death (6:1–8:3)
   b. Spread to Samaria, the Ethiopian eunuch, conversion of Paul (8:4–9:31)

4. **The Gentile Mission (9:32–15:35)**
   a. Peter's cures, conversion of Cornelius, Antioch, arrest of Peter (9:32–12:25)
   b. Mission to Asia Minor, Council of Jerusalem (13:1–15:35)

5. **Mission in Macedonia and Greece (15:36–20:38)**
   a. Paul in Asia Minor, Macedonia, Athens, Corinth (15:36–18:17)
   b. Paul revisits Asia Minor and Greece, farewell at Miletus (18:18–20:38)

6. **Paul's Arrest, Imprisonment, Journey to Rome (21:1–28:31)**
   a. Arrest in Jerusalem, Paul's defence before the Sanhedrin (21:1–23:10)
   b. Paul trial, journey to Italy, Paul and Jews in Rome (23:11–28:31)

Storyline

Like the Gospel, Acts begins (1:1–2:47) with a formal prologue and picks up where the Gospel left off. The ascension marks a turning point as Jesus sends the Spirit to guide his disciples. Jerusalem is the starting point for the mission to the ends of the earth, i.e. Rome, the capital of the empire. The need to replace Judas is dictated by the symbolism of the Twelve as the new leaders of a restored Israel. For Luke it indicates that the Christian Church is the reconstituted Israel, the people of God. He dramatises the coming of the Spirit with visual and audible manifestations that recall the Sinai event. Disciples are now empowered by the gift of the same Spirit who guided Jesus' ministry. Its first manifestation is the ability to communicate with diverse people from every nation assembled in Jerusalem. The puzzled response of the crowd sets the stage for Peter's sermon that interprets the Pentecost event. Citing the Prophet Joel, Peter interprets the outpouring of the Spirit as the beginning of the Last Days, marked by prophecy and cosmic signs, when God's salvation will be extended to all human beings. Jesus' humanity and ministry as prophet through his deeds of power are emphasised. His death is regarded as part of God's plan to reconcile all people. The result is new life already adumbrated in Psalm 16, while Psalm 110 is applied to the risen Christ as a descendant of David. At the climax of the sermon,

Jesus is given two titles – Lord and Messiah – that signify divine status and God's agent in salvation respectively. Peter's speech evokes a powerful response – a change of heart and reception of Baptism as a means of initiation into the Christian community for a large number of listeners. There follows the first of three summaries that outline the chief characteristics of the Jerusalem community: adherence to the teaching of the Twelve and centring its religious life in the Eucharistic liturgy. Wealthier Christians are led to sell their possessions when the needs of the community's poor require it, and attendance at the Temple continues. This portrait offers an ideal to which believers can aspire.

The next section (3:1–5:42) begins with the first healing story in Acts of a lame beggar that produces wonder and astonishment as it symbolises the saving power of Christ. It gives Peter an opportunity to interpret the miracle, to proclaim the Good News and to issue a call to repentance. It is by faith in the crucified and risen Jesus that the man has been restored. Peter, while affirming the Jewish involvement in the death of Jesus, exonerates them because they were unaware of his messianic dignity. Now repentance and conversion will hasten his future coming. Peter identifies Jesus with the prophet foretold by Moses and all the prophets. Christ by his resurrection has brought to the world the blessings promised to Abraham.

The Sadducees are annoyed at Peter and John not only because of their preaching of the resurrection, but also because of their success despite their lack of authority to teach. Peter's response is that salvation is now available to all people through Jesus. Since the reality of the cure cannot be denied, the apostles are duly cautioned against preaching or teaching in the name of Jesus. But they reply that they cannot obey a

THE FOUR GOSPELS: *Following in the Footsteps of Jesus*

command contrary to God's. On their release, the community joins in prayers of thanksgiving, praise and petition and their prayers are answered in a perceptible manner. A summary of their communal life emphasises the sharing of material goods. The example of Barnabas's generosity stands in sharp contrast to the deception of Ananias and Sapphira in hoarding some of their possessions (4:36–5:11). Luke again describes the unity of the Jerusalem community and highlights powerful deeds that result in greater numbers of believers and increased cures. A second action by the Sanhedrin, motivated by jealousy, is taken against the apostles because of their success and popularity, but they are miraculously released from prison and resume their public teaching. Their disregard of the Sanhedrin's prohibition infuriates the leadership who are determined to invoke the death penalty until the common sense advice of Gamaliel prevails. The apostles are scourged in a last endeavour to shake their convictions, but this only strengthens their resolve to teach and proclaim Jesus.

The following section (6:1–9:31) begins with the need for assistants arising from a conflict between Greek-speaking and Hebrew/Aramaic-speaking members within the Jerusalem Jewish/Christian community. This dispute leads to a restructuring of the community by a division of functions that would better serve its needs. Of the seven people chosen and designated to oversee the distribution of food, two of their number, Stephen and Philip, are presented as preachers of the Christian message. The real purpose of the episode seems to be to introduce Stephen as a prominent figure in the community; his long discourse and death will presently be recounted. Meanwhile, the Jerusalem community continues to expand with a large group of priests joining the disciples. A lengthy narrative regarding Stephen portrays him as filled with grace and power and working signs and wonders. Endowed with wisdom, his opponents are unable to get the better of him so they falsely accuse him of depreciating the importance of the Temple and the Mosaic Law.

Stephen's defence (7:1-53) is not a response to the charges brought against him but takes the form of a discourse that reviews the vicissitudes of God's Word in the history of Israel and ends with a plea for hearing the word announced by Christ and now preached by the Christian community. With Stephen, the differences between Judaism and Christianity begin to appear as he highlights Israel's past defections. His speech reviews salvation history, which indicts Israel for its failure to obey God's commands and his envoys, the prophets. Israel has also misunderstood God's choice of the Jerusalem Temple. By implying that the audience shares the ancestral hostility to God's prophets and that they are resisting the Spirit, Stephen fuels a rage that not only kills him but spawns persecution against Christians. He dies, like Jesus did, with words of forgiveness on his lips. The ensuing flight from persecution provides new inroads for preaching the Gospel. The evangelisation of Samaria is a stepping-stone in the narrative of the mission to the Gentiles. Philip's preaching and deeds of power provoke a favourable response. A contest ensues in which God's power prevails over that of Simon, a magician. Peter and John provide a link between the Samaritan converts and the Jerusalem community. In the account of the conversion of the Ethiopian eunuch, Luke demonstrates that the spread of Christianity outside the confines of Judaism are in accord with God's plan.

There are three accounts of Paul's conversion in Acts (chapters 9, 22, 26) with some differences in detail. The first

(9:1-19) occurs when the Word of God is first spread to the Gentiles. That Paul is divinely chosen is linked to suffering for the sake of the Gospel. Here Luke uses the story of the miraculous conversion of the persecutor of Christians to initiate the preparation for that global mission which will occupy the remainder of Acts. As apostle to the Gentiles, he will carry the Word of God 'to the ends of the earth'. His initial preaching is met with a mixed response. He visits the apostles in Jerusalem before returning to Tarsus until he is later summoned to Antioch. A summary statement presents another idyllic picture of the growth of the Spirit-empowered Church (9:31).

In the following section (9:32–15:35), Peter's miracle working in the coastal cities of Lydda and Joppa demonstrates the efficacy of his preaching and prepares for the conversion of the first Gentile. The lengthy story of the conversion of Cornelius is a major turning point in Luke's narrative (10:1–11:18). It tells of the visions of Cornelius and Peter, Peter's welcome for Cornelius's messengers, followed by his testimony in Cornelius's house and his self-defence before the Jerusalem leaders. The Baptism of Cornelius and his household opens a new chapter in the history of Christianity. For the first time, Gentiles accept the Gospel and become full members of the Church. The narrative stresses that God initiates and approves of this new missionary step. It is God who instructs Cornelius by an angel, directs Peter by a vision, and pours out the Spirit as a tangible sign of acceptance. Cornelius was among a class of devout Gentiles who admired Judaism and attended synagogue services. Lifting the Mosaic prohibition on unclean foods is a sign that the Gentiles are no longer banned from full membership of God's people. Peter now realises that God shows no favouritism to one nation above another in the new dispensation, but all stand as equal candidates for divine blessing. Peter's sermon begins with the Baptism of John, then sums up the Gospel story and ends with the commission of Jesus to preach the Good News. This is followed by a Pentecost experience for the Gentiles, who speak in different tongues and are baptised afterwards. The momentousness of this new development is retold once more as Peter defends his actions before the Jewish–Christian community in Jerusalem. God's gift of life-giving repentance, given first to Israel, is now also bestowed on the Gentiles.

The first church to include Jews and Gentiles is founded in Antioch (11:19-26) where the name 'Christians' originates. They quickly obtain the services of Barnabas and Paul who later deliver famine relief to fellow-Christians in Judea. The persecution of Christians takes a new turn when King Herod targets the apostles. James is beheaded and Peter is thrown in prison. His miraculous rescue is God's answer to the prayer of the Church, while the persecutor suffers a miserable death. Barnabas and Paul return to Antioch and embark on their first missionary journey to the Gentiles of the greater Mediterranean world (13:1–14:28). The Spirit guides their mission that begins in Cyprus with the unmasking of the magician Elymas, and continues through southern Asia Minor before returning to Antioch. Paul proclaims the Word of God first to Jews and then to Gentiles. The key event in Luke's account of this first journey is the experience in Pisidian Antioch. The preaching proclaimed by Paul in the synagogue is initially favourably received. His inaugural sermon traces biblical history from the exodus to the coming of Jesus, stressing that Christ fulfils the Davidic covenant by being raised from the dead, and supersedes the Mosaic covenant by offering divine forgiveness. The sermon ends with a warning to those who reject the message. With the arrival of Gentiles the following

Sabbath, the Jews, prompted by jealousy, contradict Paul who turns to preach to the more receptive Gentiles. The Jews' refusal frustrates God's plan for his chosen people.

At Iconium, Paul and Barnabas preach first to the Jews, and many Jews and Greeks become believers, but eventually persecution impels them to new mission territory where their cure of a cripple and the reaction of the crowd occasions Paul's first sermon to a pagan audience. This sermon is unusual in that it appeals to what can be known of God from creation (14:15-18). Rather than showing how Christianity is an outgrowth of Judaism, Paul says that God formerly permitted the pagans to stumble in the darkness of mythology and false worship. The time to enlighten all nations has now arrived with the Gospel that urges them to turn away from lifeless idols to serve the true God who, from the beginning, has made his divinity and goodness known through the beauty and blessings of the natural order. Paul is stoned by a mob before setting off to nearby cities. He appoints elders to provide guidance and stability for the new missionary communities before returning to Antioch in Syria. On their return, they recount how God has opened the door of faith to the pagans.

The Jerusalem assembly (15:1-29) marks the rejection of the view that Gentile converts are obliged to observe the complete Mosaic Law. This is a crucial turning point. Luke's account presents a model for decision-making in important matters. Testimony is first given by Paul, Barnabas and Peter about what God is doing in a new time and place. All of these events prove to the leaders that God does want them to accept Gentiles into the Church. This turn of events is interpreted in the light of Scripture by James, and a decision, guided by the Spirit, is conveyed by a letter containing the stipulations, which is positively received by the wider Church. The compromise decision made it possible for Jewish Christians, who continued to observe the Mosaic Law, to associate with Gentile believers. The significance of the Jerusalem Council lies in the way Church leaders were able to recognise and officially affirm the new direction in salvation history that would permit expansion of the Gospel to the Gentiles.

Paul now begins the journeys that will take the Gospel throughout the Roman Empire (15:36–20:38). He takes the decisive step of crossing from Asia Minor to Greece where some of the more important Pauline churches will be founded. The Gospel will be taken completely beyond Judaism, and in time these Gentile churches will be the custodians of a tradition that God has been preparing since Abraham. It will be their responsibility to see that the Good News continues to be preached to the ends of the earth. Luke shapes the traditions available to him to illustrate his understanding of the growth of the early Church. Paul revisits the communities he established on his first journey and then, at the prompting of the Spirit, crosses over to Macedonia where he establishes communities at Philippi, Thessalonica and Beroea. To escape the hostility of the Jews, he departs for Greece where he preaches at Athens before leaving for Corinth and returning to Jerusalem. Luke's account of Paul's third missionary journey is confined mainly to his work at Ephesus. After bidding farewell to the elders at Miletus, he returns to Jerusalem.

Paul and Barnabas go their separate ways (15:36-40), while Paul teams up with Silas and Timothy to revisit the converts in Syria and Asia Minor. The direction of the second journey is determined by the Spirit when Paul receives further instructions to cross over from Asia Minor to evangelise the mainland of

Europe and sojourns at Philippi (16:11-40). After the conversion of Lydia and her household, the church at Philippi later became a flourishing community. When Paul exorcises a spirit of divination from a slave-girl, those who exploited her bring Paul and Silas before authorities and they are cast into prison. Their miraculous deliverance prompts the conversion of the gaoler and his household before the apostles are requested to leave. They arrive at Thessalonica but depart quickly under a cloud of controversy and are dogged by opponents. In Beroea they have a more positive reception before they are again forced to move on.

Paul's presence in Athens sets the stage for the great discourse before a Gentile audience (17:22-31). Luke uses the occasion to advance his case for the superiority of Christianity. It is not just another religious cult; rather, Christianity rivals a philosophical understanding of the universe. The speech touches on common themes in philosophical accounts of religion. His opening words seek to make his audience more receptive. He then develops three claims about God that they have in common – God is the creator of the whole universe and so has no need of human service; he has allotted certain zones to the nations, sustains and is present to all created things; and true worship of God rejects superstitious practices. God, the omnipresent creator and sustainer of the universe, is not swayed by human ritual. Paul emphasises the unity of all humanity and its closeness to the Creator. Greek philosophers also spoke of seeking and finding God, and Paul even quotes their own poets. Only at the conclusion of the speech does he mention the resurrection, something that was not current in Greek philosophy. This God who raised Jesus from the dead now calls Paul's listeners to abandon paganism and accept the message about Jesus, whom God has appointed judge of the human race. This departure from the common ground only draws scepticism among his listeners, and Paul sets out for Corinth where he remains for some time.

Luke's account of Paul's extensive work at Corinth (18:1-17) refers to the fact that he worked at his trade of tentmaker to support himself. In his brief account of the founding of the Church there, Luke follows the line he has already established. After Paul's success in attracting influential people, hostility from the Jews forces the apostle to turn to the Gentiles. Luke also mentions Paul's associates, Priscilla and Aquila, who will later instruct Apollos more fully in the Christian faith. Paul is comforted when the Lord assures him of divine protection and success in his Corinthian ministry. The Jews bring Paul before the Roman proconsul, who refuses to hear a charge involving Jewish religious law.

The third missionary journey of Paul (18:22–20:38) concentrates on episodes concerning the mission in Ephesus, the location of the famous Temple of Artemis. Paul's confrontation with that cult occupies most of the account of his mission there. Upon his arrival in Ephesus, Paul discovers people who are believers, but had yet to receive Baptism and the Spirit. He begins by preaching in the synagogue, but when heckled, transfers to a lecture room where he holds daily discussions over a period of two years with considerable success. Some Jewish exorcists are overpowered by an evil spirit for making unauthorised use of Jesus' name. Magical practices and manuals, incompatible with belief in Jesus, are discarded and burned.

However, a riot breaks out (19:23-41) when the business of the silversmiths who sold replicas of Artemis's shrine is threatened by Paul's evangelisation. The town clerk advocates due process rather than mob action to settle the dispute. Afterwards, Paul revisits the communities he founded in Macedonia and Greece before returning by way of Troas where he raises a dead man to life. He addresses the elders of Ephesus at Miletus (20:18-35) by recalling his past service, remarks on the present situation, and appoints future leaders. He admonishes them to guard the community against false prophets and prays with them. The pattern of Paul's ministry provides a model for the leaders to follow. Paul's farewell speech provides the occasion for Luke to reflect on the transition from the generation of the apostles to the Church of his own day. Officials from the local church are to lead the community. The Spirit who guided the Church through the apostolic period will continue to direct her course.

Paul's dedication to his mission leads him to continue his journey (21:1–23:11), even in the face of suffering that awaits him in Jerusalem. On his arrival in Jerusalem, James proposes that Paul demonstrate his own piety to allay the fears of some who suspected Paul of leading Jewish Christians away from their ancestral traditions. Parenthetically, Luke notes that the evangelisation of Israel has met with great success. Ironically, participation in Jewish rituals is the occasion that leads to Paul's arrest. Luke uses this situation, in which Paul defends and explains his mission, to show that Christianity is the logical development and outgrowth of Judaism. Paul delivers four speeches in his own defence: to the Jews in Jerusalem, to the governor Felix, to the governor Festus, and to King Agrippa. His first speech to the Jerusalem crowd recalls the piety of his early years. Only the direct intervention of the risen Christ provided the evidence for God's direction of his life and ministry. This is underlined by a second vision of Christ as Paul is praying in the Temple. In his appearance before the Sanhedrin, Paul is able to defuse the situation by pitting Sadducees against Pharisees on the question of the resurrection of the dead.

Because of a Jewish conspiracy against Paul (23:12–26:32), the Romans must intervene to remove Paul to Caesarea. In his speech before Felix, the Roman procurator, Paul defends the Jewish character of his own personal conduct and stresses the continuity between Judaism and Christianity. With the arrival of the new procurator, Festus, Paul invokes the privilege of a Roman citizen to be tried in Rome. Since the Jewish king, Herod Agrippa II, is curious about Paul, Festus arranges for a final speech for Paul who defends himself by repeating the circumstances of his life as a devout Pharisee who was converted by a divine vision in which he was commissioned as a missionary to the Gentiles. The founding events of Christianity are public events of recent history. Although no grounds for legal action against Paul are found, he cannot be released since he has demanded a hearing at the imperial court.

In the sea voyage to Rome and his sojourn there (27:1– 28:31), Paul stands out as a pillar of strength and composure and encourages those around him. The story of Paul's journey is told in vivid detail and with all the high drama of ancient adventure stories. Paul gets along with his captors and his prophetic influence saves all on board. During a vicious storm that destroys the ship and has the survivors washed up on the beach at Malta, Paul demonstrates his own confidence in God. The episode associated with the stay in Malta includes the drama of the natives watching the shipwrecked party. When Paul is unharmed by a poisonous snake, they conclude that he must be a god. He wins more friends by healing the sick and the travellers are provided with everything they need to continue their journey. With Paul's arrival in Rome, the programmatic spread of the word of the Lord to 'the ends of the earth' is accomplished. In Rome, Paul is placed under house arrest, but is allowed to proclaim the word in the capital city. Paul's final words reflect a major concern of Luke's: how the salvation promised in the Old Testament, accomplished by Jesus, and offered first to Israel, has now been offered to and accepted by the Gentiles. The Jewish rejection of the Gospel message leads to its proclamation among the Gentiles. Paul's confident and unhindered proclamation of the Gospel in Rome forms the climax to the story outlined in Acts 1:8: Jesus' followers would witness to 'the ends of the earth'.

Literary Characteristics

Acts traces the story of the Church's beginning and growth from Jerusalem to imperial Rome and retains a continuing importance in shaping the identity of the contemporary Church. Acts was written as a manual for missionaries. The success of the mission testifies to the power and necessity of the proclaimed Gospel. The prophetic boldness and effectiveness of the Church's missionaries, inspired by the Spirit, is told to invigorate the missionary outreach and to teach how to convert others in continuity with the mission of the early Church. It was written by Luke as a response to the new missionary situation of his day. Acts enables future believers to locate themselves within space and time as participants in a real historical movement.

Speeches in Acts cover more than one-third of the narrative. Peter's Pentecost sermon (2:14-36), his address to the people after the cure of a lame man (3:12-26), and his defence before the Sanhedrin (4:8-12) aim to convince the Jews that Jesus is the expected Messiah. Paul's preaching before diaspora Jews (13:16-41) gives a summary of salvation history together with the claim that Jesus is the expected Messiah, and is similar to Peter's speeches. Paul's speeches at Iconium (Ac 14:15-17) and Athens (17:22-31) are examples of missionary discourses to pagan audiences. Stephen's speech (7:1-53) dwells on the conflict between Jewish and Christian traditions, while Paul's farewell speech at Miletus (20:18-35) is concerned with the succession of future leaders and their qualities. Paul's speeches before Jews and Gentiles (22:1-21; 24:10-21; 26:2-23; 28:17-20) serve to defend his spiritual authority in Christianity. All of the speeches show continuity of content to prove the trustworthiness of the Gospel's claims. God's plan of salvation has been disclosed in the Scriptures, especially through the prophets. According to these witnesses, Jesus is God's Messiah and only Saviour attested by his ministry and resurrection. All who repent and call on Jesus will be saved. They will receive the gift of the Spirit and will be incorporated into the Christian community by Baptism. Jesus' return at the end of time will effect universal restoration (cf. 3:20-21). The stories Luke recounts in Acts are meant to be models and examples of how God continually deals with his people, exemplifying how he usually acts in the lives of Christians. As pastoral leader, Luke concentrates on a few well-chosen stories and describes them in detail to provide Christian readers with examples to follow. He believes that God is active in the events he relates and so Acts becomes a presentation of the Christian way of following the risen Christ as seen in the lives of the earliest Christians.

Unity of Luke-Acts

Luke wrote his Gospel in the closing decades of the first century, several years removed from the time of Jesus. His experience of the Church at the time he wrote, a Church containing Gentiles as well as Jews, influenced his presentation of the life of Jesus with hints of openness to universal salvation not found in Mark or Matthew. Luke wants to show that the Gentile mission in Acts occurred not only because of Jewish rejection of the Good News, but principally because the groundwork for the Gentile mission was already laid in the life of Jesus. That is why Luke presents his Gospel with distinctive allusions to universal salvation. He includes passages peculiar to himself and carefully points up passages in common with Mark and Matthew so that they could be seen as anticipating Acts. In this way Luke makes his point that the life of Jesus foreshadows the Gentile mission.

Already in Simeon's prophecy he sees in the child Jesus 'a light for revelation to the Gentiles' (Lk 2:32). The quotation from Isaiah 40:3 includes: 'And all mankind shall see the salvation of God' (Lk 3:6). In his sermon at Nazareth, Jesus cites Isaiah 61:1-2 as programmatic for his entire ministry to the underprivileged in society. He also mentions Elijah's meeting with the Sidonian widow and Namaan's cure, both non-Jews. Nowhere in Israel has Jesus found such faith as that of the pagan centurion (Lk 7:9). Those entering the kingdom will come from the four corners of the earth (Lk 13:29). The healing of the Gerasene demoniac takes place in Gentile territory (Lk 8:26-39). The queen of the South who listened to Solomon, and the Ninevites who listened to Jonah, will rise at judgement to condemn this generation (Lk 11:29-32). Luke's portrayal of Jesus as seeking out the marginalised, the lost and sinners like Zacchaeus, anticipates God's seeking out the Gentiles in Acts.

The mission of the seventy-two is peculiar to Luke (Lk 10:1-20).[3] Many of this episode's details suggest anticipation of the Gentile mission. The number seventy-two represents the nations of the world (cf. Gn 10, LXX). The distinctness of the seventy-two from the sending of the Twelve (Lk 9:1-6) further suggests that their ministry anticipates the ministry of many others in

Acts, apart from the Twelve, who preach to the Gentiles. The preparation given to them by Jesus is treated in much more detail than the preparation of the Twelve. Their return is also given more attention. In Acts, an extensive set of characters appears alongside the two leading apostles, Peter and Paul, and the latter is not even one of the Twelve. Jesus' warning about wolves foreshadows the many times in Acts when 'wolves' attacked Paul, Barnabas and Silas as they preached to Jews and Gentiles. Jesus' command to 'eat what is set before you' (Lk 10:8) anticipates the breaking down of Jewish and Gentile social barriers in Acts chapters 10–11 that paved the way for mission to the Gentiles. That the seventy-two will experience rejection also foreshadows the preaching to Jews and Gentiles in Acts. On many occasions, Jews stirred up trouble for Paul and his companions, forcing them to move on. On three occasions, Paul declares that he is turning to the Gentiles because the Jews have rejected his message. The mission of the seventy-two is inserted into the Journey Narrative, which is primarily didactic in giving instructions on discipleship and only secondarily geographical. It is first of all, of course, a journey of Jesus to his death, resurrection and ascension, but it also provides, in Luke, an opportunity for Jesus' teaching of his disciples.

Furthermore, details of some of the Gospel parables are better understood in the light of Acts.[4] For example, the parable of the lamp (Lk 8:16; 11:33) – 'so that people may see the light when they come in' – can be regarded as referring to Gentiles entering the Church. In the parable of the mustard seed (Lk 13:18-19), the emphasis is on the growth of the seed and on birds nesting in the branches of the tree. The latter refers to all the nations of the world in the Old Testament, and so points towards the worldwide mission that includes Gentiles in the

Church. The parable of the great banquet (Lk 14:15-24) relates how those who had been invited to the banquet gave excuses for not attending. So the master sends his servants out on two more occasions to the streets and lanes, and then outside the city to the highways and hedges to bring in guests to fill his house. The second invitation likely refers to Jesus' ministry to outcasts in Jewish society. The third invitation, peculiar to Luke, may be taken as referring to the inclusion of Gentiles in the Church. Jesus' seeking out of Zacchaeus (Lk 19:1-10) also prefigures God's seeking out the Gentiles in Acts.

Luke is not just writing history – it is more a theology of salvation history. He wants to show that the situation of the Church in his time of writing is rooted in the ministry of Jesus. He also offers a theology of Gentile mission by establishing in the Gospel and Acts that faith in Jesus is what is required for salvation. God's plan was to bring about salvation in Jesus. Although the Gentile mission was unplanned by the apostles, Acts shows that it was in God's plan according to the Old Testament. The guidance of the Spirit and the miracles related in Acts confirm this. Luke also relativises Temple worship (Ac 7:1-54) and the Mosaic Law (Ac 15:1-21) to highlight faith in Jesus. Luke, of course, is writing about the salvation brought by Jesus, but his *presentation* of the life of Jesus in the Gospel contains several details that anticipate the Gentile mission in Acts. That is why the full meaning of Luke's Gospel becomes clear only by reading Acts. It seems that he deliberately wrote his Gospel in such a way as to prepare for his second volume, Acts. After carefully studying the traditions regarding Jesus, he deliberately shaped his Gospel in such a way as to make his task of describing the mission to the Gentiles in Acts easier. Luke-Acts is therefore a unified work because of the unifying purpose of God behind all the events that Luke narrates. The mission of Jesus and that of his disciples represent that purpose being carried out through human means. The offer of salvation to Gentiles had always been part of God's plan.

Portrait of Jesus

The key figure in Luke-Acts is of course Jesus Christ himself as the one in whom God's activity in history is now made fully manifest. The reader immediately notices the qualities of mercy, compassion, love, charm, joy and delicacy that characterise Luke's portrait of Jesus. He is presented as a Palestinian Jew, born in Bethlehem and raised in Nazareth, a human being with great concern for others. Dante has described Luke as 'the scribe of the gentleness of Christ'. Some of the most memorable stories of divine compassion are found only in Luke, for example, the Widow of Naim (Lk 7:11-17), the Prodigal Son (Lk 15:11-32), and Zacchaeus (Lk 19:1-10). Jesus lives in his Father's presence and his mission carried out in a spirit of prayer demonstrates this. His ministry is a source of joy that permeates the whole Gospel in contrast to Mark's concentration on the suffering Messiah, and Matthew's insistence on bearing fruit. Jesus is the Saviour sent to seek out and save the lost. He is the great benefactor of humanity, an attractive personality, and an example to be imitated.

Luke presents Jesus as the prophet par excellence, for nobody can speak in God's name the way he does. He also presents him as a man attested by God with mighty deeds, wonders and signs – a person transcending the normal human condition. It is Luke's combination of the human and the transcendental aspects of Jesus' existence that make up Luke's view of the person of Christ. Conceived by the Spirit and born of the Virgin Mary, he is described as Messiah, Lord and Saviour. At his

Baptism he is endowed with the Spirit and declared Son, as one having a unique relationship to God. Jesus is Son of God whose mission is described by Luke in terms of the long-awaited prophet-like-Moses, the mouthpiece of God, whose words and deeds display the characteristics of Israel's God. During his public ministry 'because God was with him, Jesus went about doing good and curing all who had fallen into the power of the devil' (Ac 10:38). He frequently celebrates meals with friends and sinners alike in a table fellowship that connotes intimacy and sharing, and readers are reminded of the Eucharist. As God's anointed, he encounters opposition, rejection and death, but his innocence is witnessed by Pilate, Herod, the good thief and the Roman centurion. The identity of Jesus is given final expression by his death as both the final act of obedience to his Father and the ultimate expression of his love for others. His resurrection is seen as validation of his claims. Luke insists on the reality of the resurrection, yet does not regard it as a mere resuscitation. Jesus has entered 'his glory' (Lk 24:26), that is, into the presence of the Father. The ascension is described as the final leave-taking, but Jesus will return again at the end of the ages. In the meantime, the form of the risen Christ's presence in his Church will be in the Spirit, whose presence through the apostles enables them to continue Christ's mission to humanity.

Portrait of Disciples[5]

Who are the Christians according to Luke? They are the ones living in continuity with the disciples whose story fills Luke-Acts. Disciples are those who accept Jesus' call to follow him, who hold certain values in common, and whose lives come together in a shared experience. They are identified by their relationship to Christ, the Teacher. Their lives are patterned on Jesus' teaching and they become an identifiable group. The disciples were first called 'Christians' at Antioch (Ac 11:26), that is, those who recognise Jesus as the Christ, the Messiah.

Disciples are those who later were called Christians. They are first mentioned in Luke 5:30 at a banquet given by the tax collector Levi in Jesus' honour. The call of Peter (Lk 5:1-11) by Jesus is emblematic of the call of disciples. Peter shows himself to be open to discipleship when, against the odds, he takes Jesus at his word. With the extraordinary catch of fish, Peter recognises who Jesus really is, and at the same time his own unworthiness. He has the necessary dispositions and when Jesus calls, Peter accepts. Disciples, therefore, are those who acknowledge Jesus as Lord in faith and recognise their own unworthiness. They are called into the reconciling presence of the Lord, and Jesus never abandons them. This *presence*, however, is more than physical. It also means awareness, openness, acceptance and attentiveness, which serve as the basis for personal communication. Disciples are those who are taught by Jesus, who listen to Jesus, the Teacher. They accept the invitation to follow Jesus (Lk 5:11), and subsequently become disciples who are willing to be taught by Jesus.

Luke uses a second term, 'followers', to designate those called by Jesus. Disciples should not be passive, they should always be active – otherwise they are no longer followers of Jesus. *Followers* are associated with Jesus, Christ and Lord, and with the Gospel narrative that tells his story. Only Jesus has followers, hence followers are only mentioned in Luke's story of Jesus. In Acts, disciples taught those who accepted their invitation to follow Jesus, the Christ, not themselves. Following Jesus means leaving everything (Lk 5:11, 28; 18:28), and turning away from a former way of living as a prerequisite for following Jesus. It is inseparable from taking up one's cross 'every day' (Lk 9:23), and connotes a change of values, attitudes and life orientation. To follow Jesus means to walk with him through suffering to glory (Lk 24:26). In taking up their own cross, followers show their *solidarity* with Christ, the perfect human being. Luke 9:57-62 stresses the implications of following Jesus – a detached way of life, saying goodbye to the dead past, joining the living in proclaiming the reign of God, and not looking back – for only those who look forward are fit for the Kingdom of God. Luke 18:18-43 develops some of the social implications of following Jesus – leaving all for the sake of the kingdom and giving to the poor (cf. Ac 2:42-47; 4:42-45 where sharing distinguishes followers of Christ). This remains an ideal for Christians, even if they sometimes fail (cf. Ac 5:1-11). It is summarised in *solidarity* with the life and mission of Jesus, becoming one with him, sharing his values and mission, even rejection. This solidarity is a response to Jesus who gave his own life, transcended death, and who will accompany them on mission through the Spirit. With Christ, followers reach out in solidarity to bring the Good News to the ends of the earth.

Disciples who become followers are also *forerunners* who prepare the way for the Lord's return in glory. It is comparatively easy to see oneself as a disciple secure in the Lord's presence, or even as a follower pursuing a life well mapped out by Christ. Forerunners, however, preparing for the future, are *open* to the new and the unforeseen even as they follow Christ. In Luke, forerunner is neither a noun nor a verb, but a prepositional phrase 'before him'. It is used of John as forerunner who prepared the way of the Lord's first coming (Lk 1:76; 7:27). Luke applies it to disciples and modifies it to 'before him', i.e. the Lord Jesus Christ (Lk 9:51-52; 10:1). 'Lord' evokes

Jesus' glorified state. Making a people ready for the Lord is the role of the Twelve (Lk 9:1-6) and of the seventy-two (10:1-20), as well as the missionaries in Acts. John's role prepares the way for missions in Acts that will continue to reach out to the ends of the earth. The role of forerunners is compared to that of John who prepared for his coming in history; disciples as forerunners are those who prepare for his final coming in glory. Forerunners are mentioned twice in the introductory section of the Journey Narrative that leads to the ascension, to heaven, where the Lord will remain until the universal restoration (Ac 3:21) that will take place at his return (Ac 1:11).

Luke's Journey Narrative operates on three levels: first, there is the historical journey to Jerusalem when the disciples related to Jesus as Teacher; second, the Gospel was written after the paschal events had taken place, so disciples are those following Jesus on that journey through suffering and death to eternal life; and third, the theme dominating 9:51–10:37, however, is that of forerunners sent before the Lord to prepare the way, so the entire journey may be seen as the life of those who prepare for the Lord's return in glory by going on mission. Forerunners need special qualities, among them openness to a presence yet to be, based on the Lord's promise and hope of fulfilment, and on the experience of how God fulfilled his promises in the past. Forerunners have the example of Jesus in his openness to God's will as it unfolded in his life, and that was fulfilled in the ascension. Fulfilment, however, may be different from one's expectations. So there is the temptation to impatience, like that of the disciples wanting to call down fire on the Samaritan town (Lk 9:52-55). The mission will be fulfilled in a different way when a Samaritan becomes a model for disciples in succouring a person in need (Lk 10:25-37). There are also tensions and problems that are difficult to bear (Lk 17:22-37), such as the danger of losing heart and taking fulfilment into one's own hands, so there is need to persevere in prayer (Lk 18:1-8) – especially in the face of disappointment. The Father will give nothing less than the Spirit to those who pray to him (Lk 11:13).

Those who heed Jesus' call are described by Luke as disciples who are taught by Jesus, as followers who pursue a path first traced by the Lord as described by Luke, and as forerunners who prepare for the Lord's final coming. They are to develop particular qualities of life that are important for living the Christian life in history as Luke envisages it. Disciples are those who gather around Jesus to learn how to live, act and pray. Followers are those who seriously try to pattern their lives on that of Christ. They are in solidarity with Christ and remain with him as they pursue their mission, which is an extension of his own. Forerunners are open to the new and the unforeseen, rather than trying to block out or control the future, or retreat into the past. They prepare the way of the Lord who will come in glory. The presence, solidarity and openness that are characteristic of Christians according to Luke are exemplified in Mary's response to the angel at the annunciation: 'I am the handmaid of the Lord,' she said, 'let what you have said be done to me' (Lk 1:38). Mary was present to the Lord. She committed herself in solidarity to God's plan of salvation as it unfolded. Regarded as humanly impossible, Mary responded with openness, trusting in the power of the Spirit. We find her finally in the company of the apostolic community (Ac 1:14) who devoted themselves to prayer as they awaited the coming of the Spirit.

The Reader

Since Christians have the responsibility of sacramentally revealing the Lord's presence to others, even though they are limited and sinful, it is only through the Spirit that they can rise to the demands of discipleship. That is why Luke concludes the Lord's response to the disciple's request with the assurance that the Father gives the Spirit to those who ask him (Lk 11:13). It is the Spirit who enables Christians to live like disciples, followers and forerunners. From the beginning of the Gospel to the end of Acts, Luke introduces the Spirit as the source of every major development of salvation history. The Spirit is the power behind Jesus' historic life and prophetic ministry. It is the same Spirit who transforms ordinary men and women into disciples, followers and forerunners of the Lord. Luke-Acts may be regarded as a commentary on the Spirit's role in the life, mission and prayer of Christians.

The Gospel highlights the role of women in the ministry of Jesus. Luke's portrayal of women as equal to men is shown in the Gospel by the parallelism of events involving men and women. Women accompany Jesus during his ministry and provide for him out of their own means (Lk 8:1-3). Martha and Mary receive Jesus into their home and Mary sits at Jesus' feet, the position of a disciple (Lk 10:38-42). In Acts, as in the Gospel, women are paired with men. The Eleven devote themselves to prayer as they await the Spirit, together with the women and Mary (Ac 1:14). Those who came to believe in the Lord were both men and women (Ac 5:14). Many women in Acts play important roles, providing charity and help in the early Church. Devout women invite the apostles into their homes.

Prayer holds an important place in Luke-Acts. Luke gives examples of prayer: the Magnificat (Lk 1:46-55); the Benedictus

(Lk 1:68-79); the Nunc Dimittis (Lk 2:29-32); the Gloria (Lk 2:14); a prayer of thanksgiving (Lk 10:21-22); and the Our Father (Lk 11:2-4). Disciples pray before choosing Judas' successor (Ac 1:24-25); they pray under persecution (Ac 4:24-30). Luke depicts Jesus praying during all significant moments of his life: after his Baptism (Lk 3:21); in the wilderness (Lk 5:16); before choosing disciples (Lk 6:12-16); on the occasion when he asked the disciples who he was (Lk 9:18-22); and at the transfiguration (Lk 9:28). He prays for Peter (Lk 22:32), and as he is dying on the cross (Lk 23:34, 46). Jesus gives instruction on prayer (Lk 11:5-13; 18:1-8, 9-14). The habit of regular prayer is instilled in the disciples and is evident throughout Acts where the disciples pray at crucial moments. The early community devoted themselves to the apostles' teaching and fellowship, to the breaking of bread and to prayers (Ac 2:42). The disciples pray frequently, having learned the importance of prayer from Jesus. In the Gospel, Jesus institutes the Eucharist (Lk 22:19-20) that in Acts becomes the 'breaking of bread' and was a daily celebration (Ac 2:42, 46). Paul also preaches and breaks bread on his missionary journeys (Ac 20:7, 11). The disciples need to pray to meet the challenges of mission. Like Jesus, they too experience persecution, deprivation and tribulation, for example, the continuous sufferings of Paul, his arrest and deportation, the execution of Stephen and James, and the imprisonment of Peter. And yet, there is a note of triumph and joy even in the presence of suffering. The apostles live by the Word of God and turn in prayer to the God who sustains them.

Luke devotes considerable attention to the danger of riches and their proper use. However, there is no idealisation of poverty. The poor are unfortunate people who are in need of material help and to whom Christians have an obligation to succour by almsgiving. In itself, poverty is an evil that must be alleviated by Christians from whom generosity is expected (Lk 3:11; 6:30, 38; 16:9). In describing the lifestyle of the early Christian community (Ac 2:42-47; 4:32-35), Luke wishes to keep before his readers an ideal of generosity that should always inspire Christians. There is the example of Barnabas and the negative example of Ananias and Sapphira (Ac 4:36-5:11). The sharing of goods is presented as an ideal, not of poverty, but of fraternal love. There is no ideal of poverty, but of fraternal love that includes love for the poor to help them out of their poverty. Far from being a Christian virtue, poverty is a scandal and an insult to the justice of God. Christians must put an end to this scandalous condition.

For Luke, riches can present a major obstacle to becoming a disciple, as the story of the rich aristocrat illustrates (Lk 18:18-23). Luke also has warnings on the danger of riches (Lk 6:24). The rich man is so self-preoccupied that he does not notice the beggar Lazarus at his gate (Lk 16:19-31). There is also a warning in the explanation of the parable of the sower: 'As for the part that fell among thorns, this is people who have heard, but as they go on their way, they are choked by the worries and riches and pleasures of life and do not reach maturity' (Lk 8:14). The danger of avarice is illustrated by the parable of the rich farmer, for the heart of one who possesses riches is attached to the goods of this world (Lk 12:16-21). Disciples, like the crafty manager, should be 'astute' in their relations with the world so as to assure their eternal recompense (Lk 16:1-13).

Other ways to deal with riches is to share possessions with the unfortunate after the manner of the Good Samaritan (Lk 10:30-36), or rather than feasting with cronies, to provide for the poor, the lame and the homeless who have no resources with which to reciprocate (Lk 14:12-24). In the parable of the pounds (Lk 19: 11-27), Luke recognises that Jesus may not return for a long time, so disciples must remain stewards and utilise the talents and resources that God has given them. Opposed to the desire for riches is trust and confidence in God in whom Christians place their security. Luke's corrective to the misuse of material things, therefore, is not non-use, but proper use. Nevertheless, Christians must be ready to sacrifice possessions should they present an obstacle to their growth in faith.

Meals have an important place in Luke's narrative. They are occasions for discussion, teaching and controversy. Sharing at table connotes fellowship and intimacy, reminding readers of the table fellowship of the Eucharist. For example, in the story of the two disciples on the road to Emmaus (Lk 24:13-35), Luke is telling us how it is possible to come into contact with the risen Christ *today*. He says that the risen Christ is forever journeying by our side, unrecognised for the most part because of self-preoccupation, false hopes or unfulfilled expectations that lead to gloom and depression – symptoms of a lack of faith and trust. But Christ is still with us even when we fail to recognise him for a long time, especially when we are assailed by doubts, disappointments and discouragement like the two disciples. That the disciples were not expecting him reminds us that the Lord may be present to us in unfamiliar guises when we least expect him. In the community Eucharist, when we listen to his word and share his meal, our hearts burn too, our eyes are opened, faith and hope are rekindled and we feel compelled to witness and to share. The Lord is risen and present, so life can never be the same again.

Conclusion

The Our Father as transmitted by Luke can serve as a concise summing-up of his two-part narrative insofar as it has a bearing on the Church's mission. It is the prayer of Christians as they journey to the Father, the prayer of the Christian exodus, and the prayer of Christian mission. It is a prayer to God, the source of life and salvation, based on the analogy of earthly fathers who are givers of life. Christians relate to God with that warmth, intimacy, love and respect that adults have for fathers or father figures. But it is through the Son that we come to know the Father by sharing in the life he has given his Son, Jesus, through the power of the Spirit (cf. Lk 10:21-22). At Pentecost, the Spirit descended on the apostolic community (Ac 2:1-4) to impart divine life. Acts may be regarded as the story of how the Christian life is to be lived in history. Life in the Spirit is a share in the life of the risen Lord. God is our Father revealed by the Son, whose life Christians share in the Spirit.

The mission of the Church is to collaborate in making holy the 'name' (personal identity as related to us) of the Father together with the Son who revealed it. All of the Christian life comes from hearing the Good News brought by Jesus; with him Christians collaborate in hallowing the Father's name when they engage in mission. Christians look forward in hope to the full hallowing of the name, when God will be 'all in all'. The Father's kingdom is his self-communication in revelation that is accepted in faith. It is manifested in the transformation of persons and society. It is essentially the Father's presence both in creation and in history. We pray for the fulfilment of the kingdom already in our midst (Lk 17:20-21). Luke's entire narrative is the story of the coming of the Father's kingdom brought and proclaimed by Jesus and embracing all people. It is given to the 'little flock' (cf. Lk 12:32) of disciples and will come into conflict with the spirit of evil, but will be upheld by Jesus' prayer (Lk 22:31-32). By giving his life on the cross as the ultimate act of service, Jesus revealed the Father's kingdom as he entered it to inaugurate a rule that will never end. 'Thy kingdom come' sums up the Christian commitment to worldwide mission that will also bring with it opposition and persecution. Luke-Acts shows us how difficult it is to break through religious and political boundaries that people erect to protect themselves and their interests. So there is need for Christians to take up their cross daily and follow Jesus into his Father's reign. This is the Christian vision.

Bread for each day addresses a fundamental need of Christians throughout history, and of those who are engaged in mission. They need sustenance as they prepare for the coming of the Lord. It is bread for those who view life as a journey to the Father as they follow Jesus. It is the bread for those who want to serve by taking part in mission rather than being served (cf. Lk 22:24-27). Only the Father can give such special bread for all who work for the spread of his kingdom. The Eucharist epitomises the Christian mission when the risen Christ is present and recognised (cf. Lk 24:13-35). Christians take part in the Eucharist and offer themselves in union with the risen Lord for the salvation of others. The Eucharist unites Christians and sends them out on mission.

Christians living their daily lives and participating in mission are aware of their brokenness and sins that separate them from God, so they ask for healing of both personal and social wounds. This petition expresses the need to be forgiven by the Father and our need to forgive others as Jesus forgave his enemies on the cross (Lk 23:34). It is difficult for Christians to forgive like the elder brother in the parable (Lk 15:25-30). It is also difficult to request forgiveness like the Pharisee who could not bring himself to pray properly (cf. Lk 18:9-14). In the parable of the Prodigal Son (Lk 15:11-32), the father illustrates the way our prayer for forgiveness is answered and the way we are to forgive others. The younger brother models the humble attitude that sinners must acquire when approaching the Father. The elder brother mirrors the difficulties we have in forgiving. Of ourselves, there is no way that we could meet the demands of Christian forgiveness. We are more like the proud Pharisee or the unforgiving elder brother. That is why we pray for forgiveness for ourselves and for the ability to be able to forgive others so that we can become effective missionaries.

Christians ask that we may not to be put to the test in the final moments of life. They make their own the prayer of Jesus at Gethsemane (cf. Lk 22:39-46) and heed his warning to 'pray not to be put to the test'. They pray that they too accept their humanity and creaturely status before God as they reach out to other people, and not fall away when tested by circumstances or persons in the course of their missionary work (cf. Lk 8:13). Christians meet the test of their human limitations and their fear of death the moment they are called to join their Father in glory.

The Our Father unlocks Luke's vision of the Christian life and the demands of discipleship for mission. Its meaning is not restricted to the author's intention or to its first readers. For Luke, the end of the story of Jesus is his Church, and the story of Jesus is the beginning of the Church. His viewpoint is that Jesus' history is the beginning of the continuing history of the Church, and he is firmly convinced of its universal character. Acts represents the breakthrough of Christianity to universality as a world religion.

NOTES

1. Luke 4:1-13; cf. Mark 1:12-13; Matthew 4:1-11. Already in the Old Testament, Ben Sira had cautioned: 'My son, if you aspire to serve the Lord prepare yourself for temptation' (2:1). Temptation or trial suggests the humanity of the 'Son of God' as he struggles to follow his mission of suffering service. In overcoming these temptations, he becomes an example for Christians in times of testing that is concretised in temptations to gluttony (stones into bread), ambition and control (the kingdoms of the world), and vainglory and attention seeking (leaping from the pinnacle of the Temple). The story of the temptations describes inward experiences that are told in symbolic language (cf. the profound psychological analysis of temptation in Gn 3:1-13). Luke and Matthew are portraying in dramatic form the type of temptations Jesus actually underwent throughout the course of his ministry. In overcoming them, he becomes a model for modern Christians by reminding them that there is more to life than pleasure, the pursuit of power, social status, or prestige in order to be popular or well-thought of.

2. The numbers seventy and seventy-two symbolise all the nations of the world in Genesis 10 in the Masoretic text (Hebrew) and Septuagint (Greek) respectively. Since Luke would have used the Septuagint rather than the Masoretic text, the original reading favours seventy-two. Luke seems to be anticipating the later mission of the Church.

3. Thomas J. Lane, *Luke and the Gentile Mission* (Frankfurt am Main: Peter Lang, 1996), pp. 86–130.

4. Ibid., pp. 131–49.

5. Eugene LaVerdiere SSS, *When We Pray ...: Meditations on the Lord's Prayer* (Notre Dame, Indiana: Ave Maria Press, 1983), pp. 33–52.

✧

CHAPTER FIVE

FOURTH MOMENT: CHRISTIAN CONTEMPLATION – THE GOSPEL OF JOHN

Introduction

The Gospel of John represents the culmination of the foundational experience of God's love in Jesus Christ and in his community. It serves as the Church's manual or guide for attaining full Christian development. The three previous stages or moments of Christian maturation have presumably already been traversed. This Gospel represents the simplicity of the vision of the Christian who has mastered the complexity of the three previous manuals. It locates the unifying principle underlying these phases of development in the gift of the Father's love, which Christians receive through the Son in the Holy Spirit. Christian faith primarily consists of the reception of that gift. Whoever possesses this faith begins to love as Christ loves us, and can hope to attain eternal life. Consequently, in John love is the only precept. All the Church's precepts, laws, rites, service, witness, etc., are sustained by the gift of this love which alone constitutes their true meaning and value. Fidelity to the grace and demand of God's love is the key to Christian authenticity, maturity and engagement with the world. John is the manual of Christian wisdom that promotes an integrated vision of the entire Christian experience in both its internal (Church) and external (world) relationships.

The Gospel of John is the result of an experience of contemplative simplicity underlined by the fundamental values of faith, hope and love. It is the contemplation of the transparency of the mystery of the historical Jesus towards God, his Father, and towards the Church animated by the Spirit. It is the Gospel for the mature Christian and is often described as the most 'spiritual' or mystical of the Gospels. John is represented in art as the eagle because his gaze into the mystery of God points to the eagle that flies directly into the sunlight. John, more than the other Gospels, attempts to capture the mystery of Jesus and its relationship to human beings. In one sense, John is timeless in his statements about light, life, love, faith and judgement. It is also timely because it reached its final form in the context of a community's spiritual growth. John is at pains to tell us what was really going on during the life and ministry of Jesus, as well as its relevance for the lives of Christians of all times.

The tradition relating to what Jesus said and did underwent considerable theological reflection as the message of Jesus was adapted to successive generations of believers. The impression given is that the Gospel of John was slowly built up over a lengthy period and that its final canonical form dates from the closing decade of the first century. The original readers already knew the basic story of Jesus and so the evangelist tells it in a new way with different accents and emphases. An aspect of his dramatic presentation is his employment of symbolism, the meaning of which is brought out by the discourses that usually accompany the signs. They are clearly linked to Jesus' work on earth. The author's purpose is to bring out their deeper dimension and so reveal the glory of the Son of God.

For John, the story of Jesus is that place in history where the ultimate truth about God is to be found ... John had more to tell about Jesus than any Gospel could hold. He had glimpsed the divine light which, all the while, irradiated the Teacher from Nazareth.[1]

John invites his readers to a more profound and stable faith directed to the living and glorified Lord, now present in his community through the Spirit. Faith in him has the power to bestow salvation.

It seems that a particular disciple of Jesus[2] stands at the beginning of the tradition, who has a different memory and interpretation of Jesus' ministry to those of the Synoptics. Preaching, reflection, debates and controversies about the identity of Jesus shaped the tradition and explains the Gospel's strong emphasis on testimony, witness and the listing of arguments. In this way it resembles a court case. Traditional deeds of Jesus have become the subject of long homilies involving theological reflection. It gradually became clear that only a correct evaluation of Jesus as divine decides one's relationship to God. That is why Jesus' divine identity is affirmed in the strongest possible terms, but of course this insistence does not obliterate his humanity. The evangelist believes that Jesus' human status does not totally define him, nor does his uniqueness as God's Son efface his humanity. John is also a Gospel of encounters. Dramatic scenes stress the one-to-one contacts with Jesus. One after the other, various characters encounter Jesus, the light that has come into the world. In this encounter they judge themselves by their decision to come to the light or remain in darkness. As well as being historical individuals, these characters also represent the faith reactions of everyone. Hence the Gospel was written for the express purpose: 'that you may believe that Jesus is the Christ, the Son of God, and that believing this you may have life through his name' (Jn 20:31).

In what is usually called the Book of Signs (chapters 2–12), the evangelist sets forth the meaning of Jesus Christ in terms of his acts: (a) Signs that Jesus brings a new order: the wedding at Cana (water turned into wine symbolises the jubilant and superabundant aspects of the new order of the Gospel that supersedes the old order of Judaism); the cleansing of the Temple (the risen Jesus is the new locus of God's presence); new birth (through divine activity symbolised by the water of Baptism); new worship (replacement of the old rituals by worship in spirit and in truth). (b) Signs that give life: Jesus as the Bread of Life and Lord of creation (multiplication of the loaves, walking on the water, and subsequent dialogue and discourse). (c) Signs that Jesus is the light of the world (in the context of Tabernacles' ritual of light and conflict with the Jews; the healing of the man born blind). (d) Sign that Jesus is the resurrection and the life (the raising of Lazarus and what it signifies). (e) Signs that Jesus brings life through death (the anointing of Jesus, triumphal entry to Jerusalem). The signs culminate in the death of Jesus and his glorification (chapters 18–21), the significance of which is explained in the farewell discourse (chapters 13–17). The signs point beyond themselves to a truth about Jesus. The death of Jesus, on the other hand, is not simply a sign – it is the reality, the love of Jesus in action. It is what it illustrates – the *reality* signified by the signs has now become an actuality.

The symbols, like the images and metaphors to which they are related, provide connecting links between two different worlds. They span the gap between sensible reality and mystery. They are the meeting point between the finite and the infinite.[3]

Symbols are drawn from everyday life, but their significance comes from the rich associations they had already acquired in the Old Testament. There is a deep relationship between the symbol and the reality it represents. For example, light naturally lends itself to symbolism, it connotes clarity and warmth, whereas darkness is something to be dreaded and is associated with evil. The Word who is God comes as the light of the world (8:12) bringing life and light to human beings (1:4; 3:19). Its coming was made necessary as a result of human wrongdoing, which brought with it a darkness that strives to overcome the light. By way of human response to the light, one either accepts or rejects it. As faith begins to take hold in the world, darkness will gradually be overcome and the real light will shine forth. Water turned into wine is the fulfilment of Jewish expectations and the replacement of Jewish festivals (Passover, Tabernacles, Dedication), as well as institutions (Temple, priesthood, Sabbath), brings with it joy and celebration.

John insists that Jesus is the revelation of God and that in him alone is salvation found. In the background are the Jewish feasts that recalled the great moments of God's saving intervention in the past history of his people. It is against these, especially in chapters 5–10, that John portrays Jesus as fulfilling and replacing the Sabbath, the Passover, the feasts of Tabernacles and Dedication of the Temple. The evangelist uses the light shed by Jesus' resurrection to illume the person, words and deeds of Jesus. There is a historical level of understanding that existed during Jesus' public life, but there is also the deeper faith understanding that is seen with hindsight. This was possible only after the paschal events and the coming of the Spirit. John presupposes a historical tradition about Jesus and is intent on emphasising what he considers relevant for his readers who are struggling with opponents who deny that Jesus is the promised Messiah.

Outline of John

1. **Prologue: A hymn adapted as an introduction and summary (1:1-18)**
2. **Ministry of Jesus (1:19–12:50)**
   a. Preparation (1:19-51)
      I. Testimony of John the Baptist (1:19-34)
      II. Call of first disciples (1:35-51)
   b. Beginnings (2:1–4:54)
      I. Miracle at Cana (2:1-12)
      II. Cleansing of Temple (2:13-25)
      III. Discourse with Nicodemus (3:1-21)
      IV. Testimony of John the Baptist (3:22-36)
      V. Discourse with Samaritan Woman (4:1-42)
      VI. Healing of Ruler's son at Cana (4:43-54)
   c. Ministry of Jesus (5:1–10:39)
      I. Cure of paralytic, discourse and debate (5:1-47)
      II. Miracle of loaves, walking on the water, discourse on Eucharist (6:1-71)
      III. Discourse and debate in Jerusalem during feast of Tabernacles (7:1-52)
      IV. The adulterous woman (7:53–8:11)
      V. Discourse and debate on light (8:12-59)
      VI. Cure of man born blind and aftermath (9:1-41)
      VII. Discourse on Good Shepherd (10:1-21)
      VIII. Discourse and debate at feast of Dedication (10:22-42)
   d. Conclusion of Ministry (11:1–12:50)
      I. Resurrection of Lazarus and decision on Jesus' death (11:1-54)

II. Journey to Jerusalem, anointing, triumphal entry, discourses (11:55–12:50)

3. **Passion, Death and Resurrection (13:1–20:31)**
   a. Last Supper, treachery of Judas foretold (13:1-30)
   b. Farewell discourses (13:31–16:33)
   c. Final prayer of Jesus (17:1-26)
   d. Arrest, interrogation before Annas, Peter's denial, Jesus before Pilate (18:1–19:16)
   e. Crucifixion, death, burial (19:17-42)
   f. Apparitions of risen Jesus, conclusion (20:1-31)
4. **Epilogue:** Apparition at Sea of Galilee, destiny of two disciples, second conclusion (21:1-25)

Storyline

The Prologue (1:1-18) functions as an overture, introducing the main themes of the Gospel: life, light, darkness, witness, faith, glory and truth. The Word, through whom the world was created, is divine and becomes known to human beings in the person of Jesus Christ. Life and light symbolise ways in which the Word is present to sustain creation. There is opposition to this light, but darkness cannot overcome it. John appears in history, sent as a witness to prepare the way for the coming of Jesus, the true light. Already in the world but unrecognised, Jesus came to his own people who, for the most part, did not accept him. To those who believed in him, Jesus gave power to become children of God, not through any natural agency, but through God who is the immediate cause of their new spiritual life. The eternal Word enters the human and time-bound sphere by becoming flesh, so the story of Jesus is the story of the Word become flesh who dwelt among us. In him, the faith community has experienced the magnificence of God's presence. The incarnate Word becomes the new mode of divine presence among his people, surpassing God's former covenant love and fidelity to his people in the Old Testament. John is a witness to this. The countenance of the true God can be seen in the face of Christ, who is the visible image of the invisible God and is therefore qualified to make him known.

The testimony of John about the Messiah and Jesus' self-revelation to the first disciples (1:19-51) introduces the Gospel proper. John's negative testimony about himself when questioned by 'the Jews'[4] is followed by his positive testimony concerning Jesus, thereby shifting attention away from himself to Jesus and leading others to faith in him. Jesus as the Lamb of God evokes the Passover lamb, the cultic symbol of Israel's deliverance (cf. Ex 12:1-13). He will baptise with the Spirit and take away the world's collective sin of alienation from God and one another. This is followed by the revelation of Jesus to Andrew and Peter and later to Philip and Nathanael, all of whom become followers of Jesus. Various Old Testament titles identify Jesus, culminating in a profession of faith in Jesus as the Son of God and King of Israel. Jesus himself becomes the place where heaven and earth meet, for no one sees God except through Jesus. Already, Jesus is gathering disciples who believe, however inadequately, in his mission.

The miracle at Cana (2:1-12) is the first act of Jesus' ministry in John. Jesus' mother identifies the problem that will evoke the miracle, but does not make a direct request. Although at first Jesus seems to reject his mother's request, she appears quite confident that he will accede to her petition. What is revealed in the wine miracle is linked to what will be revealed in his death, his 'hour'.[5] The sign of abundant excellent wine (the first of seven signs) points beyond itself to the revelation of God in Jesus, a manifestation of God's presence and power working through him, and his disciples believe. An abundance of wine is also a sign that the messianic age has arrived (cf. Is 25:6; Jl 3:18; Am 9:13) and with it the replacement of the most important Jewish feasts, institutions and customs.

The cleansing of the Temple (2:13-25) is placed at the beginning of Jesus' ministry to highlight the fact that Jesus brings a new covenant that supersedes the institutions of the old. The action of Jesus is a prophetic sign of the Temple's imminent demise, together with the termination of its rituals. Jesus challenges his critics to destroy his own body, for ironically it is destined to replace the Temple as the locus of God's presence when raised from the grave in divine glory. The end of the chapter warns against a faith based solely on miracles, for many attracted by Jesus' miracles will not remain faithful.

The discourse with Nicodemus (3:1-21) continues the self-manifestation of Jesus. It is the first of the Johannine discourses, shifting from dialogue to monologue and ending with the evangelist's reflection. Jesus instructs Nicodemus on the necessity of new birth from above. Although he is a teacher of the Law and a member of the Jewish religious leadership, Nicodemus misunderstands what Jesus is saying, assuming that he is speaking about physical birth, whereas Jesus is speaking about birth from God, which has baptismal associations. Wordplay and misunderstanding characterise the dialogue and Nicodemus disappears from the scene after this exchange. Jesus now addresses a wider audience. His descent in the incarnation and the offering of his own life on the cross makes eternal life[6] possible for those who believe. This is the new life Jesus promised to Nicodemus. Although Jesus' death is intimately linked to God's love for the world, his presence confronts people with the decision to believe or not, thus making it a moment of self-judgement. God sent Jesus to save the world and the world will judge itself in its response to him. The final testimony of John (3:22-36) recognises that his own ministry, though real, is of secondary importance compared to the saving mission of Jesus. He is content to direct his disciples to become followers of Jesus. For John is only the 'best man' who arranges and manages the wedding celebrations, and he is happy to fade into the background now that his mission is fulfilled. The remaining verses serve as the evangelist's summary of the entire chapter.

Two conversations – Jesus and the Samaritan woman; and Jesus and the disciples – form the content of the subsequent narrative (4:1-42). The dialogue with the Samaritan woman progressively reveals the truth about Jesus and his mission. It continues the theme of replacement of water and cult with the living water of revelation that Jesus brings, as well as the Spirit who enables one to worship God appropriately. Jesus is revealed as greater than the patriarch Jacob. The woman persists in treating Jesus' words literally until reference to her marital status persuades her that Jesus might be a prophet who would inform her about the proper location of worship. Jesus tells her that these disputes have now become irrelevant. The woman finally wonders if Jesus could be the Messiah and immediately sets about bringing others to Jesus. As a result of her conversation with Jesus, the woman has moved from protest and misunderstanding to confession and witness. Meanwhile, Jesus' dialogue with his disciples revolves around mission and harvest. The large numbers of Samaritans who come to believe in Jesus indicate the truth of his words about the rich harvest. They are led to Jesus on the basis of the woman's testimony, but it is their own experience of Jesus that leads them to faith. The story concludes with the affirmation that Jesus is the Saviour of the world, thus highlighting the universality of Jesus' mission.

This episode is followed by the healing of the nobleman's son at Cana (4:43-54) and takes place at a distance. The apparent rebuff of Jesus indicates that his actions will not be governed by demands for signs and wonders. It is met, however, by the father's faith in Jesus' words of life and promise before any results become known. The report of the son's recovery corroborates the knowledge that Jesus' word gives life and the experience leads both him and his whole household to faith.

Sharp confrontation between Jesus and those who do not believe is highlighted in the remainder of the public ministry of Jesus. The debates concern the identity of Jesus – his origin and destiny. This identity also concerns readers. It is important to know whether Jesus is from God and is God, otherwise John's claim that Jesus is the Saviour of the world would be brought into doubt. Two large units make up the next section (5:1-47): a Sabbath healing of a paralysed man, and the controversy following the healing – a lengthy discourse by Jesus that draws out the theological implications of the healing and controversy. Jesus provokes hostility among the religious leaders by healing a paralysed man on the Sabbath. Sabbath observance was based on God's resting on the seventh day (Gn 2:2-3), but it was also thought that God's providence remained active even on the Sabbath to keep all things in existence. This was especially true in cases of giving life at birth and taking it away at death, which also became the time of judgement, for human beings are also born and die on the Sabbath. Jesus claims the same authority to work as the Father. John uses the discourse that follows the miracle cure to draw out what the real issue is, namely, Jesus' assertion to equality with God. Opponents counter that no human being may claim to do things that only God can do, i.e. to give life and to judge. Jesus defends his claim to both by appealing to the special relationship he enjoys with God. As Son, Jesus does what the Father has instructed him to do. Furthermore, those who question his behaviour should look to the witnesses he can bring forward – (1) John the Baptist; (2) the witness of the deeds that God has enabled him to do; and (3) the witness that God has given through the Scriptures. His opponents fail to recognise that he is from God because they are more interested in human adulation and are not really concerned with the glory that belongs to God. Their confidence in Moses is misplaced, for Moses witnessed to Jesus and will condemn anyone who rejects that testimony.

The following section (6:1-71) contains two miracle stories – the miracles of the loaves and the miracle of Jesus walking on the water – followed by a dialogue with the crowd and a discourse on the bread of life that provokes different responses. The story of the multiplication of the loaves is the fourth sign, symbolising the food that is really available through Jesus and has obvious Eucharistic overtones. The abundance of the miracle is stressed. The reaction of the crowd expresses conventional messianic expectations, but Jesus withdraws since he will not answer the world's expectations of him. The fifth sign is a nature miracle, portraying Jesus as sharing in God's power. As Jesus walks on the water, he identifies himself to the disciples with the divine name 'I am'.[7] This miracle reveals Jesus' divinity because he shares in God's dominion over the waters of chaos (cf. Is 43:2; Ps 77:19; 107:23-30; Jb 9:8). The lengthy dialogue and discourse that follow interpret the two signs that immediately precede them. The discourse by Jesus is framed by conversations between Jesus and the crowd (vv. 25-34) and between Jesus and his disciples (vv. 60-71).

The conversation between Jesus and the crowd is characterised by misunderstanding. They fail to see beyond the actual feeding to the presence of God in Jesus that the miracle of the loaves reveals. Only Jesus gives the food that endures for eternal life (i.e. for living even now in the unending presence of God) and this is received in faith, not by the performance of a specific act. Jesus reinterprets the story of the manna in the wilderness (cf. Ex 16; Ps 78:24) as food that perished and did not bring the Israelites to their heavenly destiny. He explains that in the miracle of the loaves they have already received the sign they demand, namely, the gift of God's presence. When the crowd asks for this bread, Jesus proclaims: 'I am the bread of life.' This is followed by an invitation to come to Jesus and believe in him for their salvation. The 'bread of life' is a symbol of God's revelation in Jesus, who has descended from heaven to carry out the will of him who sent him. Jesus' words are the source of eternal life. Like the behaviour of the Israelites in the desert, 'the Jews' complain. Jesus' claim to be the bread from heaven is challenged, since they think they know his family background. Jesus explains that while faith in him is impossible without God's initiative, humans retain responsibility for how they respond, and that initiative is now made concrete in the revelation brought by Jesus.

In the second half of the discourse (vv. 51-58), Jesus says that he is the food that gives life, not the manna or any other bread. It is through eating his flesh and drinking his blood in the Eucharist that the believer is able to share fully in this food. Participation in the Eucharist creates a relationship between Jesus and the believer that contains the promise of new life;

they 'abide in'⁸ one another. Jesus becomes the source of life for the Christian, and the Eucharist is at the very source of that relationship. Jesus is speaking both literally and sacramentally. The future tense (v. 51) points to the cross and resurrection, and to the Eucharistic liturgy where Jesus offers himself as living bread for the life of the whole world. Jesus' words elicit a range of responses – complaint; disbelief; abandonment; confession of faith; and betrayal. In the face of Jesus' self-giving to those who believe, many of his followers turn their backs on him. An earthbound perspective is profitless in the face of divine mysteries, Jesus says (v. 63). However, only Jesus has, as Peter proclaims, the words of eternal life.

Conflict between Jesus and his opponents intensifies. Jesus manifests himself in the context of Jewish feasts embodied in Temple rituals. Jesus appropriates to himself symbols of sacred time, bread, water, light associated with the Sabbath, and the feasts of Passover, Tabernacles and Dedication. The great feasts recalled and made present the great moments of God's intervention in the history of his people. The episodes in these sections (7:1-52; 7:53–8:11; 8:12-59) are portrayed as occurring at the feast of Tabernacles. The symbols of water and light were part of the Tabernacles ritual and Jesus appropriates them to express his identity and mission. Crowds of pilgrims assembled for the feast provide the context for his relatives' suggestion that Jesus should display his works and make a name for himself. But Jesus cannot manifest the fullness of his glory until the 'hour' of his Passion, a time set by God, not by the expectations or demands of others. Jesus' secret journey to Jerusalem is independent of his relatives' demand. Opinion about him there is already divided. Throughout these sections we are reminded that officials are seeking Jesus' death. He is accused of leading people astray and being possessed by a demon. However, since Jesus' 'hour' has not yet come, all attempts to arrest, condemn and stone him come to nothing.

People are astonished at his teaching since he has never studied as a rabbi, yet Jesus maintains that he has received his teaching from God. Therefore, he does not seek his own glory as human teachers often do. He is accused of healing on the Sabbath, although the law permits activities like circumcision to take place on that day. People think they know his origins, making it impossible for him to be the Messiah. Yet Jesus' real origins are from heaven and the deeds he performs testify to this fact. Jesus now begins to speak in a symbolic way about his departure. He will go to a place where they cannot follow him. But the crowd fails to grasp his meaning and thinks he is going to the diaspora Jews, or perhaps to kill himself. The irony is that Christianity will spread beyond the confines of Palestine and that Jesus will freely give up his life on behalf of others.

On the last day of the festival, alluding to the water ceremony of the feast, Jesus proclaims that he is the source of spiritual water that quenches our deepest thirst, that is, of the Spirit poured out upon the world after his glorification. Discussion on the Davidic lineage of the Messiah and a failed attempt to arrest Jesus prompts Nicodemus to plead for due process and legal justice, only to be rebuffed by the Pharisees. The story of the adulterous woman (7:53–8:11)[9] is a test case brought by the Pharisees as a trap designed to incriminate or discredit Jesus. If he authorises stoning, he is guilty of criminal wrongdoing in the eyes of the Roman authorities. If he forbids stoning, he will be denounced as a false messiah who contradicts Moses. Jesus neither condemns the woman nor condones her sins. He forgives her past and challenges her to live uprightly in the future.

The lamp-lighting ritual of the feast is the occasion for Jesus' proclamation that he is the light of the world. This provokes another debate about the validity of Jesus' witness to his own identity and mission. But Jesus' knowledge of where he has come from and where he is going makes his testimony valid. His opponents judge solely by what is visible and do not recognise Jesus' divine origins witnessed to by God himself. This is followed by the theme of his death, and Jesus goes on to identify himself as one in whom God is visible and made known by using the divine name 'I am'. He will be recognised when he is glorified in his death. In the final verses (8:31-59) the debate intensifies and the tone becomes more adversarial. The theme of identity of the opponents' real father – Abraham, God, or the devil – predominates. Since Jesus judges them by what they do, their actions show that they have the devil for their father. The dialogue concludes with an attempt to kill him.

The story of the man born blind (9:1-41) demonstrates that it is possible for the blind man to progress from restoration of physical sight to spiritual insight and true faith in Jesus. He comes to recognise more and more clearly that Jesus cannot be a sinner and so must have come from God. This sixth sign is introduced to illustrate the saying: 'I am the light of the world.' The story contrasts Jesus, the light, with the Jews who become progressively blind in refusing to accept the testimony of others. The neighbours' disagreement about the identity of the man affords him the opportunity to serve as witness to his own healing by giving a full report of how Jesus cured him. The narrative then divides into five scenes: (1) the blind man and the Pharisees, some of whom conclude that since Jesus violated the Sabbath, he cannot be from God; (2) the Jews and the parents, the latter who refuse to get involved out of fear;

(3) the Jews who put the man under oath to tell the truth, but ironically he turns their repeated questioning about his healing back on them by pointing out the contradictions of their own position; and (4) Jesus' self-identification leads to the man's confession of faith. He has moved from naming Jesus as his healer, to acknowledging him as a prophet and a man from God. Finally (5), in response to Jesus' question, he comes to full faith in Jesus as Son of Man. Paradoxically, the Pharisees, while claiming to see clearly, become progressively blind to the revelation of God in Jesus and judge themselves thereby.

The allegory of the good shepherd (10:1-21) continues the discussion. Instead of addressing the situation of the Pharisees directly, Jesus does so indirectly. The whole illustration gives a realistic portrayal of pastoral conditions in Palestine at that time. An enclosure protected the flocks at night from thieves and predators. Only the shepherd would be recognised and admitted by the gatekeeper. Calling the sheep by name is a mark of intimacy and familiarity. The shepherd leads them out to graze and find pasture. The sheep are the disciples who hear the voice of Jesus and follow him wherever he goes. The Pharisees who are blind to the spiritual dimensions of Jesus' teaching do not understand. They are the spiritual descendants of the shepherds of Israel denounced by the prophets as worthless and evil (cf. Ezk 34:1-10). Through a series of 'I am' sayings, Jesus shows that he is the genuine shepherd. Jesus is the gate – the point of access for the flock to a place of safety and for going out to pasture. The positive image of the shepherd is then contrasted with the negative image of the hired hand. Jesus identifies himself as the good shepherd of Ezekiel 34:11-16 who fulfils God's promises and is even willing to lay down his life for his sheep. Readers are reminded that Jesus' death is a free offering on his part. Other sheep, not of his fold, express Jesus' universal outreach to include all in the one flock under the one shepherd. Finally, the evangelist tells us about the different reactions to what Jesus says.

The Jewish feast of Dedication (*Hanukkah*) is the occasion when Jesus claims to be the one whom the Father has consecrated and sent into the world (10:22-42). It resembles a formal interrogation about Jesus' identity as Messiah and Son of God, and of whether in Jesus one experiences the presence of God in the world. Jesus' work and God's work cannot be distinguished because Jesus shares fully in God's work. John's role in witnessing to Jesus is reaffirmed. Another attempt to arrest Jesus fails.

The raising of Lazarus (11:1-44) is the climax of the signs and leads directly into the decision of the Sanhedrin to kill Jesus (11:45-54). The theme of life predominates, for this is a sign of the real life that the risen Jesus will give to all who believe in him. Dialogue precedes the sign and explains it. Martha already believes that Jesus is the Messiah, the Son of God, and that her brother will rise on the last day. But Jesus leads her to a deeper faith; he is not only the resurrection but also the life, so that whoever believes in him will never die. Still, Lazarus' return to life is only a sign and that is why he emerges from the tomb still bound in burial clothes. This makes concrete the hold that death still has on him. In contrast, Jesus will give an eternal life impervious to death that is later symbolised by his emerging from the tomb leaving his burial clothes behind (cf. 20:6-7). Jesus will rise completely free from the bonds of death. He possesses the absolute sovereignty over life and death that was believed to be the sole prerogative of God himself. Ironically, the Lazarus miracle provides the catalyst for the formal death sentence given to Jesus, for the report of the miracle is the direct cause of the council meeting. Caiaphas unintentionally prophesies concerning the real meaning of Jesus' death – to gather into one all the scattered children of God.

The decision to kill Jesus is linked to the upcoming Passover (11:55–12:50). The anointing by Mary is an act of extravagant love towards Jesus that anticipates his burial, while Judas will betray him. John's version of the triumphal entry into Jerusalem highlights the title 'King of Israel', an important theme, the nature of which is redefined by Jesus and will reach its conclusion in the Passion narrative. Only after Jesus' death and resurrection will the real meaning of Jesus' kingship be fully understood. The appearance of the Greeks points to the imminent arrival of the 'hour' of Jesus. Through the image of the seed, Jesus teaches that his death will bring new life because it produces fruit – a symbol for the future community of faith that includes both Jews and Gentiles. Jesus' death is also the ultimate act of service that invites the community to serve one another with the same kind of love. His death marks the defeat of the powers of evil when he will draw all people to himself. This points to the worldwide acceptance of the Gospel. The mention of light is an appeal for faith in Jesus, given the urgency of his impending hour. As the evangelist struggles with the fact that Jesus is rejected for the most part by his own people, he reflects on the tragedy of unbelief. The public ministry concludes with the words of Jesus that summarise what went before. It succinctly states the significance of the presence of Jesus and the decision one takes as a consequence.

The theme of the remaining chapters is enunciated in 13:1 with the announcement that Jesus is aware that his 'hour' has come and that he wishes to show to the very end his love for his own who are in the world. Only 'his own' are present to hear Jesus speak of his plans for them. He prepares the disciples for the events to come as well as for their future life as a community of believers. The foot-washing scene (13:1-30) not only reflects the service he is about to perform in his death, it also sets the pattern for relationships among his disciples. By offering a morsel of bread to Judas before he departs into the night, Jesus makes explicit that one of those whose feet he has washed will betray him. The transition from the meal to Jesus' final words (14:1–16:33) is provided by 13:31-38. Jesus is now about to be glorified when he makes visible the presence of God that began when the Word became flesh. The decisive moment of glorification is the unfolding events of Jesus' 'hour'. The love modelled in the foot washing will be enacted fully in his death. His disciples are to love one another in the same way. Peter does not yet realise the full extent of Jesus' love and declares his willingness to follow him. Jesus' final words to his disciples are known as the farewell discourse. Through it, he explains the significance of his death and departure to his disciples before the events happen, so that when they occur, they will be able to interpret them through the eyes of faith and not give way to despondency. He also prepares them for the life they will lead after the events of his hour. There are recurring themes: the assurance of Jesus' abiding presence; the necessity of Jesus' return to the Father; the promise of the Spirit (Paraclete); the future of the community; the centrality of love.

The discourse begins by stressing the theme of departure. Jesus consoles his disciples by a promise to return to take them to himself so that they may be with him. Thomas's question leads to the famous response: 'I am the Way, the Truth and the Life', and Philip's question leads to Jesus' 'To have seen me is to have seen the Father ... I am in the Father and the Father is in me.' This theme of divine indwelling leads to the theme of how the Spirit, Jesus and the Father will come to dwell in the Christian. The Spirit as Paraclete will play the roles of advocate to defend Christians, and of consoler to comfort them. He also will serve as teacher, explaining the implications of what Jesus said, and as his witness. Jesus gives his gift of peace, accompanied by a warning that the prince of this world is coming.

Like the allegory of the shepherd, that of the vine and the branches (15:1-8) portrays Jesus as the vine of the new Israel. As branches united to him, Christians will bear fruit pleasing to God, the vinedresser. Withered branches will have to be removed and burned. Jesus is, therefore, the source of the community's identity and fruitfulness. The verb 'remain' (*menein*) expresses the central theme. The vine imagery symbolises how the life of the Christian community is shaped by love and intertwined with the abiding presence of God and Jesus. To bear fruit, to do the works of love, is the concrete sign of discipleship modelled on Jesus' death as the ultimate demonstration of his love. The community's relationship to the world will be characterised by hate, persecution and the possibility of death. Its treatment by the world is an external sign of their relationship with Jesus. The persecution of Jesus' followers is concretely described. Jesus' departure is a prerequisite for the coming of the Paraclete as the prosecuting attorney who will prove the world wrong. In Jesus' life, death and glorification, the ruler of the world is judged because evil is shown to be powerless before God. The Paraclete will also enable the community to hear afresh the teachings of Jesus after his departure. The disciples' confusion shows how difficult it is for them to comprehend what Jesus is teaching, and the image of childbirth illustrates how the disciples' pain and sorrow at Jesus' departure will be transformed into permanent joy. Prayer asked and answered in Jesus' name is also an occasion for joy. The discourse ends in a note of triumph, for love defeats the power of death.

Jesus' prayer (17:1-26) is the final scene of the farewell meal. He addresses his Father in prayer, highlighting the unity of Father, Son and the believing community. Jesus prays that the events of his hour will complete his revelation of God and then his Father will be glorified. He entrusts the community into his Father's care, for the community will live and work in the midst of opposition. Jesus prays for all those who in the future will come to believe through the witness of the community. His prayer for unity among his followers is grounded in the unity of Jesus and the Father and will serve as a witness to the world. Jesus concludes his prayer by reviewing his work and ministry that made known the Father's love, and provides a fitting introduction to the story of Jesus' hour.

The earthly Passion of Jesus was already well known to John's readers. It is now retold from the perspective of its ultimate purpose – as the expression of the love of Christ for human beings. He is the central figure, all-knowing and in control. At the centre is the trial before Pilate that includes the scourging and the mock coronation of Jesus as king. At Golgotha, there is no cry of abandonment, no darkening of the skies, no rending of the veil. It is the hour of triumph, of the exaltation of the dying Jesus to draw all people to himself as he hands over the Spirit. John points to the ultimate significance of the event in the plan of God.

Jesus' arrest, interrogation and trial before Pilate (18:1– 19:16) follow in quick succession. Throughout his Passion, Jesus remains in complete control of his destiny. He freely lays down his own life; nobody takes it from him. Jesus takes the initiative by approaching the soldiers who come to arrest him; he does not wait to be arrested. He also identifies himself to the arresting party against the background of his divine majesty so that those who come to arrest him fall to the ground. Peter again fails to understand how the betrayal and suffering of Christ are part of the Father's plan. In the interrogation before Annas, Jesus confronts his accusers with the evidence of his public teaching. He demands that they bring evidence against him, which they are unable to do. Meanwhile Peter denies that he is Jesus' disciple.

Jesus is brought before Pilate and the scene is turned into a highly developed drama. Seven episodes show Pilate shuttling back and forth between Jesus and 'the Jews'. Two trials are related: between Pilate and 'the Jews', and between Pilate and Jesus. The important issue is how Pilate and 'the Jews' will respond to Jesus' royal status which is at the centre – Jesus is scourged, crowned, dressed as a king and ironically proclaimed: 'Hail, the King of the Jews.' Meanwhile, Jesus explains to Pilate that his kingship is not political; moreover 'the Jews' admit that the real issue is not the charge of kingship, but that Jesus claimed to be God's Son. Pilate is challenged by Jesus as to whether he belongs to the truth and so it is Pilate who is really on trial. The leaders call for Jesus' crucifixion, despite Pilate three times declaring him innocent. Jesus does not accept Pilate's claim to authority – he gives into threats and has an innocent man condemned. Meanwhile 'the Jews' proclaim that they have no king but Caesar, thereby renouncing their status as God's people.

Jesus carries his own cross as a sign that he freely lays down his life. Details in the crucifixion scene, which fulfil the Scriptures, demonstrate that everything is happening according to God's plan. Pilate reaffirms the kingship of Jesus in the languages of the empire; Jesus is king for everybody to see. For John, the Lord reigns from the wood of the cross. Mary, his mother, and the Beloved Disciple are included among those at the foot of the cross, but the evangelist is interested mainly in their symbolism. Together they constitute the nucleus of a family of disciples. Jesus dies at a time when the paschal lambs are being slaughtered in the Temple (cf. 1:29). At the end, Jesus declares: 'It is completed' and hands over the Spirit. He calmly lays down his life for his friends when he is ready, thereby dying in a sovereign, life-giving manner. When Jesus' side is pierced, blood and water flow out. Here the evangelist seemingly intends a reference to the two channels (Eucharist and Baptism respectively) through which the Spirit is communicated to believers. The burial of Jesus also stresses his sovereignty; he is buried as befits a king. For John, it is the Passion of a sovereign king who has overcome the world.

The resurrection of Jesus is no resuscitation, but signifies that the same Jesus is now living in a whole new glorified existence. John's account of the appearances of the risen Christ (20:1-31) is really a series of encounters illustrating different degrees of faith. They remind the reader that in the range of faith there are different degrees of readiness and different factors that cause people to come to faith. The Beloved Disciple, on seeing the burial garments without the body, comes to full faith. Mary Magdalene comes to faith when the risen Jesus calls her name. Fear and hiding still mark the lives of the disciples. When the risen Jesus stands among them and shows them his hands and his side, they are filled with joy. They are commissioned like Jesus to bring life, light and truth to others, made possible through the gift of the Spirit that is connected with the forgiveness of sins. Absent when Jesus appeared to the other disciples, Thomas refuses to believe their testimony. Instead he wants to probe the wounds of Jesus to be sure. Jesus appears and invites Thomas to do so, at which point he professes a faith that gives the highest evaluation of Jesus uttered in the Gospel: 'My Lord and my God.' No greater praise can be given to Jesus' followers: 'Happy are those who have not seen and yet believe' (20:29).

The presence in John of an additional chapter (21:1-25) involving the appearance of Jesus by the lakeside seems to be totally independent of the previous appearances. Unsuccessful in their fishing, the disciples do not recognise Jesus who is suddenly present on the shore. Jesus uses their fishing trade to symbolise what they must begin to do. The miraculous catch brings about the recognition of Jesus. A subsequent meal on the shore fills out the missionary symbolism of the catch. Readers are challenged to recognise the risen Lord who is present when they celebrate the Eucharist. They are also invited to see in Peter the role of shepherding the sheep. The threefold pattern of Peter's affirmation is set against his previous threefold denial. In his care for the flock, Peter will be required to lay down his life. Still, it is the Beloved Disciple, not Peter, who vouches for the truth of what is written and his testimony is true. The conclusion challenges all attempts to enclose Jesus in neat categories and hints at the sheer inability of any written work to capture Jesus and his impact in full.

Literary Characteristics
It is possible to catch glimpses of the public life of Jesus and the Johannine community through the window of the Gospel.

However, the evangelist is not primarily writing history. Because the genre of history is so much to the fore today, the first question that enters readers' minds is: 'Did this actually happen as described?' Rather, the author is composing a literary composition and so the primary question becomes: 'What does all this mean?' Reading John's Gospel as narrative, we are invited to enter a literary world created by the evangelist from materials drawn from the historical life of Jesus that have long been reflected and meditated upon. The Gospel is a blend of historical tradition and faith. Accordingly, the most fruitful way to read John is to read it as narrative or story independent of historical considerations. To attempt to put an overall historical construction on the Gospel's highly symbolic speech is to misread it, whereas to allow the symbolism to imaginatively speak to the reader is to read it as the author meant it to be read. Too little attention has been devoted in the past to the impact the whole story makes upon the reader. The unifying principle of the composition is not the chronology or geography of a life story. Its main theme is an attempt to tell readers what God has done for them through the life, death, resurrection and glorification of Jesus, and how to respond to this gift of God both as individuals and in community. Consequently, as long as we insist on seeing the Gospel only as a window on what happened during Jesus' ministry, we will be unable to grasp the full truth that the Gospel wishes to convey. Only when the narrative is held up as a mirror to the readers' lives, as the author intended, can there be an interaction with the glory[10] of Jesus that it discloses. A major goal of the Gospel is to present a daring reinterpretation of Jesus and his ministry to give readers a deeper view of the identity and significance of Jesus. The overall purpose is to deepen authentic faith in Jesus, the Revealer of the true God, as contrasted with inauthentic or inadequate faith.

John has situated his story of Jesus in history between 'the beginning' (1:1) and 'the last day' (6:40). Jesus is the one who comes forth as the Word-made-flesh from the Father's side, and in the resurrection returns to the One who sent him. The characters that inhabit the Gospel are sharply defined by their response to Jesus, by their ability to believe, and by their progress in faith or away from it. Some reject him, others refuse to confess their faith openly, and a few are caught between Jesus and his opponents, and must choose whom to follow. The ironies evident throughout the narrative successively unmask the folly of disbelief and misperception. The disciples who react to the manifestation of his 'glory' with belief represent a variety of perceptions that must be superseded. Only the mother of Jesus and the Beloved Disciple are portrayed as responding with faith, hope and love from the very beginning. They are the true witnesses to Jesus and so become models of authentic faith. To read this Gospel with sensitivity to its characters' different responses is not only to enter into the narrative world of the author, but also to allow oneself to be challenged regarding one's own response. John's message will help readers overcome whatever lack of understanding of Jesus they still may have, so that Jesus will be able to call them both his disciples and his friends.

Revelation takes place in the person of Jesus, in his whole life and death. The content of this revelation is that God is love and that this love is manifested by Jesus for those with eyes to see. The supreme manifestation of this divine love is the laying down of his life for the sake of the world. Human beings discover the truth about life and death at the foot of the cross. There they discover the love of Christ and so discover who the true God really is: 'God loved the world so much that he gave his only Son, so that everyone who believes in him may not be lost but may have eternal life' (3:16). John did not invent this message of a loving God revealed through the gift of his Son in a supreme act of love (cf. 13:1), for the life and death of Jesus already had constituted the foundational story of Christianity. What John is doing is leading his readers into a new and deeper vision of Christianity, into an ever-developing belief in Jesus, the Son of God, and in this way enabling them to come to eternal life. In Jesus all that *we* can know about God is made known. What Jesus is in relation to human beings and the world is spelled out by means of 'I am' sayings, together with expressed predicates. He is the source of life for all (vine, life, resurrection); the means through which all find life (way, gate); the one who leads all to life (shepherd) as he reveals the truth (light, truth) which can nourish their life (bread from heaven both as revelation and Eucharist). All this is possible because Jesus and the Father are one (10:30), and Jesus possesses the life-giving power of the Father.

People are saved when they believe and live a new life marked by unselfish love. The Gospel as it has come down to us is a literary and theological whole, having a particular theology, style and structure. There is the portrayal of Jesus as a divine person who descended from above and whose divinity shines through his life in the world. His humanity is, likewise, very much in evidence particularly in his relationships with individual persons. John reaches back to before creation to identify Jesus: 'The Word was God' (1:1), and we are reminded again at the end when Thomas confesses the risen Jesus as: 'My Lord and my God' (20:28). Jesus is a divine being who comes into the world and becomes a human being. There is emphasis on the Father/Son relationship and the life-giving teaching and work that the Son carries out on behalf of the Father.

The structure and chronology of John differs from those of the Synoptics. His literary style favours lengthy discourses, dialogues and controversies that spell out the meaning of Jesus' teaching and actions. The evangelist has brought noteworthy dramatic skill to bear so that the Gospel's lengthy narratives become effective vehicles of encounters leading to a deepening of faith for readers. Although coming from heaven and speaking of what is true and real, the Word-made-flesh must use earthly language to convey his message. That is why Jesus uses metaphors and symbols to describe himself and his message. In dialogues, the questioner often misunderstands the figure of speech and takes only a literal meaning. This allows Jesus an opportunity to explain his teaching more thoroughly and thereby unfold his doctrine. Since Jesus is 'from above' and speaks of heavenly realities, he will inevitably be misunderstood by human beings 'from below', who mistakenly think he is speaking only of worldly things, the one reality they know.[11] Sometimes, interlocutors make statements about Jesus that are derogatory or incredulous in the sense intended. The irony is that these statements are often more true in a sense the speakers do not realise, but that readers come to recognise.[12] The rich field of imagery and allusions serve as pointers to the invisible, as windows into the divine. That is why readers today need to get beyond a technical rationality that accepts as true only what can be proved and that characterises the scientific age in which they live. They must activate their other faculties — memory, emotions, especially imagination, as well as intelligence and will — to profit fully from John's presentation.

His Gospel, therefore, invites multiple readings, meditation and contemplation to become familiar with its contents.

The presence of God in the world since creation and in the history of his chosen people culminates in the Word of God becoming flesh and dwelling amongst humans so that his glory can be seen. By the end of the Prologue, readers already know who Jesus is and they can now observe other characters as they struggle with the challenge posed by Jesus and his mission from the Father. These characters are both individual persons and representative characters. They represent various stages of faith, or a lack thereof, which creates division and growing hostility that eventually brings about Jesus' death. The Gospel narrates Jesus' public ministry (chapters 1–12); his private teaching to his disciples (chapters 13–17); his trial and crucifixion (chapters 18–19); and his resurrection appearances (chapters 20–21). His life and ministry reveals God's presence in our world, but also confronts human beings with a decision to be for or against the revelation he brings and that he himself is. Readers become more aware of how costly the revelation of God's love in Jesus becomes as the narrative moves towards his 'hour', that is, his Passion, death, resurrection and glorification.

Portrait of Jesus

John's Gospel narrative depends on events which precede the earthly ministry of Jesus and those which follow it. Jesus himself cannot properly be understood apart from these events. So the evangelist interprets Jesus as no contemporary observer would have been able to do. The perspective of the community of faith is necessary for an adequate understanding of who Jesus is. John tells his story from a viewpoint which is informed by memory; the interpretation of Scripture; the bringing together of historical traditions with the post-Easter experience of the early Church; consciousness of the presence of the Spirit in the community; and a re-reading of the glory of the risen Christ back into his earthly ministry. The author views Jesus from the twin perspective of his origin as pre-existent Word and as glorified Son of God. Only when these two perspectives are combined, the evangelist believes, can Jesus be properly understood. For John, the death of Jesus is of such great importance that it is carefully foreshadowed and interpreted in the discourse material, especially in the farewell discourse with his disciples.

Jesus occupies a central place in the Gospel of John. Practically the whole Gospel is taken up with what he says and does, and how others react to him. All the other characters appear only long enough to fulfil their role as respondents to Jesus. He is represented as the incarnation of the Word of God that continues the revelation already at work in creation and in the history of the chosen people. His resurrection demonstrates that his self-manifestation during his public life was that of God. Notwithstanding the blindness of most of his contemporaries, readers are able to see that all Jesus says and does points to his identity as the Word of God. In the post-resurrection period, the glorified Jesus is present and active through the Paraclete, identified with the Spirit (cf. 14:26), who dwells within the disciples to guide and teach them about Jesus, and to put the hostile world on trial (cf. chapters 14–16). The Paraclete becomes the connection between community life and Jesus of Nazareth, giving new meaning to what Jesus said, and so guides every generation in facing new situations (cf. 16:13). Through the Paraclete, the risen Jesus is present to believers. Much of what Jesus says in the farewell discourse is intended for future disciples. At the end of time, Jesus as Son of Man will raise the dead and pronounce definitive judgement, one that has already begun during Jesus' ministry.

Jesus is elaborately introduced in the Prologue, and by its end Jesus' origin, status and the significance of his life is already clear. John the Baptist bears witness to him in the face of opposition regarding who he is. The reader can expect that Jesus will be rejected by his own, but believed in by some. Jesus' first words are in the form of a question: 'What are you looking for?' What he subsequently says about himself reveals his relationship with his Father and exposes the blindness of others. The works he does have been given to him by the Father so that he should carry them out. All who see and believe in him will have eternal life. Since Jesus and the Father are one (10:30), Jesus is omniscient – he knows his 'hour' and what is in the hearts of people. He employs the divine 'I am' (*ego eimi*, 8:24, 28, 58) independently, and with predicates: Jesus is the bread of life from heaven, the light of the world, the door of the sheepfold, the good shepherd, the resurrection and the life, the way, the truth and the life, the genuine vine. Although he does not engage in political activity, he is capable of public confrontations. Still, there remains areas of shadow and mystery which is fitting since he 'is not of this world' (8:23). As the Father's emissary, he reveals the Father, so much so that to see him is to see the Father (cf. 14:9). The works he performs have been given to him by the Father who remains a transcendent presence and does not appear in the narrative. Yet, this God 'loved the world so much that he gave his only Son ...' (3:16). By believing that Jesus is from God, readers can come to know God as Father. No one has ever seen God, only Jesus has made him known (cf. 1:18). Those who believe become children of

God and both Jesus and the Father will come to abide with them (14:23).

In John, the divinity of Jesus is always in the background. The evangelist wants to say that Jesus is both fully human (1:14) and also fully the revelation of God (14:9). He is the human person who is the manifestation and presence of God in our world (cf. 10:30). The distinctiveness of John's Jesus is evident right from the beginning of his Gospel. Jesus is the incarnate Word. This majestic Word-made-flesh moves through the Gospel and his Passion is presented as the triumph of the Son of God. Already in the other Gospels there are glimpses of this other-worldliness aspect of Jesus' character. In John, however, we meet a visitor from another world. He preaches himself and in doing so makes the true God known: 'No one has ever seen God; it is the only Son, who is nearest to the Father's heart, who has made him known' (1:18). John portrays Jesus as the Father's agent, empowered to speak and act in his name. Jesus can say without contradiction: 'The Father and I are one' (10:30) and 'The Father is greater than I' (14:28) as the one who sends Jesus into the world. Jesus of Nazareth is the concrete shape and form that God's self-revelation takes, and John is concerned to bring out its deepest theological significance for us and for our salvation. In the Passion narrative we see the sheer majesty of Jesus – there is no sense that he is on trial. He says clearly that his kingdom is not of this world and tells Pilate that he has come to witness to the truth. Moreover, he reminds Pilate that he has no power over him except what is given him by God. In this dramatic trial scene we see the courage of Jesus, his free acceptance of the cross that ends in a shout of triumph as he breathes his last.

Portrait of Disciples[13]

Both collectively and individually, the disciples become models with whom readers can identify. They represent a continuum of responses to Jesus in which readers may share. They recognise who Jesus is and have faith in his claims. They have become children of God (cf. 1:12) and are called disciples. Nevertheless, they also exhibit typical misunderstandings. When John the Baptist points Jesus out to two of his followers, Jesus asks them: 'What do you want?' (1:38). They are invited to come and see where Jesus lives and they 'stayed' with him. Other disciples are brought to Jesus and confer on him a plethora of Old Testament titles, although they do not yet understand all their ramifications. The faith of the disciples is based first of all on signs (2:11), but they show a willingness to follow Jesus and stay with him. They do not yet understand everything Jesus says. A crisis appears when Jesus uses Eucharistic language in the discourse following the miracle of the loaves (6:60, 68). Many misunderstand and leave the group. Those who remain do so because Jesus has 'the message of eternal life' (6:68), and yet one of the remaining Twelve will betray him.

Jesus' conflict with 'the Jews' does not seem to discourage them, although they frequently misunderstand Jesus, e.g. his words about his body as the new Temple (2:21-22); they do not understand what sustains Jesus (4:32-33); the relationship between sin and suffering (9:2); or the experience of death (11:11-15). Neither do they understand the significance of Jesus' entry into Jerusalem (12:16), nor the meaning of the foot washing (13:7). Yet apparently their lack of understanding does not pose any threat to their discipleship. They are recognised by their love for one another. During the last discourse, the disciples' questions reveal that they have grasped little of what

Jesus has told them. They do not know where he is going, they do not know the way, nor have they recognised the Father in Jesus. Their faith is still imperfect. Jesus has his disciples released in the garden before his arrest, Peter denies his Master (18:25-27), and only the Beloved Disciple is mentioned at the foot of the cross. It seems that only after Jesus' glorification will they be able to fully understand. The post-resurrection scenes resolve the difficulties between Jesus and his disciples, and confirm their future roles when they are finally commissioned for the apostleship to continue Jesus' work (20:21-23). Thomas's doubts are resolved, which has representative value for future doubters. Peter is prepared for his twin tasks of shepherding and martyrdom (21:15-19), despite his misunderstanding of Jesus' death and his triple denial. With his protestation of triple love for Jesus, he has finished his preparation and is ready to 'follow' Jesus.

The *Beloved Disciple* plays a distinctive role in John's narrative. He is close to Jesus in the Gospel's climactic scenes and his relationship to Jesus, Peter and the community is carefully delineated. He also assumes symbolic significance for the evangelist as the ideal disciple. He is seated next to Jesus at the Last Supper (13:23) and his intimacy with Jesus makes him well qualified to make Jesus known. He alone is mentioned at the foot of the cross and it is to him that the mother of Jesus is handed over to form the nucleus of the new community of faith. It is the Beloved Disciple who arrives at the tomb first and only he believes without experiencing the risen Jesus. In the post-resurrection scene at the lake, he is the first to recognise the glorified Jesus and becomes the link with Jesus, as well as the source and authority of the traditions contained in the Gospel (21:24-25). He has borne witness by reminding others of what Jesus said and did, and has shaped their understanding with the help of the Paraclete. In him belief, love and witness are joined. He 'abides' in Jesus' love and the Paraclete works through him.

Thomas is the disciple who understands Jesus in the flesh, but not in his glory. He realises that following Jesus means risking death (cf. 11:16), and calls on others to follow Jesus even if it means dying with him. Yet he does not understand where Jesus is going (cf. 14:5) and cannot comprehend the appearance of the risen Christ (cf. 20:25). He represents those who embrace the earthly Jesus, but have not yet recognised the risen Christ. Yet there is an honesty about Thomas – he refuses to say that he believes what he does not believe, but once convinced, he goes all the way in acknowledging Jesus: 'My Lord and my God.' *Judas* in John's Gospel represents the humanisation of the forces of evil. He is picked by the devil and controlled by him (cf. 13:2, 27). After receiving the morsel from Jesus, Satan enters into him. He is the betrayer (cf. 6:64). He stands for the defector who goes out into the darkness, the *disciple* who betrays Jesus.

John's use of '*the Jews*' designates a group with unchanging hostility towards Jesus and usually refers to the religious authorities. They are closely associated with the response of unbelief. Their questions generate confrontation and demonstrate that they cannot accept the answers Jesus gives them. They seek to kill Jesus because he violates the Sabbath and commits blasphemy in claiming equality with God (cf. 5:18). After a prolonged and heated exchange, they twice take up stones against Jesus (cf. 8:59; 10:31, 33). At the trial of Jesus, they press for his execution. In the first half of the Gospel (chapters 1–12) there is a rising level of conflict and opposition between them and Jesus. Here the hostile Jews represent the response of unbelief and rejection of Jesus' revelation. They observe the Jewish festivals, but do not recognise the reality they are celebrating, being more intent on trapping Jesus in his speech. At the last Passover, they seize Jesus and hand him over to the Romans for execution. They are prepared to kill in order to defend their nation and holy place, but end up denying their heritage: 'We have no king except Caesar' (19:15). The reason John gives for their implacable opposition to Jesus is that they have never heard or seen the Father (cf. 5:37), they do not want to come to Jesus to have life (cf. 5:40), they have no love for God (cf. 5:42), they do not receive Jesus (cf. 5:43) or seek the glory of God (cf. 5:44). They are from a totally different world (8:23), a world of sin, darkness, blindness, death and Satan. They represent aspects of the universal human condition. What is amazing is that they are religious people who have had all the advantages of the heritage of Israel. As representatives of unbelief, they misunderstand Jesus' origin (cf. 6:42) and destiny (cf. 7:35), and so misunderstand his words and works and the witnesses to them. They search the Scriptures, but cannot understand or obey them. Moses himself will accuse them (cf. 5:45-47). They love darkness rather than light (cf. 3:19-21), the glory of humans rather than the glory of God (cf. 5:41-44), and their own life rather than the life Jesus gives (cf. 12:25). They are blind (cf. 9:40-41), unable to see beyond the superficial, the earthly. Their unbelief leads them to attempt to stone Jesus and to cries: 'Crucify him! Crucify him!' (19:6, 15). Closely related to 'the Jews' are the Pharisees.

The *crowds* follow Jesus in Galilee as a result of the signs he performs (cf. 6:2). The crowds in Jerusalem, however, are divided; some say he is a good man, others that he is a deceiver (cf. 7:12), yet many believe in him (cf. 7:31). They represent the struggle of those who are open to believing, but neither the Scriptures nor Jesus' signs lead them to authentic faith.

Minor Characters[14]

John the Baptist is introduced as a true witness to Jesus, a man sent from God (cf. 1:6-8, 15) with a subordinate role in relation to Jesus. He is the bridegroom's friend (cf. 3:29-30), the lamp, not the light (cf. 5:35). Once he has borne witness, he directs his followers to Jesus (cf. 1:35-36). A man without envy who knows he has not the leading role and so becomes a model of what followers of Jesus should do – he bears witness so that all may believe (cf. 1:7). *Mary* (cf. 2:1-5; 19:25-27) is not even mentioned by name in the Gospel. Her confident request, though, leads Jesus to grant her wish. She believes before any miracle occurs and is able to trust even when she does not understand. She does not know what Jesus is going to do, yet she is totally confident that her son will grant her request. She tells the servants: 'Do whatever he tells you.' Her faith is associated with the first sign of divine glory that enables the disciples to believe. She is addressed by Jesus as 'Woman'. At the foot of the cross she is given to the Beloved Disciple to become his mother so that a new beginning for the family of God can take place. She stands as prototype and exemplar of faith for all those who believe, even without miracles.

Nicodemus appears in three scenes (3:1-10; 7:50-52; 19:39-42) and is both an individual and a representative character. He believes because of signs – he is a Pharisee, a ruler of the Jews, and a religious leader, who comes to Jesus in the darkness of night. His lack of understanding is confirmed when he misses the double meanings contained in Jesus' words. He assumes that Jesus is referring to physical birth, whereas Jesus is speaking of the necessity of being born again to enter the Kingdom of God. The theme of being born again of water and the Spirit points to the most basic gift that Jesus has brought from heaven to earth, namely, eternal life. As God's Son, Jesus has come to reveal eternal life as life with God. Just as human beings receive earthly life from their parents, Jesus gives eternal life to those who believe in him, and explains how it takes place – from above, from God, through Baptism in the Spirit. Nicodemus acknowledges that Jesus is from God, but does not grasp the full implications of that origin. He asks 'How?' (3:4, 9), a question that, on the one hand, shows a man ready to believe, but on the other, one who is incapable of doing so, for Jesus does not fit into his categories of understanding. Ironically, as a teacher in Israel, he cannot understand even earthly things. Nicodemus is a puzzled man, a man of standing in society, yet aware that something is lacking in his life. He comes to Jesus in the darkness of night so that he might find light. He desires change, but apparently only on his terms. His is the misunderstanding of those who are unable or unwilling to understand, a failure to see that comes from a refusal to see. He represents people who shut their minds to truths they do not wish to accept. Nicodemus concedes that the rebirth of which Jesus speaks is possible, but doesn't understand how it comes about. Jesus reminds him that there are many things unseen, yet can be perceived in their effects, like the wind. Eventually, Nicodemus fades into the background.

In a later scene (7:50-52), Nicodemus does not yet confess faith in Jesus, but asks for the due process of law and is ridiculed for his suggestion. He is obviously attracted to Jesus and wants to protect him, but is rebuffed by the leaders. In the end he comes forward to bury Jesus and expresses his grief by using expensive ointments, but apparently finds no life in Jesus' death. Both he and Joseph of Arimathea represent those who believe but refuse to confess their faith openly. They are not far from the Kingdom of God, yet they remain outside.

The *Samaritan woman* is a half-Jew with a shameful past who meets a complete stranger in Jesus. The story (4:1-42) illustrates how difficult it is to come to Jesus in faith because of various obstacles that stand in the way. Yet apparently there is in her an unsatisfied longing, a vague discontent, a feeling of something lacking in her life. The woman is conscious of the Jewish dislike of Samaritans and comments sarcastically. Yet Jesus offers her something that will enable her to put the injustice of racial prejudice in perspective. Here we see the humanity of Jesus, his warmth and sympathy, and his ability to break down barriers. When Jesus offers her water that gives life, she misunderstands and asks dismissively if he is greater than Jacob. When Jesus explains that he is speaking of water that will permanently end thirst, she is attracted to this water of convenience. To move her to a higher level, Jesus shifts the focus to her husband, revealing that her life is far from perfect. To arrive at faith, though, she must first acknowledge where she stands. The woman is suddenly compelled to face herself and the immorality and inadequacy of her life. Readers can take hope from the fact that Jesus persists in spite of her past and the grace he is offering is meant to help her change her lifestyle.

Convinced that Jesus must be a religious figure, she questions him about the locus of worship, a ploy designed perhaps to distract from the focus on her personal life, and consequently the necessity of having to make a decision. Jesus tells her that though salvation comes from the Jews, the time is at hand when cultic issues become irrelevant, for true believers will worship in Spirit and truth. Jesus then confronts her with a present demand for faith by revealing who he is. She sets off for the village, still not fully convinced and wonders if Jesus could be the Messiah. Yet in her desire to share her discovery, she is able to set aside her feelings of shame. The Samaritans are introduced to Jesus on the strength of her personal witness. Being instrumental in bringing others to Jesus, her faith comes to completion.

The encounter between Jesus and the Samaritan woman operates on two levels: it is a well-crafted story of personal conversion, and an outreach of reconciliation with the Samaritans. The woman represents the schismatic Samaritans who, in Jewish eyes, were considered to be a breakaway group. Jesus has come to transcend the divisions and prejudices of history. Dialogue characterises the drama, and living water, misunderstood by the woman, becomes a central topic. It begins on a mundane level, and step by step the social and religious barriers separating them are overcome. As the light of understanding begins to dawn, the woman gradually perceives that this hated Jewish stranger is the giver of living water for which she asks, wonders if he is greater than Jacob, the father of Jews and Samaritans, and recognises him as a prophet and perhaps the Messiah. She becomes a missionary to her people who in turn are drawn to Jesus by her word, and the story ends by acknowledging him as the Saviour of the world. She is a model of a female disciple. She has advanced from the need for mundane things to the need for personal acceptance given her past life of broken relationships that evoked a lack of trust in people. She also felt the need to satisfy her deeper desires for something more. Only God can supply that living water to satisfy her needs through the Son (the Truth) in the Spirit.

The *Royal Official* (4:43-53), a Gentile, shows his willingness to believe apart from signs. He refuses to be discouraged when Jesus complains that people do not believe unless they see signs and wonders. His is a belief in Jesus' word of healing that gives life. He has faith, the essence of which is that he believes what Jesus says to be true. His son recovers and he and his household believe. The official represents those who believe because of signs, but who are also open to believe the words of Jesus. His is an authentic faith and he will have the life it gives, symbolised by the recovery of his son. Faith must have a deeper foundation than fascination with miracles. It demands a process of growth through the use of God to satisfy one's needs, to taking God on his own terms. As faith deepens, self-gratification is gradually purified.

The *Sick Man* at the pool (5:2-16) represents another kind of response. Jesus asks him if he wants to be healed, but it is not at all clear that he does. Perhaps he does not see how he could be healed since he has no one to help him. Instead he complains that he is unable to enter the waters of healing that would restore him to health and happiness. His negative thinking and self-pity prompt him to blame others. He doesn't even bother to learn the identity of the person who healed him. When Jesus later seeks him out, he reports him to the Jews. Questioned by the Jews, his defence is that the man who healed him told him to take up his sleeping mat, explaining that it was not his fault that he had broken the law. He represents those for whom not even signs lead to authentic faith. The man shows no gratitude, no faith and no curiosity about the person who healed him. Instead he identifies his benefactor as a Sabbath-breaker to the authorities and has no desire to witness in the face of hostility. Readers are challenged to examine their negative memories and negative thinking in order to let go of them. Since the man was cured on the Sabbath, it occasioned the subsequent controversy. Jesus' *relatives* (7:2-10) challenge him to go to Judea so that the disciples too can see his works, and in the process make a name for himself. But John remarks that not even his relatives have faith in him. They belong to the world and remain part of it.

The *Blind Man* (9:1-41) in seven scenes goes from restoration of physical sight to spiritual insight, while the blindness of the Pharisees is progressively unmasked. His faith grows amid trials, unlike the initial coming to faith of the Samaritan woman. The man blind from birth is healed because he obeyed the word of Jesus to wash in the pool of Siloam. He goes, washes and is healed. He serves as a counterpart and contrast to the sick man at the pool. Later he resists threats from the Pharisees and gradually comes to recognise Jesus as 'the man' – a prophet, someone from God, the Son of Man – and worships him. His progressive enlightenment is similar to that of the Samaritan woman. While other people talk *about* him (disciples, neighbours, parents), and authorities expel him from the synagogue, Jesus talks to him and leads him from darkness to light. The drama shows up the scepticism of the neighbours, the fear of the parents, the hostility of the authorities and the faith of the healed man. As the man grows in insight and faith, those claiming spiritual sight and leadership gradually become blind and spiritually obtuse. The cured man accepts Jesus as healer and miracle worker, but needs to learn who Jesus is. He models those who come from believing signs to authentic faith. The story traces the development of faith on the part of the healed man and unmasks the faith levels and divisions among those encountered in the story. The cured man is ready to defend his faith even at the price of being cut off from family and religious milieu, but he is not afraid to confess Jesus Christ.

Readers are reminded that at times faith grows only through testing and even suffering. The basic story of the man's healing is simply narrated, but beyond that, readers can pick out elements in their own conversion process. Water has a special link with Baptism that was also known as 'enlightenment'. Beyond the baptismal theme, readers are also taught that a series of tests may be necessary before faith matures. Only gradually, through suffering and harassment, does the blind man come to mature faith and enlightenment. Many people who are 'cradle' Christians come to believe in their hearts only when difficult decisions test their faith in God. It is only then that they understand what it really means to say: 'I do believe.' Moreover, the healing of the blind man produces a division among those who interrogate him. An encounter with Jesus or his word forces people to decide one way or another. In contrast to the blind man who, step by step, is given sight both physically and spiritually, the religious authorities, who can physically see perfectly, gradually become spiritually blind. The evangelist is also interested in those who refuse to commit themselves. The parents, for example, know the truth about their son, but refuse to say anything out of fear. They are obviously uncooperative. Readers who are baptised and nominally accept Jesus, but are not willing to confess it if it costs anything, are challenged to examine the quality of their own commitment. On the other hand, the Pharisees, religious people, are annoyed that they are unable to rebut the man's argument based on Scripture and are forced to resort to abuse and insult before they throw him out.

Martha, Mary and Lazarus (11:1-46; 12:1-11) are friends of Jesus and are loved by him. When Lazarus, their brother, falls sick they send word to Jesus to come and heal him. Martha accepts Jesus as a healer and miracle worker, but does not yet acknowledge him as the resurrection and the life for those who believe. Jesus' raising of Lazarus from the dead is meant to symbolise the giving of resurrection life to every believer. Lazarus stands for the disciple to whom life has been restored, and readers are challenged to accept that their hopes for eternal life will be realised in Jesus. Martha moves from traditional expectations to belief in Jesus as the Messiah and Son of God (cf. 11:27) – a discerning faith. Mary represents the response of devotion and love while Lazarus represents the hope of resurrected life. The three represent faith, love and hope respectively. The raising of Lazarus is the climax of Jesus' public ministry – the sign – and demands the radical call of faith. Lazarus is not raised to eternal life, but restored to mundane life. It is a sign that Jesus gives eternal life that already begins for the believer even in this life.

Whereas the Samaritan woman illustrated an initial coming to faith and the blind man an incipient faith deepened through testing, the Lazarus story illustrates that deepening of faith which comes from the prospect of facing death. The evangelist tells the story in such a way that readers are led to a more profound understanding of death. Life and death are used by John to teach about earthly and heavenly realities. Martha already believes that Jesus is the Messiah, the Son of God, and that her brother will be raised on the last day. Yet her faith is incomplete, for she wishes that her brother had never died and hesitates when Jesus orders the opening of Lazarus' tomb. Jesus does bring Lazarus back to life, but this is not his purpose in coming into the world. Instead he comes to give life that cannot be touched by death, so that those who believe in him will never die. True faith includes a belief in Jesus as the source of unending life that comes about with his own resurrection. Only when readers come to the account of Jesus' tomb (20:6-7) and compare it with the symbolism of Lazarus emerging from the tomb still wrapped in burial clothes, does it become clear that Jesus rises to eternal life, never to die again. He leaves behind his burial cloths that are no longer needed. Lazarus, however, is brought back to life but he will die again. The raising of Lazarus is only a sign meant to symbolise eternal life, the kind of life that God possesses and that Jesus makes possible even now for those who believe in him.

Facing death often constitutes a unique challenge to belief for many Christians. No human support goes with them to the grave. Each person enters the door of death alone. If Christ has not conquered death, then there is no future life for human beings. Death is the last enemy to be overcome and it is not unusual for people to have doubts as they come face to face with it. The evangelist captures this insight by placing the Lazarus story at the end of Jesus' public ministry as a challenge to readers when they hear Jesus say: 'I am the resurrection and the life. If anyone believes in me, even though he dies he will live, and whoever lives and believes in me will never die. Do you believe this?' (11:25-26).

The role of *Pilate* is explored in seven scenes (18:28–19:16) that alternate between inside and outside the Pretorium. He first of all tries to avoid hearing the case. Then he asks Jesus if he is King of the Jews; when Jesus answers that his kingdom is not political, Pilate again declares him innocent. The question now is will he defend Jesus against 'the Jews'? When they choose Barabbas, Pilate hopes to mollify them by having Jesus scourged and is followed by mockery. Pilate for the third time declares Jesus innocent, but 'the Jews' become hostile since Jesus claims to be the Son of God. At this stage, Pilate becomes anxious, asks Jesus where he comes from, but receives no reply. Instead Jesus reminds Pilate that he would have no power if it were not from God. Pilate would have liked to release Jesus but fears a charge of infidelity to Caesar. The outcome is that 'the Jews' deny their heritage and Jesus is condemned. Throughout it all, Pilate seeks desperately to avoid making a decision, but ends up condemning an innocent man. He exercises worldly power and ends up standing with the world against Jesus. Readers are reminded that there are situations in life where compromise is impossible and a decision one way or the other becomes inevitable together with the consequences. Favouring Jesus proved too costly politically for Pilate. The evangelist exposes the consequences of attempting to avoid a decision and the futility of trying to compromise. There is a miscarriage of justice by an indecisive and incompetent Roman official under severe pressure from 'the Jews'. We can trace the means Pilate took to avoid making a decision – he does not wish to condemn Jesus because he is innocent and attempts to evade responsibility. He tries to use the custom of releasing a prisoner; he strives for compromise by having Jesus scourged; he appeals to emotion and pity by presenting Jesus to the crowd. Because he doesn't have the courage to make the right decision, he abandons Jesus to the mob.

Mary Magdalene becomes a devoted follower of Jesus at the cross and at the tomb. She regards Jesus as an earthly friend and teacher. But witnessing the Passion (cf. 19:25) gives her no advantage or insight. At the empty tomb (20:1-18) she concludes that the body must have been stolen. When she eventually recognises the risen Lord, it is not through sight, but through

Jesus calling her name. She wishes to retain his presence, but from now on the relationship between the risen Lord and the believer will be different. Disciples have become his 'brothers' and so become children of God. Mary does not understand Jesus' death as glorification. Neither the empty tomb nor the vision of the risen Jesus lifts the veil – only the words of Jesus do when he calls her by name.

What kind of faith is needed to be totally committed to Jesus? In the fourth Gospel, characters are individualised by their position in society and by their interaction with Jesus and so they become types or models with whom readers can identify. They represent different kinds of responses to Jesus so that readers can see their misunderstandings and the consequences that result. The evangelist highlights particular responses that are held up to the readers' scrutiny in such a way that they are swayed in the direction of his perspective.

A. There is rejection of Jesus by a world that is hostile to him. Opponents, who love darkness and human glory, misunderstand the heritage of Israel and do not really know God, end by denying their heritage altogether and affirming instead the lordship of Caesar. Neither do the relatives of Jesus move beyond their unbelief.

B. There is acceptance without open commitment in the cases of Joseph of Arimathea and Nicodemus. They refuse to make the sacrifices that open belief demands. Nicodemus stands to lose his social standing and the accompanying prestige. The security of his position prevents him from fully accepting Jesus.

C. There is acceptance of Jesus as a worker of signs and miracles, but Jesus does not trust himself to such people.

Many of the disciples cease to follow Jesus beyond this level. The sick man at the pool recognises Jesus as a healer, but makes little progress towards faith. He falls back to remain part of the world opposed to Jesus.

D. There is belief in Jesus' words. The Samaritan woman, the royal official and the blind man each find faith because they are willing to trust the word of Jesus. The result is that the official's household believes, the Samaritan villagers comes to faith, and the blind man has the courage to witness to Jesus. Trust in Jesus' words leads to authentic faith.

E. There is commitment in spite of misunderstandings. The disciples believe, yet misunderstand. Peter cannot accept Jesus' death, while Thomas has difficulty believing his resurrection. Philip does not understand that Jesus is the revelation of the Father. Martha and Mary do not comprehend that Jesus is the resurrection and the life. Mary Magdalene does not comprehend the resurrection, the empty tomb, or the new relationship of the risen Lord to his followers. None of them understand perfectly, and yet they follow the Revealer.

F. There is paradigmatic discipleship exemplified by Mary and the Beloved Disciple. Neither one has a history of misunderstanding. Mary trusts Jesus and is given into the Beloved Disciple's care. The Beloved Disciple abides in Jesus' love and is a true witness in handing on the Johannine tradition.

G. There is also defection when Judas, one of the Twelve, goes out into the darkness, and some of the disciples withdraw and walk no more with Jesus following the discourse on the Bread of Life. On the other hand, Peter denies Jesus, but is restored and is given a pastoral role. It seems then that characters can either regress or make progress during the course of their life.

The characters in the Gospel of John represent a variety of responses that allow readers to ponder the alternatives. The evangelist is sympathetic to those whose response is positive but less than adequate. Through his Gospel, conceived as a narrative composition, the evangelist leads readers towards the responses he deems preferable.

The Reader
DEATH OF JESUS

In John, the death of Jesus is ironically not the hour of darkness, but of elevation on the cross, the return to the Father and his glorification. Jesus is portrayed as being in total control of all that is happening to him. Revelation is the central theme of Jesus' life and ministry in John, reaching its high point in the Passion narrative. The manner of his death is a declaration of God's love for the world (cf. 3:16). The purpose of the Passion narrative is not only for historical information, but to explore the significance and meaning of the Passion as the final hour of the Father's revelation in Jesus, and its implications for the salvation of the human race.

Early on, the nascent Christian Church had to face the scandal of the cross. Jesus' crucifixion as a common criminal and the apparent failure of his mission as God's Messiah called for explanation. His terrible agony and disgraceful death were stumbling blocks to those Jews who looked for signs of God's power in Jesus to overcome their enemies and to be freed from foreign domination. Later on, as the Church spread to the

Gentile world, sophisticated pagans regarded the preaching of a crucified Messiah as foolishness. They looked instead for a wisdom teacher or philosopher who would teach them how they ought to live. Still, the message of the cross – suffering – is one of the greatest of human mysteries. This mystery, expressed in Jesus' Passion, is at the centre of the Gospel preaching. Since the cross does not follow the logic of human reason, it becomes an obstacle, a scandal, for those who expect a powerful Messiah to liberate them from foreign oppression, or for those who expect a teacher of wisdom to guide them in the ups and downs of life. Such expectations can blind them so that they are unable to see that the folly of the cross confounds the wise and empowers the foolish for salvation (cf. 1 Co 1:21-25). Belief in Jesus crucified and risen is regarded by Christian preachers as the greatest wisdom, something already foretold by God in the Old Testament: '"Was it not ordained that the Messiah should suffer and so enter into his glory?" Then, starting with Moses and going through all the prophets, he explained to them the passages throughout the scriptures that were about himself' (Lk 24:26-27).

The different Passion narratives in the Gospels emphasise diverse facets of the Passion for their readers, seen in the light of the Old Testament, the resurrection and the coming of the Spirit.[15] In Mark and Matthew, Jesus plumbs the depths of abandonment only to be subsequently vindicated; the Lucan Jesus shows concern for others and dispenses forgiveness; in John, Jesus reigns victoriously from the cross, fully in control of all that happens and freely offers up his life for the sake of others. No one portrait exhausts the meaning of Jesus. A true picture of the whole emerges only because the viewpoints are different. And so it is important for readers to be able to see

Jesus bowed in dejection (Mk, Mt); at other times, Jesus' arms stretched out in forgiveness; and in other instances to see in the cross the proclamation of a reigning king. There are times in the lives of readers when they desperately need to cry out with Jesus in Matthew and Mark: 'My God, my God, why have you deserted me?', only to find that despite appearances, God does listen and can reverse the tragedy. At other times, suffering may be linked to being able to say with Jesus in Luke: 'Father, forgive them, they do not know what they are doing', and being able to entrust oneself confidently into God's hands. At still other times, Christians see with Johannine faith that suffering and evil have no real power over those whom Jesus has enabled to become God's children. To exclude one or other perspective would deprive the cross of much of its meaning.

FAITH

For John, belief and discipleship are interchangeable, for faith is the primary factor in following Jesus. The verb 'to believe' occurs more often in chapters 1–12 (the Book of Signs) because Jesus is presenting people with the choice of believing. In the Book of Glory (chapters 13–20, 21), Jesus is speaking to those who already believe. The emphasis here is on that love which is the perfection of faith. This role is explained in detail in chapters 13–17, when Jesus speaks of the union of the disciples with himself, and is carried out in the Passion narrative. The first half of the Gospel discusses faith in great detail and love in relation to faith. Faith is nothing more than the human response to the love of God. Furthermore, a certain type of love accompanies faith and another stands in opposition to it. John uses the verb 'to believe' because he wants to stress that faith is more an active commitment to the person of Jesus that is also susceptible to growth. It means more than trust or confidence and involves a willingness to respond to God's demands as presented in and by Jesus. There is therefore no conflict between faith and good works. To have faith in Jesus whom God has sent is the work demanded by God (cf. 6:29). To believe means to receive and accept Jesus' self-revelation, to attach oneself to him in a personal union in order to receive eternal life from him. That is why the believer 'abides' in Jesus. Faith is a form of knowledge, insight, vision and truth. It is not just a one-off decision, but rather a process of union with Jesus that incorporates Christians into the very unity of Father and Son.

Only by believing in Jesus can one become a disciple and have eternal life. Faith also means accepting truths about Jesus, in particular his identity (cf. 6:69; 11:27). Christian faith means accepting Jesus for what he is as Messiah and Son of God who has come into the world. By entering the world in human form, he automatically becomes God's self-revelation to human beings, the revelation of the transcendent God whom no one has ever seen (cf. 1:18; 14:9). To accept or reject God's self-revelation in Jesus means to accept or reject God (cf. 5:10-12). Jesus comes to reveal God's inner life to human beings by offering them a share in it. God's offer of himself in Jesus results in the intimacy (cf. 17:3) of the children of God (cf. 1:12). Through faith, Christians accept God's self-revelation in Christ, but it is God who makes them his children. Faith is human beings' first step towards salvation and that is why the verb 'to believe' is used to emphasise its dynamic aspect. Only in the act of full and perfect acceptance of Christ can it be said that one has fully believed.

Christ, the light, has come into the world and people must choose to accept or reject him; many refuse, though some accept by faith and are saved. Chapters 1–12 tell the story of this initial choice being made by Christ's contemporaries to his offer to become his disciples. John also describes what holds people back from making such a commitment to Jesus. They love darkness rather than the light because their works are evil (cf. 3:19). To live and walk in darkness means to live in a state of separation from God (cf. 8:12; 12:35) and to refuse to give up evil ways. They prefer the honour, praise and approval given by human beings (cf. 5:41, 44); they are interested only in self-advancement and self-glorification (cf. 7:18; 8:50). So love of darkness, separation from God, an over-attachment to self, self-exaltation and inordinate self-love, makes acceptance of Christ by faith impossible.

LOVE

Love is closely associated with faith in John. By living as they ought to, Christians manifest in the very way they live their lives the divine life they have received through Christ. They are the ones who 'live by the truth' and whose works are done 'in God' (3:21). Love for God is the ultimate explanation of that love that accompanies faith (cf. 5:40-44). It is presented as above all 'remaining' in Jesus, a total dedication to his person that is characterised by permanency. It is a union of persons based on the union that exists between Father and Son. Divine indwelling in the Christian is a dynamic union that expresses itself in a way of life lived in love. That is why faith and love are almost interchangeable in John. To abide in Jesus is also intimately associated with keeping the commandments in a spirit of love (cf. 15:10), with the struggle against the world, and with bearing fruit (cf. 15:5). All of these are basic Christian duties and are not confined to some elite or to mystics.

There is one fundamental decision to be made – to believe in the One whom God has sent. This faith rightly understood includes love for God, Christ and the community, and faith turned towards the future, including the hope of eternal life. It also means the fulfilment of the moral duties arising from love and the rejection of all the works of darkness. Faith and discipleship are perfected in love, a love for Jesus confirmed by keeping his commandments (cf. 14:15, 21). Active love for brothers and sisters in Christ is proof of communion with God and Christ: 'I give you a new commandment: love one another; just as I have loved you, you also must love one another. By this love you have for one another, everyone will know that you are my disciples' (13:34-35; cf. 15:12-13). Jesus' washing of the disciples' feet is intended to be the pre-eminent sign of this love, a model of love only when seen in connection with his sacrificial death. John's emphasis on love, with its highlighting of fraternal charity, means that Christians should not want to be in heaven before their time. This is the concrete mark of the new life, the tangible manifestation to the world of what Christianity really is.

HOPE

It is the relationship with Christ, in whom we have the fullness of life and salvation, that gives hope in the face of the darkness of a world estranged from God. John's ethical teaching may be synthesised in faith, love and hope – the reduction of the Christian life to three fundamental attitudes. Although John insists that 'eternal life' is already offered in this life, he recognises that physical death must still intervene (cf. 11:25).

Death, however, cannot destroy the eternal life already present, but obviously there must be an aspect of completeness to eternal life after death that is lacking in those who have yet to pass through physical death. Jesus passes through death to resurrection so that he may prepare dwelling places in his Father's house (cf. 14:2-3). There is a future vision of glory to be granted when Christians join Jesus in his Father's presence (cf. 17:24). There is also a Second Coming, a resurrection of the dead and a final judgement on the last day (cf. 5:28-29; 6:39-40, 44; 12:48). Jesus speaks of a final manifestation of divine power yet to come. Although John lays emphasis on the attainment of eternal life in the here and now, it is carefully balanced with the traditional view that looks to the future for fulfilment. Jesus also mentions the last day: 'Now the will of him who sent me is that I should lose nothing of all that he has given me, and that I should raise it up on the last day' (6:39; cf. 11:24; 12:48). He speaks about coming back: 'After I have prepared a place for you I shall return to take you with me, so that where I am you may be too' (14:3); of a future resurrection: 'For the hour is coming when the dead will leave their graves at the sound of his voice: those who did good will rise to life and those who did evil to condemnation' (5:28-29; cf. 11:24); and 'Anyone who believes in the Son has eternal life, but anyone who refuses to believe in the Son will never see life' (3:36). Although believers already have eternal life – that quality of life proper to God, the result of divine indwelling (cf. 5:24; 14:23) – it will reach perfection in a life beyond death. The historical appearance of Jesus that is central to John's narrative, therefore, is not final. The reigning presence of God is still to come in power and glory. In the meantime, Christians walk by faith, not by sight. They perceive God dimly as in a mirror (a metal plate which did show a dull reflection of sorts, cf. 1 Co 13:12). Faith is often lived in darkness and is subject to being tested.

Conclusion

The fourth Gospel aims at leading its readers to a deeper faith, specifically to an understanding of Jesus as the divine Revealer that elicits a faith, making them out as 'children of God'. By showing Jesus confronting a wide variety of individuals in everyday situations, the Gospel dramatises the message that the Word has become flesh and dwelt among us. The various characters are defined by their response to Jesus, by their ability to believe and progress along the path of faith. They mirror the struggles, dilemmas and misperceptions of those who are confronted by the Revealer and must respond. Readers see ordinary people come step by step to behold the glory of God, enfleshed in the person of Jesus of Nazareth. As a result of reading the Gospel, readers are persuaded to join the company of those who profess authentic faith. They are given identity with the past, hope for the future in the experience of salvation in a life beyond the grave, and the promise of the Spirit in the present.

John has made a synthesis of his own special emphases and insights in a language intelligible to his audience. Many would agree that the Gospel of John is the least 'dated' work in the New Testament. It transcends the barriers of time and culture and so can still speak to our problems today. There is an air of universality and timelessness about it. No other book has so influenced the faith and life of Christians with its in-depth presentation of the person and work of Jesus, its championing of the Gospel of life, and its exploration of the existential challenge that the person of Jesus poses to those who encounter him. It is a profound meditation on the historical life and meaning of Jesus of Nazareth, giving a penetrating presentation of his person and life. This is accomplished against the background of a highly original and challenging reflection on the Old Testament, and of Jesus as the fulfilment of the hopes and destiny of Israel. John records fewer incidents from the ministry of Jesus, but supplies a lengthy explanation in the form of discourses. Jesus' awareness of himself as the Son of God is a constant theme. The Father is mentioned over one hundred times and the Spirit is treated as completing Jesus' historical presence as one who remembers, recalls, guides, comforts and defends. Only then will the Gospel be fully appreciated, and people will realise the love that the Triune God has for each person, and adequately respond with an ever-growing faith, love and hope. Since Jesus is pre-eminently the revelation of the Father's love for the world (cf. 3:16), it is not surprising that John stresses that love is the essence of what it means to be a Christian, a disciple of Christ. Love is shown in the obedience of faith to God and to his revelation in Jesus.

The Gospel of John encourages every Christian to an ever-deepening search for the meaning and relevance of Jesus of Nazareth, to penetrate below the surface to the love that lies behind all the confusion and darkness of our world. It is an invitation to reflect on Jesus whom Christians too often take for granted. John is more concerned with the meaning of the facts of Jesus' life than with the facts themselves, but it is only the Spirit that can teach us to apprehend it (cf. 16:12-15). In the historical Jesus we are given the ultimate truth about God and human beings, society and the world. Salvation becomes an ongoing exodus from this world through death to the heavenly mansions prepared by the Son for his own.

NOTES

1. Wilfrid J. Harrington OP, *John: Spiritual Theologian* (Dublin: The Columba Press, 1999), p. 18.

2. Known as the Beloved Disciple and traditionally associated with John the apostle, one of the Twelve, although this association is sometimes challenged by scholars. He became the source of the traditions that have gone into the making of the fourth Gospel (21:24). We shall continue to refer to John as the author of the fourth Gospel, despite the fact that the author managed to maintain his anonymity as the story is being unfolded. However, the authority of the Gospel flows from its message and its reception by the Church, not from the identity of its author.

3. See R. Alan Culpepper, *Anatomy of the Fourth Gospel* (Fortress Press: Philadelphia, 1983), pp. 180–202.

4. Mentioned throughout the Gospel, 'the Jews' does not refer to the Jewish people as such, but mainly to authorities who refuse to believe in Jesus. They are representatives of a world hostile to Jesus.

5. The 'hour' is the period in Jesus' life when he returns to the Father (13:1). It is accomplished in his Passion, death, resurrection and ascension. Glorification is the goal of the hour (12:23; 17:1).

6. 'Life' is a favourite Johannine word, so much so that John may be called the Gospel of Life, the chief purpose for which it was written: 'that you may have life through his name' (20:31). Natural life becomes a symbol for the spiritual gift of God, since natural life is humans' most treasured possession; it becomes a suitable symbol to indicate the most precious of divine gifts. 'Eternal life' is the life by which God himself lives and is communicated by the Son to those who believe (3:16; 5:24). The communication of this gift is associated with Baptism in the Spirit and is qualitatively different from natural life, for it is a life that not even death can destroy (11:26). Already possessed by believers, it will be perfected when physical death is no more (5:28-29).

7. Jesus is presented as speaking in the same manner as God speaks in Second-Isaiah (chapters 40–55). John is drawing attention to the divinity of Jesus by his use of the divine 'I am' (*ego eimi*).

8. To 'abide in' (*menein en*) is to be intimately united with Jesus (cf. 6:56). Divine indwelling is an intimate union that expresses itself in a way of life characterised by love.

9. This episode is a later insertion into the Gospel of John and is missing from early Greek manuscripts. It is found in different contexts in various manuscripts. However, it is accepted as part of canonical Scripture and does fit into the present context.

10. In the Old Testament, the 'glory of God' (*kebod Yahweh*) signified the felt presence of a loving, saving and guiding God among his people. This presence is now enfleshed and made visible in the person of Jesus. We look to the story of Jesus to see how this glory becomes manifest, especially at his 'hour'. The cross of Jesus is the pre-eminent place where the glory of God shines forth drawing all people to himself (cf. 12:32).

11. For example: 2:19-21; 3:3-4; 4:10-11; 6:26-27; 8:33-35; 11:11-13.

12. For example: 3:2; 4:12; 6:42; 7:35; 9:40-41; 11:50.

13. R. Alan Culpepper, *Anatomy of the Fourth Gospel* (Philadelphia: Fortress Press, 1983), pp. 115–132.

14. Ibid., pp. 132–48.

15. Raymond Brown, *Christ in the Gospels of the Liturgical Year* (Philippines: St Pauls, 2008; Collegeville, MN: Liturgical Press, 2008), pp. 192–4.

CONCLUDING REMARKS

What is a Gospel?

The Gospels are first and foremost Good News in narrative form, regarded as the preferred means to communicate the mystery of Christ and his implications for discipleship. Good News became shorthand for the revelation and salvation brought about through the life, death and resurrection of Jesus Christ. The Gospels present the origins of the Good News in the life and ministry of Jesus who embodied the Good News in his own person. They are literary and theological productions that endeavour to link the identity between the Jesus of Nazareth and the risen Christ now alive and active at the heart of Christian communities – someone whose earthly life and glorified presence are still relevant to readers today. The four Gospels function to shape the identity of and guide the readers' way of life. Their purpose is not simply to inform; they also perform and transform the lives of readers (cf. Is 55:10-11) by involving them in their story of Jesus and calling them to be his disciples. The Word of God always accomplishes something; it transforms hearts and even entire cultures wherever it is faithfully proclaimed.

The writing of the Gospels represents the third stage in handing on the Good News. It follows from the second stage – the oral, pastoral, liturgical and missionary stage of transmission. Behind both these stages stands the first stage, namely, the historical ministry of Jesus in which his person, words and deeds, death and resurrection made a profound impact on his original audience. The third stage was committing to writing the traditions that had developed in the second stage, reflected upon in the light of the Old Testament and applied in a variety of pastoral situations. Each of the Gospels tells the story within a broad biographical framework as a literary means of relating the remembered and interpreted story of Jesus in the light of the resurrection and the coming of the Spirit. The experiences, insights and problems of the early communities for whom the evangelists wrote also played a not insignificant part in the telling of the story, while the Old Testament provided the religious vocabulary and literary genres to aid in the task of writing. The continuity of God's plan of salvation, that has now reached its culmination and fulfilment in the person of Jesus, is also highlighted.

Each of the Gospels is a literary and theological whole, whose individual parts cannot be understood apart from the whole. As stories, they are meant to engage the reader personally. The Gospels are distinctive in that they are narratives about a person whom the evangelists believe to be alive and active after his death. The story of Jesus related in the Gospels is historical insofar as it tells of a historical person. At a deeper level, though, it is a story that history cannot fully assess, for example, Jesus being sent by the Father, his resurrection and glorification. These lie beyond the competence of historians and yet they form the most important part of the story. Each evangelist took the traditions that made up the story of Jesus and cast them in the form of a coherent narrative as the best means to convey the meaning and significance of the Christ-event. The Gospels tell their story, each in their own manner and from a believer's point of view, in order to guide readers to share in that same belief.

The Gospels take on a life of their own as literary works independent of their authors and their originally intended readers. Readers today inhabit a very different worldview from the one reflected in the Gospels. Accordingly, there is a need to bridge the gap created by time, place and culture. Contemporary readers also come with their own outlook, experience, understanding, educational background, prejudices and different degrees of faith commitment. A basic self-awareness as they approach the narratives is necessary. The Gospels are also an integral part of the canon of Scripture established by the Church and are best understood within that community. That is why a faith seeking understanding and nourished by the liturgy and prayer of the believing community gives readers the support and guidance needed to avoid misinterpreting and misunderstanding the meaning and purpose of the Gospel narratives.

Christology

The call to discipleship, today as ever, is intimately bound up with the identity of Jesus. In the Gospels, this identity is for the most part presented in terms of titles adopted from the Old Testament and the early Christian tradition, and adapted for use in accordance with the theological outlook of each of the evangelists. Jesus not only announced the Good News, he himself became the embodiment of the Good News communicated through the impact of his person, words, deeds, death, resurrection and glorification. Each evangelist incorporated these insights into his narrative, mainly through the use of various Christological titles that interpret and correct misunderstandings and false expectations. However, these titles cannot be properly understood apart from the individual narratives in which they are embedded. It is in the light of each narrative viewed as a whole that the titles are properly interpreted and understood.[1]

The evangelists employ three principal Christological titles for Jesus – Messiah, Son of Man, Son of God – often in combination. The title Messiah/Christ and related terms – Son of David, King of the Jews, King of Israel – are correct but inadequate for describing Jesus in view of the widely differing hopes and expectations that were current in first-century Palestine. For Pilate, Messiah signified a political pretender to royal status; for the religious leaders, King of Israel recalled to mind a divine agent who would free Israel from its political enemies and establish the reign of God. In the Gospel of Mark, Jesus repeatedly forbids disciples and others from making his messiahship public to offset false expectations, but also in part because of his unusual lifestyle, the apparent failure of his mission, and the dishonourable death he was about to undergo. A proper understanding only becomes possible in the light of his suffering and death, together with the resurrection that was regarded as divine vindication.

The title *Son of Man* occurs in different contexts that refer to Jesus' earthly activity as a human being, or his suffering and death, or his future coming in glory. In the Old Testament, 'Son of Man' signified a human being (cf. Ezk 2:1; 3:1), or a superhuman figure appearing in the clouds of heaven and receiving power, glory and a kingdom (cf. Dn 7:13). As Son of Man, Jesus uses the title as a self-designation as well as claiming the power to forgive sins, lordship over the Sabbath, and a model of service for others to imitate. The title is also used in connection with his approaching death, resurrection and his coming in glory at the end of time.

In the Old Testament, the title 'Son of God' was commonly used of kings, prophets, righteous persons and the people of Israel as a whole. In the Gospels, *Son of God* in a unique sense is used for Jesus at his Baptism and transfiguration; it identifies Jesus as beloved Son with a close relationship to God, his Father. Demons declare his divine sonship, and the centurion at the foot of the cross recognises him as Son of God. The evangelists give the title a new level of meaning in keeping with the Christian belief in Jesus' unique relationship with God, his Father, revealed during his ministry and vindicated in his Passion and resurrection.

Other titles employed by the evangelists include Son of Abraham through whom all the nations will be blessed; Emmanuel (God-with-us); Jesus (the one who saves); Lord (*Kyrios*), a title used for God in the Old Testament and a common way of addressing Jesus by people of faith; and a Moses-like figure portraying Jesus as the definitive Teacher of the Law, obedience to which is summed up as doing the will of God. Jesus is also a prophet like Moses, or the eschatological prophet endowed with the Spirit to bring Good News to the poor; the Saviour who alone brings salvation from the alienation that is sin, and from sickness, evil and death. He is the Word (*Logos*) of God, the One sent, a divine person who descends from above to reveal the true God and is identified with him by his use of the divine name 'I am' (*ego eimi*).

Discipleship

Readers have an opportunity to observe the different characters in the Gospels and, as a result, their own understanding of discipleship is challenged. This is particularly true in the case of the disciples, as readers observe their initial repudiation of all they know to follow Jesus, through to their lack of understanding, fears, confusions and ultimate abandonment of Jesus at the hour of his Passion. Because their response is deemed inadequate, a tension develops in readers who are initially inclined to identify with them. Furthermore, readers are challenged to monitor their own reactions and responses and often find themselves in a dilemma; they feel the attraction and challenge of Jesus and his message on the one hand, and, at the same time, they identify with the reactions of the disciples.

Mark in particular tells his story in this manner because he wants readers to reflect on their own appraisal of Jesus, his mission and their understanding of Christian discipleship. He hopes that this self-examination will bring about changed attitudes and behaviour in his readers. As Mark's narrative progresses, readers' initial identification with the disciples is challenged. They are forced to distance themselves as the disciples become more and more unresponsive to the challenges presented by Jesus. A choice must be made between Jesus and his challenging demands, and the disciples with whom readers have already formed a positive attachment.

At the beginning, after being summoned by Jesus, disciples leave behind old ties and embrace the new family of Jesus. They are sent on mission and instructed to imitate Jesus in mutual service, in the renunciation of power and prestige. They are to trust in God in the face of suffering and death. However, readers' confidence in the disciples is undermined when Jesus himself applies the whole catalogue of outsider characteristics to the disciples (cf. 8:14-21). Whatever confidence remains is shattered during the events surrounding the Passion. Judas betrays his Master, and three of the disciples sleep at Gethsemane. All of them desert Jesus at the moment of his arrest, and Peter denies ever having known him. It is the disciples' inability to come to terms with suffering and death and their repeated failure to understand that gives Jesus the opportunity to enunciate the standards of Christian conduct. Mark's failing discipleship becomes part of a Christology grounded in the resurrection. Jesus' injunctions to silence operate to prevent him becoming fully known during his lifetime, and points towards Easter as the time of full disclosure. Disciples play the role of pre-Easter people, unfinished and superficial in faith. It is with the resurrection that the veil of obscurity is removed and clarity of perception is restored. However, the suspense created by the disciples' failure to understand is not resolved within the narrative itself. According to predictions (9:9; 14:28; 16:7), the resolution becomes a possibility in connection with the post-resurrection meeting between Jesus and the disciples in Galilee.

Matthew's portrayal of the disciples is more sympathetic than Mark's. The latter's critical comments have either been eliminated or toned down. This enables the disciples to function as a positive example of faithful followers of Jesus. Although at times Matthew indicates that they do not understand what Jesus is saying, he prefers to describe them as those 'of little faith', as having an incipient faith, and Jesus speaks positively of them as brothers. They are referred to as disciples or learners when Jesus sits down on the mountain to teach them and, despite their failures, he continues to have confidence in them. They become recipients of authority to act in his name, and are blessed because they see and hear. After the explanation of the parables in chapter 13, they reply positively to Jesus' question.

It is important for Matthew that the disciples understand and perceive the deeper meaning of Jesus' sayings and actions. Although they fail at the time of the Passion, the risen Lord calls them his brethren and they respond to his final call to meet him in Galilee. It is there that Jesus commissions them to make disciples and they are commanded to teach all that he has taught them.

In *Luke-Acts*, discipleship consists of being moulded by a tradition, being empowered by an experience, and becoming a participant in a community. But above all, it involves a mission to be carried out. There is a whole series of correspondences between what Jesus does and says in the Gospel, and what the disciples do and say in Acts. The disciples are shaped by what Jesus says and does. Luke tells the story of the life of Jesus in such a way that Jesus is depicted as the founder of the Christian community who also provides for its continuation after his departure. The disciples are shaped by the tradition surrounding Jesus. His public life is presented in such a way that events become models for disciples to follow, and his life as a whole becomes an example for followers to emulate. Disciples are first and foremost witnesses (Lk 24:44-49; Ac 1:8) and the Gospel foreshadows the evangelistic outreach of the post-Easter disciples. As well as a tradition that shapes their lifestyles, they fulfil their role as missionaries only when they are empowered, guided and protected through the ongoing experience of the Spirit. It is the Spirit that enables them to endure hardships, opposition, persecution, imprisonment and threats of death. Furthermore, disciples are not solitary individuals, they are members of a community (Ac 2:44; 4:32), and the mission they are to fulfil is corporate in nature. Christians are those living in continuity with the disciples whose stories fill Luke-Acts. They follow the path laid out by Jesus and are in solidarity with him, sharing his values and mission. They also prepare the way of the Lord and are open to the future and the unforeseen, trusting in the Spirit who accompanies them.

In *John*, followers of Jesus are called 'disciples' more often than any other Gospel, and belief plays a central role in discipleship. Faith is portrayed as something that evolves. The disciples' perception of Jesus, while correct and adequate despite their inability to comprehend who he really is, remains incomplete prior to his 'hour'. Yet in the midst of mounting opposition, the disciples continue to follow Jesus and they reaffirm their earlier belief in him. After his death, Jesus does return and bestows on them the Spirit. They now become aware of the significance of the 'hour' and perceive Jesus' full status as God's unique representative. John also presents a sustained contrast between disciples and non-disciples throughout the narrative. Central to this contrast is the belief and acceptance of Jesus' claims vis-à-vis his Father. Such belief is portrayed as necessitating a process of gradual understanding and perception. Disciples themselves represent a continuum of responses as well as typical misunderstandings. Various minor characters are also introduced to challenge the reader. From among all the characters in John's narrative, Mary and the Beloved Disciple are held up as prime examples to imitate. For the post-Easter community, the 'hour' has passed, the Spirit has come and abides with the community, and Jesus' full status has been grasped and accepted. The peace that is bestowed by Jesus through the Spirit is one that survives rejection, open antagonism and even the possibility of death in a hostile world. It is truly a peace 'not of this world'.

Christians have four Gospels to guide them through the essential stages on the road to Christian maturity. The Gospels fulfil the need to explain in-depth both to oneself and to others what the Christian faith is all about and how it is solidly founded. The four Gospels articulate the Christological (centred on Christ – Mark), ecclesiological (lived out in community – Matthew), missionary (for the sake of the world – Luke-Acts), and contemplative ('remaining' in Christ in faith, hope and love – John); all are dimensions of the Christian life that are necessary to traverse in order to become a mature Christian. In this way Christians are equipped to explain their hopes, convictions and lifestyle to those who inquire: 'Always have your answer ready for people who ask you the reason for the *hope* that you all have. But give it with courtesy and respect and with a clear conscience' (1 P 3:15-16).

Readers who have worked their way through each of the four Gospels can readily appreciate the lyrical heights to which Paul rises in a triumphant concluding paragraph in Romans. He says that *nothing* can separate us from the love of God manifested in Jesus. The love of Christ shown in the Christ-event is, for him, the embodiment and concretisation of the love of God for each one of us. It is a vision of life that looks at the present with a clear faith and to the future with a sure hope:

> After saying this, what can we add? With God on our side who can be against us? Since God did not spare his own Son, but gave him up to benefit us all, we may be certain, after such a gift, that he will not refuse anything he can give ... Nothing therefore can come between us and the love of Christ, even if we are troubled or worried, or being persecuted, or lacking food or clothes, or being threatened

or even attacked ... These are the trials through which we triumph, by the power of him who loved us ... For I am certain that ... no created thing, can ever come between us and the love of God made visible in Christ Jesus our Lord. (Rm 8:31-39)

NOTE

1. Maurice Hogan SSC, *Seeking Jesus of Nazareth* (Dublin: The Columba Press, 2001), p. 65.

FURTHER READING

General

Brown, R. E., *An Introduction to the New Testament*, New York: Doubleday, 1997.

Hogan, M., *Seeking Jesus of Nazareth: An Introduction to the Christology of the Four Gospels*, Dublin: The Columba Press, 2001.

Kingsbury, J. D., *Jesus Christ in Matthew, Mark, and Luke*, Philadelphia: Fortress Press, 1981.

Lofink, G., *Jesus of Nazareth: What He Wanted, Who He Was*, Collegeville, MN: Liturgical Press, 2012.

O'Grady, J. F., *The Four Gospels and the Jesus Tradition*, New York: Paulist Press, 1989.

Pagola, J., *Jesus: An Historical Approximation*, fifth edition, Miami, FL: Convivium Press, 2014.

Ratzinger, J., *Jesus of Nazareth*, three volumes, New York: Doubleday, 2007; San Francisco: Ignatius Press, 2011; London: Bloomsbury, 2012.

Ryder SCJ, A., *Following Christ: Models of Discipleship in the New Testament*, Franklin, WI: Sheed & Ward, 1999.

Schnackenburg, R., *Jesus in the Gospels: A Biblical Christology*, Louisville, KY: Westminster John Knox, 1995.

Senior CP, D. and Collins, J. J., eds., *The Catholic Study Bible*, second edition, New York: Oxford University Press, 2006.

Senior CP, D., *Jesus: A Gospel Portrait*, new and revised edition, New York: Paulist Press, 1992.

The New Community Bible, Catholic edition, New York: Alba House, 2013.

Mark

Achtemeier, P. J., *Mark*, from the *Proclamation Commentaries* series, Philadelphia: Fortress Press, 1975.

Best, E., *Disciples and Discipleship: Studies in the Gospel According to Mark*, Edinburgh: T&T Clarke, 1986.

Best, E., *Mark: The Gospel as Story*, Edinburgh: T&T Clark, 1983.

Doohan, L., *Mark: Visionary of Early Christianity*, Santa Fe, NM: Bear & Company, 1986.

Donahue, J. R. and Harrington, D. J., *The Gospel of Mark*, from the *Sacra Pagina* series, Collegeville, MN: The Liturgical Press, 2002.

Harrington OP, W. J., *Mark*, Dublin: Veritas, 1979.

Harrington OP, W. J., *Mark: Realistic Theologian*, Dublin: The Columba Press, 1996, 2002.

Hooker, M. D., *The Message of Mark*, London: Epworth Press, 1983.

McBride, D., *The Gospel of Mark: A Reflective Commentary*, Dublin: Dominican Publications, 1996.

Montague, G. T., *Mark: Good News for Hard Times*, Ann Arbor, MI: Servant Books, 1981.

Rhoads, D., Dewey, J. and Michie, D., *Mark as Story*, second edition, Minneapolis: Fortress Press, 1999.

Stock, OSB, A., *Call to Discipleship: A Literary Study of Mark's Gospel*, Dublin: Veritas, 1982.

Sweetland, D. M., *Our Journey with Jesus: Discipleship According to Mark*, Wilmington, DE: Michael Glazier, 1987.

Van Iersel, B., *Reading Mark*, Edinburgh: T&T Clark, 1989.

Matthew

Bosetti, E., *Matthew: The Journey Towards Hope*, Boston: Pauline Books & Media, 1997.

Doohan, L., *Matthew*, Santa Fe, New Mexico: Bear & Company, 1985.

Hahn, S., *Understanding 'Our Father'*, Steubenville, OH: Emmaus Road Publishing, 2002.

Harrington OP, W. J., *Matthew: Sage Theologian*, Dublin: The Columba Press, 1998.

Harrington SJ, D. J., *The Gospel of Matthew*, from the *Sacra Pagina* series, Collegeville, MN: The Liturgical Press, 1991.

Hendrickx, H., *The Sermon on the Mount*, London: Geoffrey Chapman, 1984.

Kingsbury, J. D., *Matthew*, from the *Proclamation Commentaries* series, Philadelphia: Fortress Press, 1977.

Luz, U., *The Theology of the Gospel of Matthew*, Cambridge: University Press, 1995.

Meier, J. P., *Matthew*, Dublin: Veritas, 1980.

Meier, J. P., *The Vision of Matthew*, New York: Paulist Press, 1979.

Mullins, M., *The Gospel of Matthew*, Dublin: The Columba Press, 2007.

O'Collins SJ, G., *The Lord's Prayer*, New York: Paulist Press, 2007.

Senior CP, D., *The Gospel of Matthew*, Nashville: Abingdon Press, 1997.

Senior CP, D., *Matthew*, Nashville: Abingdon Press, 1998.

Talbert, C. H., *Reading the Sermon on the Mount*, South Carolina: University of South Carolina, 2004.

Yeomans, W., *The Gospel of Matthew: A Spiritual Commentary*, Dublin: Dominican Publications, 1993.

Luke-Acts

Alday, S. C., *Power from on High: The Holy Spirit in the Gospels and Acts*, Ann Arbor, MI: Servant Books, 1978.

Barclay, W., *The Gospel of Luke*, from *The New Daily Study Bible* series, revised edition, Edinburgh: The Saint Andrew Press, 1975.

Brown, R. E., *A Once and Coming Spirit at Pentecost*, Collegeville, MN: The Liturgical Press, 1994.

Byrne, B., *The Hospitality of God: A Reading of Luke's Gospel*, Collegeville, MN: The Liturgical Press, 2000.

Crowe CP, J., *The Acts*, volume 8, New Testament Message, Wilmington, DE: Michael Glazier, 1979.

Danker, F. W., *Luke*, from the *Proclamation Commentaries* series, Philadelphia: Fortress Press, 1976.

Doohan, L., *Luke: The Perennial Spirituality*, Santa Fe, NM: Bear & Company, 1985.

Dupont OSB, J., *The Salvation of the Gentiles: Studies in the Acts of the Apostles*, New York: Paulist Press, 1979.

Edwards, O. C., Jr., *Luke's Story of Jesus*, Philadelphia: Fortress Press, 1981.

Fitzmeyer, J. A., *Luke the Theologian: Aspects of His Teaching*, New York: Paulist Press, 1989.

Green, J. B., *The Theology of the Gospel of Luke*, Cambridge: University Press, 1995.

Hahn, S. and Curtis, M., *Acts of the Apostles*, San Francisco: Ignatius Press, 2002.

Harrington OP, W. J., *Luke: Gracious Theologian*, Dublin: The Columba Press, 1997.

Johnson, L. T., *Luke*, from the *Sacra Pagina* series, Collegeville, MN: The Liturgical Press, 1993.

Johnson, L.T., *The Acts of the Apostles*, from the *Sacra Pagina* series, Collegeville, MN: The Liturgical Press, 1992.

Kealy CSSp, J. P., *The Gospel of Luke*, Denville, NJ: Dimension Books, 1979.

Kee, H. C., *Good News to the Ends of the Earth: The Theology of Acts*, London: SCM Press, 1990.

Krodel, G., *Acts*, from the *Proclamation Commentaries* series, Philadelphia: Fortress Press, 1981.

Kurz SJ, W., *Following Jesus: A Disciple's Guide to Luke and Acts*, Ann Arbor, MI: Servant Publications, 2003.

Lane, T. J., *Luke and the Gentile Mission: Gospel Anticipates Acts*, Frankfurt am Main: Peter Lang, 1996.

LaVerdiere SSS, E., *Luke*, Dublin: Veritas, 1980.

LaVerdiere SSS, E., *When We Pray ...: Meditations on the Lord's Prayer*, Notre Dame, IN: Ave Maria Press, 1983.

McBride, A., *The Gospel of the Holy Spirit: A Commentary on the Acts of the Apostles*, New York: Hawthorn Books, 1975.

McBride, D., *The Gospel of Luke: A Reflective Commentary*, Dublin: Dominican Publications, 1991.

Mullins, M., *The Acts of the Apostles*, Dublin: The Columba Press, 2013.

Mullins, M., *The Gospel of Luke*, Dublin: The Columba Press, 2010.

O'Collins SJ, G. and Marconi, G., eds., *Luke and Acts*, New York: Paulist Press, 1991.

O'Toole, R. F., *The Unity of Luke's Theology: An Analysis of Luke-Acts*, Wilmington, DE: Michael Glazier, 1984.

Patella, M. F., *The Gospel According to Luke*, Collegeville, MN: Liturgical Press, 2005.

Tannehill, R. C., *Luke*, Nashville: Abingdon Press, 1996.

Tannehill, R. C., *The Narrative Unity of Luke-Acts: A Literary Interpretation*, two volumes, Philadelphia: Fortress Press, 1991, 1994.

Van Linden CM, P., *The Gospel of Luke & Acts*, Wilmington, DE: Michael Glazier, 1986.

John

Brown, R. E., *The Gospel and Epistles of St John*, Collegeville, MN: The Liturgical Press, 1988.

Collins, R. F., *John and His Witness*, Collegeville, MN: The Liturgical Press, 1991.

Culpepper, R. A., *Anatomy of the Fourth Gospel: A Study in Literary Design*, Philadelphia: Fortress Press, 1983.

Culpepper, R. A., *The Gospel and Letters of John*, Nashville: Abingdon Press, 1998.

Doohan, L., *John: Gospel for a New Age*, Santa Fe, NM: Bear & Company, 1988.

Fenton, J., *Finding the Way through John*, Oxford: A. R. Mowbray, 1988.

Grenier CFC, B., *St John's Gospel: A Self-Directed Retreat*, Homebush, NSW: St Paul Publications, 1991.

Harrington OP, W. J., *John: Spiritual Theologian*, Dublin: The Columba Press, 1999.

Harrington SJ, D. J., *John's Thought and Theology: An Introduction*, Wilmington, DE: Michael Glazier, 1990.

Kealy, S. P., *That You May Believe: The Gospel According to John*, Slough: St Paul Publications, 1978.

Kysar, R., *John's Story of Jesus*, Philadelphia: Fortress Press, 1988.

McPolin SJ, J., *John,* New Testament Message 6, Dublin: Veritas, 1979.

Moloney SDB, F. J., *Reading John,* North Blackburn, Victoria: HarperCollins, 1995.

Moloney SDB, F. J., *The Gospel of John*, from the *Sacra Pagina* series, Collegeville, MN: The Liturgical Press, 1998.

Moody Smith Jr, D., *John*, Nashville: Abingdon Press, 1999.

Morris, L., *Jesus is the Christ: Studies in the Theology of John*, Grand Rapids, MI: William B. Eerdmans, 1989.

O'Flynn OFM Cap, S., *Come and See: Lectio Divina with John's Gospel*, Dublin: The Columba Press, 1999.

O'Grady, J. F., *According to John: The Witness of the Beloved Disciple*, New York: Paulist Press, 1999.

Talbert, C. H., *Reading John: A Literary and Theological Commentary*, New York: Crossroad, 1992.

Taylor SJ, M. J., *A Companion to John: Readings in Johannine Theology*, New York: Alba House, 1977.

Taylor SJ, M. J., *John: The Different Gospel*, New York: Alba House, 1983.